MY JOURNEY TO PARADISE

(Book I)

SUSAN HAYWARD

Copyright © 2024 Susan Hayward

All rights reserved. No part of this publication may be reproduced, distributed, or transmitted in any form or by any means, including photocopying, recording, or other electronic or mechanical methods, without the prior written permission of the author/publisher, except in the case of brief quotations embodied in critical reviews and certain other non-commercial uses permitted by copyright law.

For permission requests, write to the Author at
sharedjourneys2024@gmail.com

Website: www.creatingparadise.org

ISBN: 9798340056757

Imprint: Independently published

First printing edition: October 2024

DEDICATION

I dedicate this book to all the Souls who have existed since the beginning of their creation, in their numerous roles and avatars, throughout the many timelines and dimensions.

ACKNOWLEDGEMENTS

I am very grateful to my children and grandchildren for putting up with me wanting to share the information I come across when they find it too deep for them to fully understand and would rather hear anything else.

I am also grateful for the friends who were willing to discuss various subjects with me, one of whom is battling cancer; one still tries to convert me to Islam, another who doesn't believe in God as such but Mother Nature.

I would also like to thank Jan Frost for her constructive criticism, plus her collection of books is even greater than mine on history, law and theology subjects. I have had great discussions with you all, learning whilst amicably disagreeing on some things. I appreciate your open minds.

Thank you all for caring about me and my efforts in writing this book. Most of all I want to thank the many authors and researchers, all seekers of truth, for sharing their findings. Many are still unknown to me but collating this information is a huge task and I love every minute I spend on it.

CONTENTS

INTRODUCTION	1
JW BASIC TEACHINGS	12
1 - A PARADISE EARTH – FACT OR FICTION?	14
2 - EARLY CIVILISATIONS, RELIGIONS & PHILOSOPHIES	53
3 - THE BIBLE & OTHER BOOKS	107
4 - WHO IS GOD?	184
5 - SOURCE, THE LOGOS & THE HOLY SPIRIT	204
6 - WHO IS JESUS?	231
7 - WHO IS SATAN?	279
CONCLUSION	299
SOURCES OF INFORMATION	303
BIBLIOGRAPHY	309
WEB LINKS	311
INDEX	315

INTRODUCTION

All the world's a stage, and all the men and women merely players; they have their exits and their entrances and one man in his time play many parts, his acts being seven ages
William Shakespeare

Jehovah's Witnesses (JWs) are a cult, there's no denying this now although I would have done so vehemently if I were still a Witness.

For nearly 50 years I believed that the Bible was inspired by Jehovah/Yahweh, the God of the Bible. That mankind was only around 6,000 years old, Adam and Eve being the first humans.

I had always thought being sceptic was not good – how naïve was I? Now I know that being a sceptic but with an open mind is the best way to be. This book is my first attempt to present the result of my research on whether the things I had been taught by Jehovah's Witnesses were true or not.

Having read about the early Christians in Foxe's Book of Martyrs, I had always wondered about the faith these early Christians had, and they were willing to die for it.

I have questioned EVERYTHING, no matter how plausible it sounds, and I have likened writing this book to doing a jigsaw puzzle. As all the jigsaw puzzle pieces come together, the picture I see is more beautiful than I ever envisaged.

HOW I BECAME ONE OF JEHOVAH'S WITNESSES

I first became aware of Jehovah's Witnesses in 1969 after watching the film, **Life for Ruth** starring Patrick McGoohan. Still, although I admired the JWs for their strong beliefs, I never wanted to be one. Mind you, when as a teenager, I said to my parents, 'I'll never get divorced', but ended up doing so three times, so I've learnt - never say never.

In 1970, my husband, son, and I went to start a new life in Nicosia, Cyprus with my mother and stepfather, but my husband returned to the UK alone. As I was on my own often during the day, I had a lot of time to think. At this time, I was an idealistic eighteen-year-old with a young son. I wanted a better future for him and saw myself standing on a literal soapbox sorting out housing for the homeless, food for the hungry, getting rid of weapons and armies, healing people – I had a vivid imagination.

What with Mum being Jewish (and me too by birth), Dad was Greek Orthodox, my stepfather was Roman Catholic, his mother was Gregorian, my mother-in-law was Church of England, and I vaguely remembered a girl at school who was a Seventh Day Adventist – I was perplexed.

One day I picked up my King James Bible. I opened the pages of Revelation which talked about a new heaven and Earth, but the description of the Wild Beast and other horrors scared me, so I closed the book. I prayed to God to direct me to His true religion because I couldn't make up my mind about what religion to baptize my son and I wanted nothing but the best for him.

A couple of weeks later, two women knocked on the front door. One woman, B, spoke with a soft Scottish accent and showed me the book, **The Truth that Leads to Eternal Life** and magazines, and I devoured them.

I thought my prayer was answered and I started studying with B, who was a missionary from Palmers Green, London, married to the Greek Cyprus Branch Overseer and living in Nicosia. Everything I was learning was explained from the Bible. I even had access to the Headquarters Library where I sat every day reading all the books from one end of the room to the other.

My Roman Catholic stepfather would get very angry with me for associating with the Witnesses but would never explain why. He told me I'd get paid for going from door to door but of course, I never did.

My mother told me that she had studied with them before I was born, and some Greek relatives were JWs, but they had never convinced her to become one. Neither adult wanted to discuss anything with me, nor would they try to put me right, so thanks to their opposition, I stubbornly remained convinced I had found "the Truth".

My sister also living with us in Cyprus, started studying with B too. After a few months, I returned to England with my son to save my marriage, and my sister returned with me. A few weeks later, we were baptized in the swimming pool in Hornsey Town Hall and our story was included in the 1971 Yearbook. From then on, we looked forward to living forever on Earth with other faithful ones. Sadly, things didn't work out with my first husband, and I returned to Cyprus where my daughter was born, but my sister stayed in the UK and married a JW.

I returned to England to get a divorce when my daughter was six months old. I was living in a bedsit when I made friends with another housemate who was to become my second husband. Little did I know he was an alcoholic (he hid it very well) and eventually we divorced because I ended up staying in a Women's Aid Refuge after my husband had attacked me with a sheath knife.

After we divorced, I worked full-time to pay the bills whilst bringing up two children and slowly stopped going to meetings. I was able to buy my own house but when and took in lodgers when I lost my job a month later. I wasn't an active Witness at the time, but I still believed what I'd been taught was true.

I even turned down a blood transfusion when I had to have an emergency operation to remove a cyst on a fallopian tube. Thankfully I had a brilliant lodger who helped take care of my children whilst I was in hospital. A few months later I took in another lodger who was to become my second husband. We both started studying with the Witnesses and things were going well when we married but I never realised he was an alcoholic and a gambler. He hid it very well.

He never became a JW, and I thought at the time I'd made another mistake. Over the years my third marriage deteriorated as I found it difficult to cope with my husband's excessive drinking, but it was because I was a Witness that I did everything I stay in the marriage. I felt couldn't just leave him as I had two more children, also the home we lived in was in my name. Also, I still thought I loved him although we split up several times in the twenty years we were married.

My health deteriorated due to the stress, but it wasn't until years later that I was eventually diagnosed as having Post Viral/Chronic Fatigue and Fibromyalgia. By this time, I was going to meetings again. The sad part was that although I was a practising JW, there was no one to advise or support me.

I thought it served me right for not marrying in "the Truth" it seemed. Also, Post Viral/Chronic Fatigue Syndrome was not recognised as a proper illness until much later so no one believed I was really ill. Some days I had no energy to even lift a pen.

I can't say I have always been a good Jehovah's Witness, but despite the problems I did my best to live up to what I believed did Christ's teachings believe I was a true Christian. Obviously, I had no idea how to make good choice as far as men were concerned. When I finally went for counseling, I found out it was because I'd married men like my father and stepfather.

WHY I LEFT JWS - SEPTEMBER 1997

I'll never forget the weekend Princess Diana died. I had spent the past week helping my eldest daughter with her court case against her ex-fiancé. Her solicitor could no longer work for her because she did not have Legal Aid. We had lived her case for five months up until the 3-day Court Hearing during which time I didn't sleep at all. This was because she could not have any more Legal Aid and so I ended up representing her in Court.

Due to lack of sleep, my brain went into overdrive, and I was talking a lot of nonsense. It seemed to me that I was going back and forth into the future. I knew I just needed to catch up on some sleep, but everyone around me was scared. At the time the Elders thought I was demon-possessed and would not let me have any association with anyone in my congregation or go out in the ministry.

A few days later, my husband persuaded me to attend a Psychiatric Unit, and when there the doctor told me that if I didn't stay willingly, I would be sectioned. I replied, 'Well, I don't have much choice then, do I?' and remained in the Unit under observation. In-patients were not allowed to sleep during the day, and I was so tired that I just wanted to sleep. In the evening, I went to bed but was suddenly woken up around 11.30 pm by a loud knock on the door but there was no one outside.

Then I heard the woman opposite me opening and closing her bedroom door. I was desperate to get more sleep but as I couldn't because of her, I went to sit with her and held her hand. She was about to doze off when a nurse came and told me to return to my room. I had very little sleep after that. In the morning, during breakfast, the fire alarm just above me went off. I was still tired from lack of sleep and the noise made my head hurt so much, I cried with pain.

I begged the nurses to let me sleep and I finally was allowed to do so. When my husband came to see me in the afternoon, I was back to normal. When he left, I rang my solicitor to find out if I had been sectioned because I wanted to go home and when I rang him again, he told me I could leave at any time. I then phoned a non-Witness friend, and she agreed to come to the unit to take me away from it.

When I told the nurse on duty I intended to leave, she said I needed to be discharged by the doctor. The staff kept trying to delay me, so I fled as soon as my friend turned up. I had rung my husband telling him I wanted to return home, but he told me that if I did, he would send me back to the Unit so obviously I couldn't go back home. It was a very scary time.

My friend left me at a local police station to find out where the nearest Women's Aid Refuge was, but being a Friday night, I was told the police were too busy dealing with drunkards to help me. I phoned another JW friend who said I could stay with her. She was from another congregation and unaffected by the ban on associating with me.

Within a few days, I found that my husband had taken out an Injunction against me so I could not go home or see my two youngest girls without supervision. Meanwhile, I went to meetings with my friend but was told I still couldn't go out in the ministry, although the Elders in that congregation could not understand why the Elders in my congregation insisted on that.

My family would not talk to me saying that I should return to the Unit first, so I was completely alone apart from my Witness friend and her congregation. It was such a stressful time, and I was very hurt and angry with how I was being treated by the family and Elders, when all I needed was to rest so my mind could stop being over-active.

I contacted MIND, a mental health charity, to try and make some sense of what had happened and deal with my feelings. Then I managed to find a part-time job too as I had no money or transport plus none of my family or friends would talk to me apart from the one I was living with. My congregation Elders didn't seem interested in me but were more supportive of my non-witness husband. In the end, I decided to stop going

to meetings and after several weeks was allowed to return home. My husband and I separated a few months later. I still loved Jehovah and believed in the

Witness's teachings, but I couldn't believe how I had been treated by the Elders who supported my unbelieving husband more than me.

What was I to do and believe? Where do I go for answers? I didn't fit in with any of these people but could not understand why. One girl said she had been very wary of me when she first met me because I was so friendly'!

The elders thought me too strong-willed although I was a "doormat" with my husband. When I left the organisation, I was like someone on a boat floating in the middle of a vast ocean. A voice in my head (which I thought was Jehovah at that time) would say, 'Don't worry, I will show you'. No. I wasn't schizophrenic.

So, I stopped worrying and continued my spiritual journey. I'd been shown one route but now I had to go along another path to my destination.

JULY 2019 - STARTING THIS BOOK

I came across some information on YouTube that made me question my beliefs. I decided to investigate what I had been taught and believed for so many years.

As with many people, the situation with COVID meant that I could use this time to research. I decided to look at the JW teachings that made them behave in an unchristian way, whilst proclaiming they were Christians. This, of course, was nothing new; the hypocrisy of most religions has been obvious throughout history. I wanted to understand how people get brainwashed into thinking they are doing good things when they are not. Twenty-two years have passed since I was an active JW, so I believe I need to explain a little about the mindset I had when researching this book. I had written articles before but never a book, although I had started a few and they're now on my "To Do" list.

ANOTHER BIG CHANGE

In 2020 I learnt how to use a Pendulum, and I write more about this further in the book. It was all going well, but then came the spanner in the works – on 10th September 2021 I had a stroke; my left arm, hand, and leg were affected which meant I could not type or even walk properly.

This was a great shock to me, especially as I was unsure how I was going to live when I could hardly look after myself. I gradually moved to be nearer to one of my daughters and her family so they could care for me.

Again, my whole life changed. The good thing was that I now had plenty of time to indulge my love of learning and gaining knowledge. I found it hard to read any books after the stroke, so I spent time watching YouTube, Gaia, and sometimes Netflix.

I also listened to Audible books. Slowly I started typing again with my right hand until I had completed twelve chapters. Even now in October 2024, I am still typing mainly with my right hand. I paid someone to edit and format the book for me. It was uploaded to Amazon in July 2024 but after buying a copy, I found many badly formatted pages. I learnt how to use Word to reformat the pages and after hundreds of attempts during the months of August and October, I managed to create the version you are now reading. It was an expensive lesson to learn but hopefully I'll be able to create future books easier.

I apologize if some web links no longer work. I've checked them several times, but they may be broken, or the website no longer exists. Also, some of the information I've quoted might not be the same as the source because it may have been updated or deleted.

JW BASIC TEACHINGS

I list fifteen Basic Jehovah's Witness Teachings and the relevant chapters where I share my findings, some of which shocked and surprised me.

TEACHING	CHAPTER
1 Belief in one God, Jehovah is the God of Abraham, Moses and Jesus	4, 5
2 That the Bible is the inspired Word of God and accept it entirely but do not claim to be Fundamentalists	2, 3
3 Jesus - honouring him as Saviour and the Son of God	6
4 Kingdom of God - a heavenly Government which will replace human governments and accomplish God's plan for the Earth	6
5 Salvation - deliverance from sin and death through the ransom sacrifice of Jesus through faith and works	6
6 Heaven - Jehovah God, Jesus and faithful angels reside in the spirit realm	6
7 Earth - God created the Earth to be mankind's eternal home where people live in peace and perfect health forever	1, 3
8 Evil & Suffering - this began when one of God's angel's rebelled and became known as Satan the Devil who is allowed to rule the earth for a limited time	7

9 Death – when humans pass out of existence. They do not believe in hell and fiery torment for unbelievers or evil doers. Millions will be who refuse to follow these will be destroyed forever.   7

10 Family – they adhere to God's original standard of marriage with sexual immorality being the only grounds for divorce   3

11 Constructing Kingdom Halls and other facilities to further their worldwide Bible education work, sharing in disaster relief   3

12 The organization – consisting of congregations overseen by a body of Elders (not a clergy class and unsalaried). There is no tithing but support their activities by anonymous donations. The Governing body serves at the world headquarters and provides direction for them worldwide.   3

13 Unity- this allows for personal choice with no social, ethnic, racial or class divisions. They endeavor to make their decisions based on their own Bible-trained conscience   3

14 Conduct – They aim to show unselfish love in all their actions and avoid practices that they believe displease God including taking blood transfusions, taking part in wars, respecting governments except when its law are not in conflict with God's Laws   3

15 Relationship with others – they endeavour to follow Jesus' command to love their neighbours, to be neutral in political affairs and not affiliate with other religions whilst respecting the choices made by non-JWs   3

1 - A PARADISE EARTH – FACT OR FICTION?

BASIC TEACHING 7: EARTH – GOD CREATED THE EARTH TO BE MANKIND'S ETERNAL HOME WHERE PEOPLE LIVE IN PEACE AND PERFECT HEALTH FOREVER

The following is from the JW website (*www.jw.org*) about the Paradise Earth:

JEHOVAH PROMISES THESE THINGS:

> *Jehovah will completely undo all the bad that Satan has done. Jehovah has made Jesus the King over all the Earth. Under his rulership, the Earth will be made into a paradise. (Daniel 7:13, 14; Luke 23:4)*
>
> **PLENTY OF FOOD**: *The Earth itself will certainly give its produce; God, our God, will bless us. There will come to be plenty of grain on the Earth; on the top of the mountains there will be an overflow. (Psalm 67:6; 72:16)*
>
> **NO BAD PEOPLE**: *For evildoers themselves will be cut off. And just a little while longer, and the wicked one will be no more; and you will certainly give attention to his place, and he will not be. (Psalm 37:9, 10)*

NO SICKNESS, SORROW OR DEATH: *At that time the eyes of the blind ones will be opened, and the very ears of the deaf ones will be unstopped. At that time the lame one will climb up just as a tag does, and the tongue of the speechless one will cry out in gladness (Isaiah 35:5, 6)*

NO MORE WAR: *Come, you people, behold the activities of Jehovah, how he has set astonishing events on the Earth. He is making wars to cease to the extremity of the Earth. (Psalm 46:8, 9)*

And God himself will be with them. And he will wipe out every tear from their eyes, and death will be no more, neither will mourning nor outcry nor pain be anymore. The former things have passed away. (Revelation 21:3, 4)

---oOo—

I had checked many things but once baptized, didn't look outside my religion or query anything I had been told. I trusted them and as far as I was concerned, I had all the answers, the Truth, at my fingertips and wanted to share these with everyone so they could look forward to the same lovely future as me.

Perhaps you can now understand how those who became Jehovah's Witnesses became hooked on these biblical teachings about living in a paradise Earth and try to share these with others. Naively, their intention was to "save" people for a paradise Earth, not to annoy them.

And this is the magic of this collection of 66 books consisting of Hebrew and Greek scriptures compiled by the Council of Nicaea in 325 CE. You can find a scripture to justify anything you want, and history proves this.

MY NOT-FOR PROFIT

In 2002, I set up a website called **Residents Associations in the UK** after becoming disillusioned with the voluntary sector, finding it was as corrupt as the business world. There are thousands of residents' associations in the UK alone, let alone worldwide. My reasoning at the time was that if we could work together to improve our immediate neighbourhood, in the end we could have our paradise Earth.

I provided a free helpline to assist with problems in the community and RA committees at my own expense and with very little help, but I wanted to help create better communities. Until 2018 I dealt with hundreds of enquiries and saw that the biggest problems were caused by greed and the lack of consideration for neighbours.

THE LAW OF ATTRACTION

In 2006, after learning about the Law of Attraction from the film, [1]**The Secret**, I thought that maybe this was how the New Earth would come about if everyone could think differently, but I've found that this was going to be easier said than done. I still wanted to be someone who would help bring this about, but HOW?

At the time, I could never understand why Christians rejected the concept of the Law of Attraction as it was Universal Law (ie. one of God's Laws). Now I do. They seem to oppose anything "New Age" and I write about the New Age Movement at the end of this chapter. I know from my own personal experiences that the Law of Attraction works, but I haven't learnt how to use it deliberately; it's usually by chance that I manage to manifest things.

In 2014 I attracted like-minded people and wanted to have a Conference to bring chairpersons from around the country together. I was looking for guest speakers and came across Bruce Nixon, author of **A Better World Is Possible**, published in 2011. The back of his book states:

> *[I am a veteran "change agent", former sustainability and organisation development consultant and business schoolteacher, author, speaker, activist, researcher and mentor. I gained corporate experience in many sectors, first in HR, later in strategic leadership development and internal consulting.*
>
> *In 1987 I started my own business as an independent management consultant, helping senior people lead strategic change and create better workplaces, providing training and development for consultants. The focus of my work has changed: my main interest is*

sustainability, in the broadest sense, and how we can bring about system change in global society.]

On his website, *www.brucenixon.com*, he says:

[We face the biggest challenge in our history. We are heading for an environmental disaster. The global economic system is unsustainable and unjust and leads to war and violence. It transfers wealth from those who create it to rich and powerful elites. Measures to restore "business as usual" bear down on those least responsible for the crisis, the young and most vulnerable.]

He agreed to be one of my speakers. Unfortunately, I ran out of steam and money, so the conference never happened, maybe one day....

In 2012, I felt something in the world was changing but I just couldn't say what. Many others did too and maybe you felt the same. Since then, I have looked at hundreds of videos and read numerous books and articles but can only summarise some of them. I hope that you want to know more to answer all the questions you may have.

Until 2023, I hadn't looked at many ex-Witnesses and their findings because I wanted to do my own research first. I had been quite narrow-minded as a JW; the Bible was the only true source of information and everything else was satanic.

My spiritual journey was going to be quite an eye-opening adventure, although I didn't know this when I first started writing this book. With my research, I came across so much information which completely threw me. It was so different to my beliefs. I was both shocked and enthralled as things started to make sense to me.

I wanted to include as much as I could in this book without infringing copyright laws so that you could see straight away what I had come across without having to look at the back of this book each time. I also tried to put as much in my own words except where it would mean leaving out the numerous details in the original article, book or website. There is so much contradictory information which is why I show different points of views. I apologise if it gets a bit boring, but I want you to see that I've done my best to look at a variety of opinions and give you as much information as possible.

OUR PLANET EARTH

There's so much evidence to prove that the Earth and its habitants are much older. This topic has been debated by scientists and scholars for centuries and here are many different theories about how the Earth was formed. Some even think that we are living in an AI simulation which was created more than 6,000 years ago but I needed to look into this theory more, especially since watching the film, **The Matrix** and how life began on our planet.

I thought the best thing to do was to go back to the very beginning of our Earth's creation. Looking up the origins of the Earth, I came across an article entitled [2]**Origin of Earth – Early Theories** which mentions five different theories. There are many other theories involved in the Earth's formation, but these are the most accepted ones.:

1. **THE NEBULAR HYPOTHESIS**

   This theory was first proposed by Immanuel Kant and Pierre-Simon Laplace.

2. **THE NEBULAR HYPOTHESIS**

   This theory was first proposed by Johannes Kepler in the 17th Century.

3. **THE GRAVITATIONAL INSTABILITY HYPOTHESIS**

   This theory was first proposed by Viktor Safronov in the 1960s.

4. **THE STELLAR NURSERY HYPOTHESIS**

   This theory was first proposed by Carl Sagan in the 1970s.

5. **THE BIG BANG THEORY**

   This theory was first proposed by Georges Lamaitre in the 1930s.

First, JWs do not think the Earth and its inhabitants were created in six 24hr days. They teach that each creative day was 7,000 years long and that we are living in the seventh day and Jehovah is resting and evolution was the construct of Satan. JWs always speak about the end of the corrupt system, not the end of the world. They seemed to have the answer based on the Bible, that God's Kingdom with Jesus Christ as

King would make this world new. If this basic teaching was true, when will this all come about?

IDEAS OF PARADISE

There are many different ideas of paradise; the religious view is that it's in heaven and a place of exceptional happiness and delight. Christians and Jews think of an Earthly paradise, as a synonym for the Garden of Eden before the expulsion of Adam and Eve. Muslims also think it is in heaven and is where Adam and Eve lived before being cast down to the Earth. It is a pleasure garden in which the blessed experience the greatest sensual and spiritual happiness.

This was when heaven and Earth were very close together or touching, and when humans and God had a free and happy association without suffering and complete satisfaction of bodily desires. It was a place of rest and refreshment in which the righteous dead enjoyed the glorious presence of God.

Yet others think of Paradise as being a golden age of human society at the beginning of each cycle of human existence in union with the divine (Hinduism), or an eternal condition of peace and changelessness (Buddhism).

We have an inbuilt desire to live in "paradise", whether it's on Earth or in heaven. Did this idea come from religions or was it in our DNA? This made me investigate whether there had been previous "paradises" and I was so surprised with what I found.

1ST PARADISE - 5D PLANET TARA

My next bit of research took me to various "New Age" websites where I learnt that our Earth originally came from Tara, a 5D planet in the second Harmonic Universe that exploded millions of years ago and then imploded into a black hole.

Some of the fragments were pulled into the lower dimensions to become our 3D planet and our Solar System consisting of twelve planetary bodies **Mercury, Venus, Earth, Mars, Maldek, Jupiter, Saturn, Uranus, Neptune, Pluto, Nibiru** and then the **Sun star**. Current science recognizes only seven planets of the twelve in our Solar System, along with dwarf planets.

So now you're most probably wondering what is meant by 3D, 5D and 7D. If the first version of our planet had the high frequency of the fifth dimension and was intended to be a world where the teachings of the universe were integrated holistically, then why can't this be a reality again? Let's see what happens next.

GALACTIC WARS

Many of us have been entertained by sci-fi novels and films such as Star Wars, Star Trek, the Stargate Series and many others. As much as I enjoy watching sci-fi films, I never really thought that ETs existed or had been part of Earth's history for millions of years. Those who dared to say they saw ETs or were abducted by them were either ridiculed or declared insane and locked up. What we didn't know was that these books and films disclosed to us what has happened in the past, what is happening now, and what will happen in the future.

In answer to my questions on who created the universe, I came across a website with so much information on it. It ties in beautifully with other information I have found. Although there will most probably be some truth there, it may not have been revealed by the "good guys" and you will see why I wrote this as you read on.

Lisa Reed claims to be a Starseed and receives her information from Ascended Masters. Starseeds are souls which lived or originate from other planets, other galaxies, on spacecraft, or in other dimensions and interlocking world spaces, who have volunteered to assist in bringing in the Ascension Cycle and assist Earth through her next phase of evolution. This topic of Ascension and Starseeds became her soul purpose, inspired passion and pervaded every waking moment of her adult life.

> *www.ascensionglossary.com/index.php/Lyran Wars* explains:

> *[The main battles in human Galactic history were started over territories in the constellation of Lyra. They were fought in the constellation of Orion, and so these many wars are also referred to as the Orion Wars. The Lyrans are the advanced races that created the Elohim in the Avatar Matrix. But soon the Lyran Wars spread to the constellation of Orion, and it became a war*

> *between the False King of Tyranny mindset and ideologies; and the ideology of the Service to Others which follows the Law of One...Even the writings of the Buddhists and Hindus hinted at galactic wars between light and darkness and the mention of blue gods (native Pleiadians), was dismissed as genetic hatred generated from the Orion Group by those in the Abrahamic religions as pagan (worship of the Devil).]*

So, there were battles between "good" and "evil" beings thousands of years before the concepts taught by the Abrahamic religions about "God", Christ, the Holy Spirit and the "Devil". Such concepts are quite new as I will show in this book. Well, as you can imagine, learning this raised loads of questions, especially as I tried to get the concept of ETs and galactic events into my mind.

What sort of rabbit hole was I being led into? All this information was like reading a storyline from Star Wars, but I persisted and tried to make sense of it all. I read the following on a website that no longer exists, but I felt the information good enough to share:

> *[...planet Earth already exists in all twelve-dimensional levels of this universe. 3D Earth is not moving into the fifth dimension; the sentient human beings of Earth are! ...Starseeds are souls which lived or originate from other planets, other galaxies, on spacecraft, or in other dimensions and interlocking world spaces, who have volunteered to assist in bringing in the Ascension Cycle and assist Earth through her next phase of evolution. Two more paradises were created on our 3D Earth. The first was Lemuria and the*

second Atlantis. There were also three floods. Beings from the future would be the saviours of those living in the past. This was how the Cycles proceeded.]

Like the days of the week, all the planets, except for Earth were named after Greek and Roman gods and goddesses. The name 'Earth' is allegedly an English/German name which simple means ground but the other thought is that Earth was named after Ea/Enki who was originally 'Lord of the Earth', until his half-brother, Enlil, took over.

HISTORY OF 5D EARTH TARA, THE ORIGINAL HUMAN AVATARS, TIAMAT & MALDEK, NIBIRU, DRACONIANS & ANUNNAKI
www.youtube.com/watch?v=Uv6bU3PzDe4

2ND PARADISE ON 3D EARTH TERRA

The second paradise was when the Earth was settling down and recovering from the explosion and separation from 5D Tara. First the Earth had to be habitable for plant life so that the air could be clean.

www.dynamicearth.org.uk/geological-timeline-pack.pdf states:

[...4,600 million years ago (mya) when dust left over from the birth of the sun clumped together to form planet Earth. The other planets in our solar system were also formed in this way at about the same time.

Between 4500 – 1500 mya, Earth's core and crust

formed, oceans too, and oxygen began to accumulate in the Earth's atmosphere when the free iron ran out.

3850 mya – the first life appeared on Earth. It was a very simple single-celled organisms. Exactly how life first arose is a mystery.

700 mya - the first animals evolved

530 mya the first vertebrates (fish) evolved

400 mya the first land plants evolved

350 mya – the first land vertebrates evolved with plants present on the land to provide a food source, animals rapidly followed.

The first to venture onto the land were primitive amphibians, and reptiles evolved soon afterwards.]

WHAT HAPPENED TO THE DINOSOURS

I felt I had to include what I had read in Frederick Dodson's book, **The Pleiades & Our Secret Destiny**.

On p.181-184, he wrote about another life and time when he lived on Mars and that Beings from the spiritual plane, The Creators, formed those human-like civilisations on Mars and another planet called Phaeton (also known as Maldek). Mars was invaded by a Serpent Race (Reptilians?) and deep crevices were created on the planet. He fell into a precipice and died, and his wife died from rocks falling on her head. Dodson wrote that hundreds of thousands of years ago this Serpent race destroyed other planets in our solar system with their technology.

This ties in with what I wrote previously from another viewpoint. By the time the counterforce arrived, it was too late. Phaeton had become the asteroid belt, and Mars was controlled by the Serpent race but was finally expelled, although some managed to hide underground, deep within the interior of Mars.

> *[P.184...The Creators proceeded to create Planet Earth...In this example, the creation story is merely transposed to a greater context. I believe religious creation stories area accurate, but they are short-hand versions of what happened, told to an audience that wouldn't understand the details.*
>
> *In a similar vein, "religious" people claim that the ancient alien theory contradicts the idea of a Creator God because it claims we were created by aliens. But the idea of ancient aliens does not contradict the God idea, it merely transposes it.*
>
> *Even if we were created by aliens, who created the aliens? And who created those who created the aliens? Whichever way you put it things always go back to an originating Source. Our Souls were created by the Highest Source...*

I compared what was written in the PDF with what Elena Danaan had written in her book, **The Seeders** (p. 491-500) that 200 million years ago, a Reptiloid species, (The Naga) from the Alpha Draconis system found Earth before anyone else. They started a terraforming program to modify the atmosphere, so it was better for them. This caused many large land animals to die out. The dinosaurs had lived on Earth for 165 million years and were members of a subclass of reptiles called Archosaurs ("ruling reptiles").

[225 mya – The first dinosaurs evolved from lizards.]

65 million years BCE, a cell of the Intergalactic Confederation, known as the "Seeders", "Founders" or "Pa-Taal" came to Earth and took DNA samples of all the Earth's flora and fauna before removing the great reptiles.

[65 mya – The dinosaurs went extinct. The dinosaurs, and many other species with them, were wiped out by the after-effects of a meteorite impact, or perhaps several impacts. The impact(s) set off chains of earthquakes, tsunamis and volcanic eruptions, which threw lots of dust and acid into the atmosphere, creating an impact winter. The dust blocked out the sunlight so plants could no longer photosynthesis, and food chains collapsed. After the extinction of the dinosaurs, mammals evolved rapidly and filled the evolutionary niches they left behind.]

Thereafter, the Seeders began modifying the original molecules in the DNA of some indigenous primates so that they could become the humans of today. 130,000 years ago (0.13 mya) – Modern humans evolved. Homo sapiens evolved in Africa from earlier humans. they left Africa around 35,000 years ago and spread around the globe. Human evolution is still pretty mysterious, due to gaps in the fossil record. The Seeders kept going back and forth improving all life on Earth and then the Anunnaki came c.372,000 BCE.

On p. 197, Dodson wrote that in the early days of Earth, space travel to and from Earth was as casual as our aeroplane travel today. We have relatives all over the Universe. Most of our human ancestors fled to the Pleiadian star system. The humans that stayed behind on Earth were enslaved by the Serpent Empire.

On p.191, Dodson wrote that approximately 30,000 years ago (according to Australian Aboriginal mythology), the Reptilian beings arrived on Planet Earth. Many of our ancestors fled the planet and the entire solar system. Others escaped to the Pleiades because they were familiar with them, having travelled there on several occasions. It was their contingency plan.

Recovering from the war, the peaceful blue-skinned Pleiadians seeing that the technological, combat-ready humans would be a blessing to them, gave the human-skinned ones some of their higher consciousness, who in return provided military defence.

On p.193 he explains that the human-Pleiadians' defence technology was superior to that of the Serpent, but they were taken by surprise. Most of the human-populated planets around the Pleiades are now well-equipped and ready for any surprise.

In chapter 5, he describes the experience another author, Michael Harner, had whilst under the influence of Ayahuasca and met some bird-headed people. Ayahuasca is a South American psychoactive beverage. It was traditionally used by Indigenous cultures and folk healers for spiritual ceremonies, divination, and healing a variety of psychosomatic complaints.

> *[I could only vaguely see them in what seemed to be gloomy, dark depths. Then they projected a visual scene in front of me. First, they showed me the planet Earth as it was eons ago, before there was any life on it.*
>
> *I saw an ocean, barren land, and a bright blue sky. Then black specks dropped from the sky by the hundreds and landed in front of me on the barren landscape. I could see that the "specks" were actually large shiny, black creatures with stubby pterodactyl-like wings and huge whale-like bodies.*
>
> *Their heads were not visible to me. They flopped down, utterly exhausted from their trip, resting for eons. They explained to me in a kind of thought language that they were fleeing from something out in space. They had come to planet Earth to escape their enemy. The creatures then showed me how they created life on the planet to hide within the multitudinous forms and thus disguise their presence.*
>
> *I learnt that the dragon-like creatures were thus inside of all forms of life, including man. They were the true masters of humanity and the entire*

planet, they told me. We humans were but the receptacles and servants of these creatures. For this reason, they could speak to me from within myself.... I began to struggle against the returning to the ancient ones, who were beginning to feel increasingly alien and possibly evil...]

He managed to ask for the antidote and when he recovered, he wrote that he went back to the blind shaman who had made many excursions into the spirit world with the aid of the ayahuasca drink.

[It seemed only proper that a blind man might be able to be my guide to the world of darkness' and described his visions to him segment by segment and told him about the dragon-like creatures who said they were the true masters of this world. He stared up towards me with his sightless eyes and said with a grin, "Oh, they're always saying that. But they are only the Masters of Outer Darkness".

He waved his hand casually toward the sky. I felt a chill along the lower part of my spine, for I had not told him that I had seen them, in my trance, coming from outer space.

3RD PARADISE – LEMURIA (AKA MU)

www.elementalbeings.co.uk/lemuria states:

[...In Lemuria, the development of the human race was such that people lived a telepathic existence very connected to the emotional self, very connected to the Oneness of all.... The Lemurian Dolphins held the codes and communication with the Dolphin realm and the whales were telepathic

and intuitive. Humanity learnt a lot from the Dolphin realm and still to this day, many humans remember this and feel great joy and elation when connecting with the Dolphin realm...Dolphins are believed to carry Lemurian light codes of profound healing vibrations... to activate our dormant vibrations to discover love and heal our heart chakra to bring us closer to the Divine.]

RUDOLPH STEINER

Years ago, my friend, Maria, had spoken of him and had sent her daughter to a Steiner school. As I was a JW at the time, I wasn't interested in anyone else's philosophy; the Bible was enough for me. Steiner was able to look at the Akashic Records and find out about Lemuria and Atlantis; links to the chapters in his book, 3**Atlantis & Lemuria**:

1. *From the Âkâshic Records*
2. *Our Atlantean Forefathers*
3. *Transition of the Atlantean into the Âryan Root-Race*
4. *The Lemurian Era*
5. *Woman in the Third Root-Race*
6. *Humanity Before the Division of Sex*
7. *The Beginnings of Sex Duality*
8. *Man's First Ancestors*
9. *The First, or Polar, Race*
10. *The Second, or Hyperborean, Race*

Then I came across an Indian Tamil writer, Devaneya Pavanar. He was a staunch proponent of the "Pure Tamil movement". He initiated the Etymological Dictionary Project primarily to bring out the roots of Tamil words and their connections and ramifications.

In his book, **Primary Classical Language of the World (1966)**, he argued that the Tamil language is the most natural" and the oldest language from which all other major languages of the world are derived. In another of his articles, he wrote that the Tamil language is a highly developed classical language of Lemurian origin, suppressed by a systematic and coordinated effort by the Sanskritists both in the public and private sectors.

More research led me to Frederick Spencer Oliver who published **A Dweller on Two Planets (1894)**. He claimed that survivors from Lemuria were living in a complex of tunnels beneath the mountain of Mount Shasta in Northern California. This city is known as *'Telos: City of Light'*.

Prof. Masaaki Kimura, a Japanese geologist, has suggested that certain underwater features located off the coast of Yonaguni Island, Japan are ruins of Mu. The link to [4]**Page One of the Exclusive Interview with Professor Masaaki Kimura** is on the website in the footnote.

Volcanic eruptions, Earthquakes and the collapsing of subterranean gas belts caused Lemuria to sink into the sea. Some colonists migrated to America forming a racial core of the earliest Indian tribes, while others reached India and from there travelled to Mesopotamia and Egypt. Pure Lemurians later became Californian Indians.

Other writers such as Augustus Le Plongeon, James Churchward, John Newbrough, Max Heindel and

Louis Jacolliot also wrote about areas that may have been Lemuria. James Bramwell and William Scott-Elliot claimed that the cataclysmic events on Lemuria (Mu) began 800,000 years ago and went on until the last catastrophe, which occurred in precisely 9,564 BCE.

Going back to Frederick Dodson's book, **The Pleiades & Our Secret Destiny**, on p194 he writes that there was another Reptilian invasion on Earth. Again, humans fled leaving behind farmers and hunters that had no interest in abandoning Earth. These Earthbound people were not interested in technology and space travel, but they were nonetheless attuned to the overall cosmos, so much more than we are today.

On P.196 he wrote that these peaceful people had built beautiful spiritual societies without the use of technology or even electricity (as we know it) and in perfect harmony with their surroundings. These people were Lemurians, and we are the offspring of those left behind.

As we live on a planet with duality, there will be some who believe that Lemuria existed and others who relegate the idea of Lemuria as pure fiction, but that's OK. I'm just relating the information I discovered with my research.

4TH PARADISE – ATLANTIS

Now I will share what I found about Atlantis. Around 32,000 BCE, a new contingent of Alteans from the

Intergalactic Confederation arrived in our star system. They settled in an island continent in the Atlantic Ocean where Enki (half-human, half-Reptilian, a Geneticist) had lived for eons of time. He welcomed them to share rulership until he left Earth. (See **The Seeders**, p 304).

The first Greek person to bring up Atlantis was Plato (c.424–328 BCE) who heard about Atlantis from his grandfather, Solon who had been told this story by Egyptian priests whilst living in Egypt. Plato describes Atlantis as a powerful and advanced kingdom that sank, in a night and a day, into the ocean around 9,600 BC.

He said the lost city lay beyond the Pillars of Hercules—two rocks in the Strait of Gibraltar. The island of Spartel once sat there. Passing sailors may have seen it vanish at the end of the last ice age, but if so, they left no records. The ancient Greeks were divided as to whether Plato's story was to be taken as history or mere metaphor.

In another book by Frederick Dodson, **Atlantis and the Garden of Eden**, on page 6, he writes about the several veils which prevent a clear view of Atlantis.

Veil 1. The 'sceptical-academic-Darwinist' view
Veil 2. The dogmatic-religious' view ....
Veil 3. The 'modernist-psychological' view ...
Veil 4. The 'ancient-alien' view ...
Veil 5. The 'gullible view' ...
Veil 6. The 'politically ideological' view ...

On p.7 he wrote that whilst researching, every time he hit upon some falsehood it could be traced back to one of those veils. Understanding Atlantis more completely requires you to suspend all of these filters for the time being and look at the evidence with fresh eyes. If one stays confined to one position, the big picture is missed...

> *[p.8...I respect modern science and all it has done for civilisation but the 'history department' appears to have gotten one little thing wrong. This one little thing shifts the entire context of history – the existence of the supernatural. So, the only very slight difference between a pseudo-scientist such as myself and the actual scientist of these subjects, is that the scientist considers mythology fiction and I consider mythology real.]*

He then shared the Chinese myth, **The Archer and the Moon Goddess**, which tells the story of how one of the "gods" took his "firebird" and flew to the moon where the moon's surface was found to be "cold, grey and desolate".

He asked, 'How could the ancients know something that ASA only "discovered" in the 1960s? He also mentions the Tamils.

> *[p.153...that The Tamils who live in southern India, Sri Lanka and Indonesia spoke the Dravidian language and are one of the oldest cultures on Earth. He says there was a flood 18,000 years ago which sunk the kingdom of Kumari Kandam (part of Lemuria) and another flood 12,000 years ago which sunk Atlantis.]*

On p.165 he says that the ancient Egyptians, the African Berbers, the Basques, the extinct Iberians and Etruscans, the original builders of Malta; the native American Algonquin, the Maya and Aztec, the Hittites, the Celts, the Phoenicians and others, are descendants of a mysterious people that survived a gigantic flood that sank both Atlantis and created the Mediterranean.

Around 32,000 BCE, a new contingent of Alteans from the Intergalactic Confederation arrived in our star system. They settled in an island continent in the Atlantic Ocean where Enki (half-human, half-Reptilian, a Geneticist) had lived for eons of time. He welcomed them to share rulership until he left Earth. (See **The Seeders**, p 304).

The ancient Greeks were divided as to whether Plato's story was to be taken as history or mere metaphor. Since the 19th century, there has been renewed interest in linking Plato's Atlantis to historical locations, most commonly the Greek island of Santorini, which was destroyed by a volcanic eruption around 1,600 BCE.

Since the 19th century, there has been renewed interest in linking Plato's Atlantis to historical locations, most commonly the Greek island of Santorini, which was destroyed by a volcanic eruption around 1,600 BCE.

It is now thought that Atlantis was not merely an island, but a continent which included places that are now islands. Despite all the negative opinions about

Lemuria and Atlantis ever existing, channellers like Edgar Cayce and hypnotists like Dolores Cannon and Sarah Breskman Cosme, have revealed a lot of information during their work. None of them claimed to be spirit mediums.

EDGAR CAYCE

Well, when I learnt about him, I was interested, especially as I too was being led by my higher self – something I would have completely rejected as one of Jehovah's Witnesses.

Edgar Cayce was an American Clairvoyant (not a medium) and a devout Christian who claimed to speak from his higher self. His words were recorded by his friend, Al Layne, his wife, Gertrude Evans, and later by his secretary, Gladys Davis Turner. During the sessions, Cayce would answer questions on a variety of subjects such as healing, reincarnation, dreams, the afterlife, past lives, nutrition, Atlantis, and future events.

He said that his readings came from his subconscious mind while in a trance-like state, exploring the dream realm, where he said all minds were timelessly connected. He spoke frequently of Atlantis during his "life readings" and claimed that many of his subjects were reincarnations of people who had lived there.

Like Steiner, by tapping into the collective consciousness, the "Akashic Records" (a term borrowed from Theosophy), Cayce declared that he was able to give detailed descriptions of the lost continent. Cayce also asserted that Atlantis would "rise" again in the 1960s (sparking much popularity of the myth in that decade) and that there is a "Hall of Records" beneath the Egyptian Sphinx which holds the historical texts of Atlantis.

According to **Atlantis isn't real, but here are all the places it could have been** (_www.popsci.com_):

1. **BIMINI ROAD**: In the mid-'60s, divers encountered a remarkably straight half mile of evenly spaced, uniform stones. Carbon dating and a lack of tool marks suggest natural erosion is responsible, but some believe it's from a sunken civilization.

2. **SOUSS MASSA PLAIN**: A 2008 analysis of 51 Platonic descriptors of Atlantis identified several possible co-ordinates, including these coastal dunes, which feature intriguing concentric dry riverbeds. Unfortunately, there's scant evidence of any empire.

3. **SPARTEL BANK**: Plato said the lost city lay beyond the pillars of Hercules—two rocks in the Strait of Gibraltar. The island of Spartel once sat there. Passing sailors may have seen it vanish at the end of the
last ice age, but if so, they left no records.

4. **DOGGERLAND**: The British Isles were once connected to Europe by a low-lying landmass. But when a megatsunami struck around 6000 BCE, the region disappeared, leaving bones and tools from local hunter-gatherers embedded in the seafloor.

5. **HELIKE**: A tsunami walloped this Greek town in Plato's day, and many assumed its remains lay in the Corinthian Gulf. But in the 1990s, archaeologists found it half a mile inland, buried under a few dozen

feet of sediment by a process called soil liquefaction.

6. **ANTARCTICA**: Historian Charles Hapgood argued the southern continent was once a northern landmass with Atlantis on its shore. Then, 12,000 years ago, a shift in the crust sent it south. Antarctica did make that trip—some 30 million years ago.

7. **MARSHALL ISLANDS**: We may have another "Atlantis" someday. Sea level rise threatens coastal communities, including this network of atolls with an average elevation of just six feet. Without intervention, they'll likely be underwater by mid-century

Elena Danaan claims to have lived in Atlantis and died there. Her video on Crowdcast is about the true, epic and beautiful history of Atlantis, how it began and how it ended, who founded it, who lived there and what technologies were in use. In it she explains that it was the colonies of Atlantis that caused problems, not the rulers.

The trailer is on YouTube
www.youtube.com/watch?v=2ilkaEQbFo

THE NEW AGE MOVEMENT[5]

It seems that this Movement developed from the teachings of the Theosophical Society founded in 1875. Theosophy is a philosophy combining mysticism and spiritualism (with heavy influences from Buddhist and Hindu thought) with metaphysics. The Society was fashioned as a 'brotherhood' promoting unity and concerned with preparing for when he arrived on Earth. One of the co-founders, a wealthy woman called Helena Petrovna Blavatsky, often known as Madame Blavatsky, was a Russian and American mystic and author announced a coming New Age.

> *[She believed that theosophists (who embraced Buddhist and Hindu notions such as reincarnation) should assist the evolution of the human race and prepare to co-operate with one of the Ascended Masters of the Great White Brotherhood. She believed they were the world's hidden leaders guiding the destiny of Earth and their arrival was imminent and brought forth a New Age.*
>
> *This New Age, known as the Age of Aquarius, promised a period of brotherhood and enlightenment. Various people in Wu-yang County received messages from these beings, including most notably Aleister Crowley (Thelema), Alice Bailey (New Group of World Servers), Guy Ballard ("I AM" Activity), Geraldine Innocente (The Bridge to Freedom), Mark L]*

Of course, now I wanted to know about the Ascended Masters of the Great White Brotherhood.

ASCENDED MASTERS OF THE GREAT WHITE BROTHERHOOD (GWB)

The Great White Brotherhood are said to be supernatural beings with great power that spread spiritual teachings through certain humans. Above them is the Council of Light. The GWB is also known as the Great Brotherhood of Light or the Spiritual

Hierarchy of Earth. They are also known as the Masters of Ancient Wisdom, the Ascended Masters, the Church Invisible, or the Hierarchy. The GWB has nothing to do with skin colour, instead it represents purity and light, their Earth base is somewhere in the Himalayas. The ascended masters receive the ray of light from this hidden command post. They are also known as the Great Brotherhood of Light or the Spiritual Hierarchy of Earth. They are also known as the Masters of Ancient Wisdom, the Ascended Masters, the Church Invisible, or the Hierarchy. This group works in secret, accelerating humanity's spiritual growth and elevating consciousness.

Some members claim to use telepathy and visions to establish contact with entities outside Earth's orbit so that they can channel the divine plan prepared for each human being on Earth. It is said that Members display positive characteristics like compassion, wisdom, and energy healing powers. You need only look on the internet to find numerous people claiming to channel various Ascended Masters, angels or other entities.

At first, I didn't think there was anything negative about GWB until I read George Kavassilas's book, **Our Universal Journey.** On p.92 he wrote about the time he worked with the GWB and explained that Saturn is the base planet for The Saturnian Council, also known as The Great White Brotherhood. He said they are a Council of Beings who embody and manage synthetic positive white love and light energy. They also implement and manage passive-aggressive programs. Inter-dimensional beings and Extraterrestrial groups function under the auspice of this Being known as Jehovah / Yahweh / Shiva/ Allah/Cronus and the Archons. It turns out then that this Being is the *False King of Tyranny*. Kavassilas also calls him the *God of Religions*.

Elena Danaan claims to be a Contactee and Emissary for the Galactic Federation of Worlds and I remembered her warning people on her website, www.elenadanaan.org/debunk, about galactic groups and organisations claiming to be of the light, also about channelling entities.

There is a big difference between channellers and contactees and she is considered someone to be genuine by several people including Dr Michael Salla, Alex Collier (another contactee) and Dan Winter. I had never been interested in such things before and was extremely sceptical when I came across such topics too, but I decided to keep an open mind and continue researching.

Having read books and watched videos by Elena Danaan, George Kavassilas and those who support them, I now extremely wary of anything that is labelled "White" or "Light". Now I take the stance that the 'proof of the pudding is in the eating' as the saying goes and watch with great interest as more things get revealed. Hopefully, I haven't lost your interest now that I've mentioned such things and that you will continue reading.

I wanted to know more about this movement which had started when I was a teenager during the 1960s.

Many young people rebelled against their parents' values and lifestyle creating the "Hippie Movement" centred largely in the United Kingdom. The New Age Movement asserts that we save ourselves by "self-fulfillment, self-realization, self-redemption". I enjoyed listening to Dr Wayne Dyer who was part of this movement, also, the film, *The Secret*, came under this movement too.

As I now believe there is a bit of truth in every belief system, I wanted to know more about this movement and its teachings. The New Age movement affected occult, metaphysical and religious communities in the 1970s and '80s. It offered a foretaste of the coming era through personal transformation and healing looking forward to a "New Age" of love and light.

The [6]**Findhorn Foundation**, which founded the Findhorn Ecovillage, in Moray, Scotland in 1962 was one of the most prominent groups during this time. When American theosophist, David Spangler, joined the Findhorn Foundation in 1970, he developed the fundamental idea of the New Age movement that certain astrological changes were bringing us into the Age of Aquarius) releasing new waves of spiritual energy. He suggested that people use this new energy to manifest the New Age, shifting responsibility for the coming of the New Age to those who believed in it.

This attracted many diverse believers who looked forward to this New Age of heightened spiritual consciousness, international peace which would bring an end to racism, poverty, sickness, hunger, and war. Had I known about this when I was younger, I might have joined them instead of becoming one of Jehovah's Witnesses. By the 1980s, this Movement had lost its momentum and by the mid-1990s, it was evident that the movement was dying, despite having been derided for its acceptance of unscientific ideas and practices (especially its advocacy of crystals and channelling) 3-5 million Americans identified themselves as New Agers.

More than one-fifth of adults in the West give credence to astrology; an equal number have practised some form of meditation. The continuing presence of New Age thought in the post-New Age era is evident in the number of New Age bookstores, periodicals, and organizations that are around.

I realised that JWs had some New Age ideas mixed with biblical "truths" but say the raising of consciousness would be brought about with Jehovah's Holy Spirit and Jesus Christ would be ruling as King to bring about the New Earth. Again, there are some truths found in the New Age Movement, but you must be able to discern what they are, just as there are in all religions.

CHRISTIANITY -V- NEW AGE

If Jesus said in Luke 21:17 (KJV), that 'the Kingdom of God is within you', (then surely that encompasses how you think and feel which is what the Law of Attraction is about). Surely, the Christian translation should have read "among you" not within you", meaning that the kingdom was present because Jesus was present. The English Standard Version says, 'the kingdom is in the midst of you'. The meaning of a "kingdom" (Collins Dictionary) is "a country, state, or territory ruled by a king or queen". Therefore, my thought is that Jesus would have said "The King is with you" in that case, not the "kingdom" because a kingdom refers to an area, not a person.

3D, 5D & CHRIST-CONSCIOUSNESS

So why is it important to understand the difference between a 3D consciousness and a 5D one? This is because there is a small, enlightened group telling us that no one is coming to save us and create this New Earth, just as David Spangler said, 'It's not that Jesus is coming back but the Christ (consciousness) is coming back'. More is coming out into the public arena that we can do this ourselves. How? By raising our consciousness to develop a Christ-consciousness that is real unselfish love for ourselves and others. This is not the same as following the Jesus Christ as promoted in Christianity.

> *www.institutechristconsciousness.org/what-is-christ-consciousness.html states:*
>
> *["Christed" is not a term used exclusively in the Christian religion, nor does it mean you must adhere to the Christian belief system to attain this state. All the world's religious traditions offer a path to achieving "Christed" status, and people are free to find their way in the context of their chosen religion, or no religion. Remember, we each have our own unique journey to finding Deity. Our*

Indwelling Spirits encourage us to grow organically on our own path. Sometimes people find their way within the context of a belief system held by one of the world's major religions; some people will find their way by blending belief systems in a unique and innovative way.

All ways and paths are honoured if they lead a person to become more loving, forgiving, patient, kind, compassionate, tolerant, and joyful. All paths of love lead to the same Divine Source of all that exists. We each share the same Deity Creator Parent Source as an individual expression of that Source Personality. We are all moving toward unification with our Source.]

Living on a 3D planet means that most of us can only discern time as being the past, present or future and we can be very judgmental. With a 5D consciousness, we will be able to see everything as linear, at the same time. Our perception won't see actions (our own or someone else's) as good or bad, right or wrong. Instead, we will have the perception to understand the history and motives behind them.

www.bodyandsoulascension.com/post/energy-frequency explains much more, but to summarise:

[Energy frequency and spiritual vibration are inter-connected aspects of human experience that affect our overall well-being. By understanding the energy frequencies and spiritual vibrations, you can elevate your consciousness, promote healing, and enhance personal growth. Everything in the universe, including our thoughts, emotions, and physical bodies, consists

of energy that vibrates at different frequencies. The frequency range of energies that science can measure is very narrow compared to the universe's energies around us. Spiritual vibration, on the other hand, refers to the quality and resonance level of an individual's energy field and one would use the chakra scale to measure it. It is influenced by a person's thoughts, emotions, and spiritual practices. Higher spiritual vibrations are associated with positive emotions, love, and enlightenment, while lower vibrations correlate with negative emotions, fear, and limited consciousness.]

Having a 3D frequency means:

[... being filled the majority of the time by survival fears like fear of death, not having enough money, fear of illness, fear of old age, an impulse for reproduction, etc....These emotions create a low spiritual vibration, you identify with your body and hence attract negativity and stagnation in life.

There is little room to progress in such circumstances. ...you find yourself filled the majority of the time by feelings and emotions belonging to intense emotions which are generally related to intimate relationships, sexual relationships, obsession with food, drugs, and the like...a material level where you are mostly led by your body instincts...

Again, since you are rather identified with your body and feel close only to some persons like lovers and family members, there is not too much room for soul evolution and personal growth....you find yourself filled the majority of the time by feelings and emotions belonging to material ambitions, fear, guilt, competition, shame, envy, anger...Love at this level is rather transactional and includes specific interests from both partners like safety, sex, caring for the house, money, fame, representation in society, need for heirs, etc.

This is the average level of the majority of people now on Earth like +90%; we are a 3D vibration civilization ultimately. If you can turn these feelings into courage, openness, altruism, and willingness to evolve and therefore take your ego under control, you get into the process of self-discovery and personal growth, leading to a more balanced spiritual vibration.]

The higher spiritual vibrations are the frequencies of 5D and higher. These are shown briefly as:

[...Interest for a higher understanding of Universal laws and mechanisms, soul awareness, body awareness level, and the like...Communication becomes important, both on the Horizontal so with other people, nature, and animals, and also on the Vertical belonging to understanding messages from higher vibrations like from God, spiritual guides and so on... Love starts to manifest not only toward other people but also toward higher vibrations and dimensions.

These individuals have transcended the majority of ego limitations and are in tune with their true spiritual nature, leading to higher spiritual vibrations in 5D. At this level your feelings should belong to discerning the spiritual causes of why things and events are as they are, helping others smaller souls to reach into higher vibrations, starting to control energies for the greater good, helping nature, etc. At this level, the feeling of Love is extended both horizontally and vertically. These individuals have mostly transcended their self and are more interested in the greater good of all!]

I often wondered why people are not interested in knowing more about our past or why things are not as good as they should be. Those of us who always want to learn and know more are considered "weird" by family and friends, as much as they love us. We feel so frustrated not being able to share the new things we are finding out. It's as if we are speaking a foreign language and the gap is increasing, but this is also happening because our frequencies are changing.

I keep asking myself, how can I believe that what I have been learning is true? How do I use my critical thinking ability and not take everything I read or hear as gospel? I hope I learnt my lesson with the JWs. I wanted to see a paradise Earth so much that I accepted all the other teachings without doing any in-depth research – the Bible was the authority and everyone else in the organisation around me knew much more than I did, so I thought.

One of my daughters and a friend told me they don't believe anything unless they see it with their own eyes. Another friend says she relies on her faith and personal experiences. All viewpoints are valid and if I wasn't seeing the picture that is forming, and had my personal experiences too, I wouldn't have the faith that my hope for a better world is not just a case of wishful thinking and New Age ideas.

To understand what is taking place today, we need to understand the nature of the recurring political-religious cycles called [4]"Great Awakenings." Each lasting about 100 years, Great Awakenings consists of three phases, each about a generation long. These cycles overlap, the end of one cycle coinciding with the beginning of the next.

A cycle begins with a phase of religious revival, propelled by the tendency of new technological advances to outpace the human capacity to cope with the ethical and practical complexities that those new technologies entail.

There are four types[7] of awakenings:

- First Great Awakening, 1730-1830 CE
- Second Great Awakening, 1800-1920 CE
- Third Great Awakening, 1890 CE-?
- Fourth, and Current, Great Awakening, 1960 CE-?

There are many like me who, although not Jehovah's Witnesses, have the hope that there will one day be a Golden Age on Earth again, but first the nefarious beings and the humans who align with them must be exposed. And this is where the Starseeds come in.

We are told that their souls have incarnated on Earth to help with what is called "The Great Awakening" to raise our consciousness. The first stage of the disclosure will be to gain knowledge about the UFOs and ETs that have been involved with Earth for eons and to this day.

Many military whistleblowers have been coming forward daily at the time of my writing this in 2023, but very little has been reported in the media 'so as not to scare the public'. The main source of disclosure will be, therefore, from members of the public.

2 - EARLY CIVILISATIONS, RELIGIONS & PHILOSOPHIES

Once you eliminate the impossible, whatever remains, no matter how improbable, must be the truth

Arthur Conan Doyle

An avid reader at the age of eleven, I visited my local library each week to borrow books on etiquette, psychology, myths, fairy tales, historical novels, and religion using all my family's library cards. I remember one week coming home with sixteen books - how I managed to carry them all, I forget.

The JWs' book, **Mankind's Search for God**, went back only about 6,000 years to Ancient Babylon where all religions were supposed to have originated. Looking at previous civilisations, we can understand how much has changed from the beginning of life on Earth to our lives today.

As a Witness, I learnt about seven different world powers, Egypt, Assyria, Medo-Persia, Greece, Rome, and Anglo-America as foretold in the book of Daniel, chapters 2 & 7.

Since then, I've learnt of many more civilisations including those of Lemuria and Atlantis already mentioned in Chapter 1.

WORLD POWERS

According to Joshua Baron's book, Great Power Peace and American Primacy (published in 2014), China, France, Russia, Germany, Japan, the UK and the USA were the great powers. In 2020, Business Insider ranked the USA, Russia, and China as the world's most powerful countries. However, if you're looking for inspiration for your upcoming travels and like the idea of travelling to a place where happiness is in ample supply, then according to the 2024 WORLD HAPPINESS REPORT here are the 30 happiest countries in the world.

1	FINLAND	16	CANADA
2	DENMARK	17	CZECHIA
3	ICELAND	18	IRELAND
4	SWEDEN	19	UNITED KINGDOM
5	ISRAEL	20	LITHUANIA
6	NETHERLANDS	21	UNITED ARAB EMIRATES
7	NORWAY	22	SLOVENIA
8	LUXEMBOURG	23	GERMANY
9	SWITZERLAND	24	UNITED STATES
10	AUSTRALIA	25	URUGUAY
11	COSTA RICA	26	MEXICO
12	NEW ZEALAND	27	SAUDI ARABIA
13	AUSTRIA	28	FRANCE
14	KUWAIT	29	SINGAPORE
15	BELGIUM	30	KOSOVO

EARLY CIVILISATIONS

Then I came across another book, **The Stage of Time** by Matthew LaCroix. He says on pages 6-11, under the heading, Mysteries of Ancient History:

[... Across the Earth, ancient ruins and megalithic structures such as Sacsayhuaman in Peru, the Temple of Jupiter in Lebanon, or Gobekli Tepe in Turkey... has been radiocarbon dated to be over 11,000 years old..... This evidence greatly contradicts what society has been taught about the timeline of human history and helps to paint a far different picture of our past.... The most important question is - why isn't this important information part of our education system?'

P.7... One of the most significant of these deceptions revolves around the incorrect information that's been provided by many of the mainstream archaeologists about the true age and purpose of the pyramids of Giza, Egypt. We're told by many of these "experts" that the largest structures on Earth were built to honour the great pharaohs of Egypt. This lie is generally accepted by the majority of society, who is often too busy to take the time to research alternate theories for themselves. Yet today, not one pharaoh has ever been found in the pyramids of Giza, or in most of the other pyramids located around the world.'

P.11... Furthermore, the particular way that society perceives evolution, human origins, and their purpose in the universe, has been manipulated and conditioned for so long, that most have become unbalanced and ignorant of what the truth is.]

I found some interesting information on the *(Ancient Civilizations Timeline: The Complete List from Aboriginals to Incans | History Cooperative)* in an article by Jana Louise Smit:

CIVILISATION	TIME PERIOD
1. Australian Aboriginals	50,000BCE – present
2. The Çatalhöyük Settlement	7,500 – 5,700 CE
3. Ain Ghazal	7,200 – 5,000 BCE
4. The Jiahu Culture	7,000 – 5,700 CE
5. The Indus Valley Civilization	2,600 – 1,900 BCE
6. The Mesopotamian Civilization	6,500 – 539 BCE
7. The Danubian Culture, or Linearbandkeramik Culture	5,500 – 3,500 BCE
8. The Norte Chico Civilization	3,000 – 1,800 BCE
9. The Ancient Egyptian Civilization	3,150 BCE – 30C
10 The Ancient Greek Civilization	2,700 – 479 BCE
11 The Mayan Civilisation	2,600 – 900 CE
12 The Indus Valley Civilisation	2,600 – 1,900 BCE
13 The Chinese Civilization	1,600 – 1,046 BCE
14 The Roman Civilization	753 BCE – 476 CE
15 The Persian Civilization	550 – 331 BCE
16 The Aztec Civilization	1,325 –1,521 CE
17 The Incan Civilization	1,438 – 1,532 CE

The beliefs of ancient civilisations are dismissed as being pagan and therefore, not to be believed, so this is where we miss out on what has been termed paleo contact", also known as "ancient astronaut" narratives with the idea that extraterrestrials or "ancient astronauts" visited Earth and influenced early human culture.

By delving into the origins of different religions, especially the Abrahamic ones, we can find the common thread. We find they had the same basic beliefs such as the existence of creator beings, the soul and reincarnation.

Some say that we will never know the complete truth until we die. However, I'm convinced that the truth has always been right in front of us and that we've had our minds blinded so that we've been unable to discern truth from lies but read on and see what you think.

1. AUSTRALIAN ABORIGINES

Geological research shows that these people were around as long as 80,000 – 65,000 years ago and dated the formative volcanic explosions described by Aboriginal myth tellers as having occurred more than 10,000 years ago. The stories of their creation are the basis of Aboriginal lore that all living things were either the ancestors themselves or were made by the ancestors. That is, a river may be an ancestor and may also be a creation snake.

[8]**The Dreamtime** is the period in which life was created according to Aboriginal culture. Dreaming is the word used to explain how life came to be; it is the stories and beliefs behind creation by spiritual beings/ancestors. The Dreaming explains how things came to be – why a rock is in a certain place or a particular got their tails, also the rules and ways of being in Aboriginal culture.

Dreaming stories explain these beliefs, such as the lesson not to hurt animals, who one should marry and bear children with (according to the Aboriginal skin system), whom one should not talk to (according to the Aboriginal skin system), how one should show respect in another's country, how one should welcome strangers to your own country. It dictates how one should behave in certain circumstances. Like other religions,

Aborigines had gods who created people and the surrounding environment during a particular creation period at the beginning of time. They believe that many animals and plants are interchangeable with human life through the reincarnation of the spirit or soul and that this relates to the Creation Period when these animals and plants were once people. Based on their primary role, deities fall into three main categories, and any one deity may belong to one, two or all three of these categories, Creation Beings, Ancestral Beings and Totemic Beings.

THE BUNYIP[9]

In July 1845, The Geelong Advertiser announced the discovery of fossils found near Geelong, under the headline **"Wonderful Discovery of a new Animal"** and was a continuation of a story on 'fossil remains' from the previous issue.

> *[It was identified by a local man as the Bunyip, represented with the characteristics of a bird and of an alligator. Its head resembled an emu with a long bill, at the extremity of which is a transverse projection on each side, with serrated edges like*

the bone of the stingray. Its body and legs partake of the nature of the alligator, the hind legs thick and strong, and the forelegs much longer, but still of great strength. The extremities were furnished with long claws, but the aborigines say its usual method of killing its prey is by hugging it to death. When in the water it swims like a frog, and when on shore it walks on its hind legs with its head erect, in which position it measures twelve or thirteen feet in height. More accounts were made in 1846 and 1852, 1857 about similar creatures.]

Serpent mythology around the world had a common origin as I hope to show; especially the inference that "the Serpent" was evil, when the original belief was it represented wisdom

PHILOSOPHY

Aboriginal society has operated on a core set of values and beliefs that are complex. They form the basis for religious practice and ways of being and doing. This philosophy constitutes a set of "truths" for people that define their knowledge, reality and cultural practices was very "mixed up" and not at all like it is in modern times and this is reflected in their original religious beliefs.

2. THE ÇATALHÖYÜK SETTLEMENT

James Mellaart first excavated this site in 1958, and he continued between 1961 and 1965. It's located near the modern city of Konya, south-central Turkey. It was inhabited 9,000 years ago by up to 8,000 people in the town that overlooked the Konya Plain approx.

140 km from the twin-coned volcano of Mount Hasan in southern Anatolia. This society has never been static, but it has been essentially non-materialistic and extremely caring of the environment.

There were large numbers of buildings clustered together with their inhabitants living in mud brick houses in an aggregate structure. The rooftops were effectively streets as no footpaths or streets were used between the dwellings.

Most of these streets were accessed by holes in the ceiling and doors on the side of the houses, with upper levels reached by ladders and stairs. Each home had extensive art and adornments, such as bull horns, leopard sculptures and plastered skulls. Some homes more elaborately decorated than others and occupied the longest amount of time, had contained the most burials.

There were no public plazas, temples, or other administrative buildings. There was no evidence of any centralized institutions to "govern" thousands of people. They were not subservient to a ruler; there were no police and no courts. This was not a band of hunter-gatherers. It was a small-scale, independent society that managed completely by themselves.

PHILOSOPHY

The community had a fascinating way of relating to death. It's not known if there were any philosophers in Çatalhöyük, but their way of thinking was reflected in how they lived in a period of pre-religion or organised religion. We can be more confident that these people knew stories that explained the world they inhabited. See also

www.templeton.org/news/catalhoyuk-a-city-of-gardeners-hippies-and-home-decorators-circa-7000-bc'

3. AIN GHAZAL

Gary Rollefson, an American anthropologist led the archaeological work at １０Ain Ghazal. The archaeological site is near Amman, Jordan and showed a Pre-pottery Neolithic settlement that was active from about 7,250-5,000 BCE. It is one of the largest early villages known in the Near East. In the earlier level, there were small ceramic figurines of both animals and people that seem to have been used as personal or familial ritual figures.

The animal figures are of horned animals and the front part of the animal is the most clearly modelled. They give the impression of dynamic force. Some animal figures have been stabbed in their vital parts. These figures were buried in the houses. Ritual buildings housed large figurines or statues. Ain Ghazal people buried some of their dead beneath the floors of their houses, with figurines. Others were buried outside in the surrounding terrain.

There is evidence of class in the way the dead were treated. Often the head was later retrieved, and the skull was buried in a separate shallow pit beneath the house floor. After the flesh had disintegrated, some of the skulls were disinterred and decorated. This was either a form of respect or so that they could impart their power to the house and the people in it.

Adult burials were found in trash pits in a variety of postures and always with the skull present. They may have been the newcomers as a lower class indicating that not every deceased was ceremoniously put to rest

> *[A typical burial for non-infants was below the floor of a house or in a courtyard, deposited in a flexed position with the skull removed after the initial burial. Burials seem to have taken place approximately every 15–20 years, indicating a rate of one burial per generation, though gender and age were not constant in this practice. Caches of skulls disarticulated from their bodies were found intentionally buried in groups, oriented in the same direction (Rollefson and Kafafi: fig. 16).*
>
> *Of the fourteen skulls excavated from the site, many were found to have been buried beneath the floors of domestic structures...*
>
> *Many of the buried skulls were treated with plaster which was molded into soft and naturalistic facial features... Some of the skulls were also painted. This practice may point towards the presence of an ancestor cult, a hero worshipper cult, enemy trophies, or apotropaic function...]*

PHILOSOPHY

From their burial rites, one can get an idea of how they thought about life and death. These rites were very much like those practised in Çatalhöyük.

Differences in these burials may suggest varied treatment and reverence of individuals, and therefore the practice of making social distinctions.

4. THE JIAHU CULTURE

Jiahu was discovered by Zhu Zhi in 1962, but extensive excavation of the site did not occur until the 1980s. This site was of a Neolithic settlement based in the central plain of ancient China, near the Yellow River. It is located between the floodplains of the Ni River to the north, and the Sha River to the south, 22 km north of the modern city of Wuyang, Henan Province. The Jiahu culture is the first peak of Chinese prehistoric culture, and these ruins are an important part of tracing the origins of Chinese civilization.

> *www.globaltimes.cn/page/202303/1286735.shtml* states:
>
> *[More than 9,000 years ago, a group of people lived in a prehistoric settlement located in what is today a village in Wu-yang County, Central China's Henan Province. These people were not only hunters, fishermen and artisans, but also excellent musicians who created a splendid Neolithic culture.*
>
> *They constructed houses, cultivated rice, domesticated livestock, and made pottery wares and bone flutes, building a homeland of idyllic beauty full of the fragrance of rice and the melodious sound of music.*

While their songs may no longer be heard, the relics they left behind made the Jiahu ruins one of the 100 major Chinese national archaeological discoveries of the 20th century...Pictograms and signs carved on tortoise shells, were also uncovered at the ruins. In later Chinese culture dating to around 3,500 BC, shells were used as a form of divination.

They were subjected to intense heat, and the cracks that formed were read as omens. Inscriptions in Chinese characters were then carved as permanent marks on the surface of the shell. The evidence of shell pictograms may indicate that this tradition has much deeper roots than previously thought.]

PHILOSOPHY

The Jiahu people were not warlike in nature but could defend themselves if the need arose. During the excavations, researchers found that the spiritual and cultural life of the Jiahu people was particularly advanced, especially when it came to rituals and music. Archaeologists believe that the Peiligang culture was egalitarian, with little political organization. I could find nothing else in their philosophy.

5. THE INDUS VALLEY CIVILIZATION

This civilisation alongside ancient Egypt and Mesopotamia, were early civilisations of the Near East and South Asia, and of the three, the most widespread. It lasted from c. 3,300-1,900 BCE. Its sites span an area from much of Pakistan to northeast Afghanistan, and northwestern India.

The cities of the ancient Indus were noted for their urban planning, baked brick houses, elaborate drainage systems, water supply systems, clusters of large non-residential buildings, and techniques of handicraft and metallurgy.

METALLURGY

The Harappans evolved some new techniques in metallurgy and produced copper, bronze, lead, and tin. A touchstone bearing gold streaks was found in Banawali, which was probably used for testing the purity of gold (such a technique is still used in some parts of India).

RELIGION OF THE INDUS VALLEY CIVILISATIONS

John Marshall, in 1931 identified the deification or veneration of animals and plants; a symbolic representation of the phallus (linga) and vulva (yoni); and use of baths and water in religious practice as worship objects of a Great Male God and a Mother Goddess. Terracotta statuettes have been identified as figurines of a "mother goddess" and goddess of fertility.

The seal showing an animal depicted as part bull, part zebra with a majestic horn, found at one site has been a source of speculation. Another seal shows a seated figure with a horned headdress, surrounded by animals was identified as an early form of the Hindu god Shiva (or Rudra regarded as a lord of animals, and often depicted as having three eyes.

PHILOSOPHY

The Indus Valley Civilisations were known for using cosmetics, hair care products, etc. made from Ayurvedic beauty recipies based on herbs and without side effects. *(www.indusvalleyuk.com)*

6. THE MESOPOTAMIAN CIVILIZATION

The word Mesopotamia means "between rivers" in Greek. Mesopotamia (modern-day Iraq and Kuwait) is generally considered the cradle of civilization. Around 10,000 BCE, Ancient Sumer was the first of the ancient Mesopotamian civilizations to develop the Tigris-Euphrates River system. The name comes from Akkadian, the language of the north of Mesopotamia, and means "land of the civilized kings". The people of the ancient civilizations of Sumer, Assyria, and Babylonia are credited with influencing mathematics and astronomy.

THE UBAIDIANS

Although never mentioned by the Sumerians themselves, the Ubaidians are assumed by modern-day scholars to have been the first civilizing force in Sumer. They were prehistoric people living in the region before the Sumerians and it is thought they evolved from the Samarra culture of northern Mesopotamia. They had drained the marshes for agriculture, developed trade, and established industries, including weaving, leatherwork, metalwork, masonry and pottery.

RULERS OF MESOPOTAMIA

Kings ruled in the name of a god and were owners of the property of the state. Priests used to influence administrative affairs. Governors were appointed to run the provincial government.

URUK

Uruk was one of the most important cities (at one time, the most important) in Ancient Mesopotamia. At its peak, around 2800 BCE, Uruk was most likely the largest city in the world.

> *www.worldhistory.org/uruk* explains:
>
> *[... According to the Sumerian King List, it was founded by King Enmerkar c. 4500 BCE. Uruk is best known as the birthplace of writing c. 3200 BCE as well as for its architecture and other cultural innovations. This was a thriving trading hub that boasted six miles of defensive walls and a population of between 40,000 and 80,000.]*

AKKADIAN EMPIRE

In Chapter 4, I show King Enmarkar's aliases, one of which was Sargon (although some think it was his grandson, Naram-Sin). He was the first monarch of the Akkadian Empire which saw the development of writing and the formation of the first cities and states.

This development ultimately led to the unification of much of Mesopotamia. The Sumerian Ziggurat of Ur was in one of the first great cities of ancient Mesopotamia. It was here that the first written languages appeared in the form of Cuneiform writing. In this region, some of the most important inventions occurred that would shape mankind such as the wheel, the idea of minutes, hours and seconds, and many other aspects of modern daily life.

THE ANUNNAKI

When I first started writing this book, I learnt about the Anunnaki, a class of gods within the ancient Mesopotamian pantheon.

> www.britannica.com/topic/Anunnaki *explains:*
>
> *[...The precise meaning of the term ("princely seed" in Sumerian) remains ill-defined, as the number of these gods, their names, and their functions vary according to the limited historical texts scholars have recovered. Among the gods named in some texts are members of the Anunnaki - Enlil, Ea (Enki), Ninhursag, Inanna (Nanna), Shamash (Utu), and Ishtar (Inanna).*
>
> *Enlil, the god of air who separated heaven and Earth, is generally regarded as the most prominent of these. The ancient Hittites and Hurrians, whose mythologies refer to a set of "former gods" banished to the netherworld by a newer generation, eventually identified the former gods with the Anunnaki. In treaties they were invoked as witnesses to ensure that oaths were kept. The Anunnaki had several functions in*

Mesopotamian mythology. The Sumerian myth of Enki and the World Order suggests that one of their main functions in early mythology was to decide the fates of human beings. They were initially associated with the heavens, but over time both literary and administrative texts reflected an increased role for the Anunnaki in Earthly affairs.

In the Babylonian creation epic, the Enuma Elish, the chief Babylonian god Marduk has authority over some 600 Anunnaki gods. He directs 300 of these gods to reside in the heavens and 300 to reside on Earth.]

THE SUMERIANS

The origins of the Sumerians are unclear, but many scholars have suggested that they may have arrived from the south. Others suggested that they descended from the mountains of the northeast. This civilization first took form in Uruk around 4,000 BCE, continuing into the Jemdet Nasr and Early Dynastic periods. The Sumerian writing system revolutionised the way humans communicate and has influenced the world dramatically. The Sumerians also paved the way for the formation of religions.

> ***SUMARIAN - NAMMU (NAMMA) NAMMU*** *was the primeval Sumerian mother goddess who gave birth to the gods and created humanity.*
> ***EGYPTIAN** - Isfet*
> ***GREEK** - Chaos is depicted as an empty void*
> ***ROMAN** - Khaos*
> ***BIBLICAL** – The Spirit of God*

SUMERIAN– AN (ANU) *was the ancient Sumerian god of the heavens. He was the ancestor of all the other major deities and the original patron deity of Uruk and the son and consort of Nammu.*
EGYPTIAN *– Nu*
GREEK *– Uranus*
ROMAN *– Caelus*
BIBLICAL *- El*

SUMERIAN - ENLIL *was the god of air, wind, and storm and the chief god of the Sumerian pantheon. He was also the patron deity of the city of Nippur. His primary consort was Ninlil, the goddess of the south wind who His primary consort was Ninlil, the goddess of the south wind who was one of the patron deities of Nippur and was believed to reside in the same temple as Enlil.*
EGYPTIAN *- Amun-Ra, Set*
GREEK *- Zeus*
ROMAN *– Jupiter*
BIBLICAL *- Yahweh, Jehovah, El–Shaddai*

You can see that these "gods" had their names changed by whichever civilisation was in power. The big question is, did they ever leave Earth? At the time of writing this, I'm not sure if they retained the same body or whether they reincarnated into another one or took on another form.

During this period of my research, I ended up creating Excel sheets of all the different gods of the world and how they related to the original ones. Once complete, I will make it available.

7. THE DANUBIAN CULTURE OR LINEARBANDKERAMIK CULTURE

It's estimated that this highly sophisticated, prehistoric Danubian culture began around 7,800 – 7,500 years ago. It lasted more than a thousand years, after which most settlements were destroyed and abandoned. Along the banks of the Danube River was once the largest civilisation in Europe, known as the Vinča culture but has been largely forgotten today. It existed long before others appeared in Mesopotamia or Egypt, and many of its innovations, writing, farming and copper metallurgy, are some of the earliest examples of technological advancements, not just in Europe, but in the world.

> *[They developed the first known cereal agriculture, especially of wheat, oat and barley. In addition to farming, villagers relied on hunting, fishing and foraging for sources of food. Weaving textiles were generally common in this culture, with the basic material probably flax, though perhaps nettle or wool was also used.*
>
> *Small weights found at some excavation sites give evidence that vertical loom weaving was used, where small weights – made of clay and marked with signs or a number – were placed at the ends to weigh down threads. Many female figurines, figures of males and animals, as well as vases, amulets and various altars were found in the excavations. Strange hybrid figurines, such as female statuettes with bird faces, were typical of the Vinča culture.*

What is still not understood about the Vinča is why the culture vanished nearly 6,200 years ago. One reason may have been the beginning of the Indo-European migration of the Kurgan people from the eastern steppes to the west. Some researchers believe that much of that knowledge shifted to Greece and supported the development of Greek culture.

Equally puzzling is how it was possible for such a sophisticated culture to develop isolated in the Danube region. Most likely, the skills developed by the Vinča, and other Danube cultures were based on existing knowledge, perhaps with some influence coming from Anatolia or further east.]

It seems that wherever the influence came from, the innovations of the Vinča culture – in writing, farming, metallurgy – were phenomenal for this Old European Danube Civilisation.

8. THE NORTE CHICO CIVILIZATION

A city called Huaricanga was founded in the fertile Fortaleza Valley on the north central coast of Peru, nearly 1,000 years before the first pyramids were raised in Egypt, civilization flourished for 1,300 years during which time it expanded into the nearby Pativilca and Supe valleys.

The inhabitants developed trading routes, extensive fishing operations and grew cotton to spin into textiles and fishing nets. They also managed to create some of the oldest pyramids in the world and it seems to have been a highly collaborative and motivated culture with dense, sophisticated settlements. In Caral, an elaborate complex of temples, an Amphitheatre, three sunken, circular plazas and residential buildings span 370 acres were discovered.

www.arthistoryproject.com/timeline/prehistory/norte-chico-civilization states:

> *[Evidence regarding the Norte Chico religion is limited. An image of the Staff God, a leering, cartoon-like figure, with a hood and fangs, has been found on a gourd dated to 2250 BCE. The Staff God is a major deity of later Andean cultures and suggests the find points to worship of common symbols of gods...This ancient civilization takes us back to the formation of one of the oldest organized human societies. The lack of written records means that this is part of the pre-historical period.]*

It is thought by some that the pyramids in this area were built long before this civilisation and were part of Atlantis.

9. THE ANCIENT EGYPTIAN CIVILISATION

Several names were used for Egypt. A popular ancient name for Egypt was "Kemet," which means the "black land." Scholars generally believe that this name is derived from the fertile soil that was left over when the Nile flood receded in August. They were ruled by kings and queens called pharaohs. Many monuments, objects and artifacts have been recovered from archaeological sites, covered with hieroglyphs that have only recently been deciphered. The picture that emerges is of a culture with few equals in the beauty of its art, the accomplishment of its architecture or the richness of its religious traditions.

The ancient Egyptians were experts at farming and construction because they were very inventive. They invented a solar calendar (a calendar based on the sun) and a writing system called hieroglyphs. Egypt's climate was much wetter in prehistoric times than it is today, and some areas that are now barren desert were once fertile.

The ancient Egyptian civilisation began after this set period ended around 5,000 years ago, the deserts of Egypt have remained how they are now. One famous archaeological site where this can be seen is in the rock art at the "cave of swimmers," as it is called today on the Gilf Kebir plateau in southwest Egypt. The cave is now surrounded by miles of barren desert; however, it has rock art showing what some scholars interpret as people swimming.

The fact that the rock art is between 6-9,000 years old, shows that part of Egypt may well have been part of Atlantis. Religion was an important part of their civilisation. They worshipped over 2,000 gods and goddesses. Formal religious practices centred on the pharaoh, or ruler, of Egypt, who was believed to be divine, and acted as intermediary between the people and the gods. His role was to sustain the gods so that they could maintain order in the universe.

The religion of Ancient Egypt lasted for more than 3,000 years, and there were a multitude of deities, who were believed to reside within and control the forces of nature. They also believed in a never-ending afterlife.

They thought it was more important than their life on Earth, so they spent a lot of time planning for their death. The Egyptian universe centred on Ma'at, which has several meanings in English, including truth, justice and order. It was fixed and eternal; without it, the world would fall apart.

DJEHUTI/THOTH– A moon god and patron deity of Hermopolis. He had many roles in Egyptian mythology and served as a scribe of the gods, credited with the invention of writing and Egyptian hieroglyphs. He is also known as the writer of the Emerald Tablets as 'Thoth the Atlantean' (aka Enoch, Hermes/Hermes Trismegistus, Mercury and Ningishzidda, the son of Enki, and some think he was also Moses/Akhenaten, Quetzalcoatl (Mayan), a feathered serpent god).

The burial of Tutankhamun (c 1,400 BCE) in which his penis was mummified, is but one example of how important fertility was in the rituals and beliefs of the ancient Egyptians. During the rule of Akhenaton (aka Moses – see Chapter 4), his wife Nefertiti played an important political and religious role in the monotheistic cult of the sun god Aten (c.1,353–1,336 BCE).

10. THE ANCIENT GREEK CIVILIZATION

Ancient Greece was a civilization spanning over 1,400 years. After the fall of the Mycenaean civilization around (1,200 BCE), Greece entered the Dark Ages, and any advances in literacy and writing were lost. Three centuries later, in c 800 BCE, Greece started emerging from the Dark Ages, adopting and later modifying the Phoenician alphabet, thus creating the Greek alphabet.

Greece was divided in small communities, following the geographical pattern of the region. Most had overthrown their hereditary kings, or basileus, and were ruled by a small number of wealthy aristocrats. These people monopolized political power. (For example, they refused to let ordinary people serve on councils or assemblies.)

These small communities were self-sufficient and were called polis or city-states which became the defining feature of Greek political life for hundreds of years. During this time there were advances in art, poetry and technology. They also monopolized the best farmland, and some even claimed to be descended from the Greek gods.

> *["The poor with their wives and children were enslaved to the rich and had no political rights," Aristotle said, "There was conflict between the nobles and the people for a long time". In the 7th century BCE, after the rise of the mercantile class, considerable tension was created among those*

city-states, regularly resulting in conflict and war. The social classes also created tension, particularly due to the increasing population and shortage of land.]

THE CONFLICT BETWEEN SPARTA AND ATHENS

Sparta, also known as Lacedaemon, was an ancient Greek city-state. It was a warrior society, located primarily in a region of southern Greece called Laconia, with a culture that was centred on loyalty to the state and military service. Sparta's population consisted of three main groups: the Spartans (or Spartiates) who were full citizens; the Helots, or serfs/slaves; and the Perioeci whose name means "dwellers-around," worked as craftsmen and traders, and made weapons for the Spartans who were neither slaves nor citizens.

SPARTAN WOMEN

Although Spartan women were not active in the military, they were educated and enjoyed more status and freedom than other Greek women.

[Spartan women had a reputation for being independent-minded and enjoyed more freedoms and power than their counterparts throughout ancient Greece. While they played no role in the military, female Spartans often received a formal education, although separate from boys and not at boarding schools. In part to attract mates, females engaged in athletic competitions, including javelin-throwing and wrestling and

they also sang and danced competitively. As adults, Spartan women were allowed to own and manage property. Additionally, they were typically unencumbered by domestic responsibilities such as cooking, cleaning and making clothing, tasks which were handled by the Helots.]

SPARTAN MEN

All healthy male Spartan citizens participated in the compulsory state-sponsored education system, the Agoge, which emphasized obedience, endurance, courage and self-control. Spartan men devoted their lives to military service and lived communally well into adulthood. A Spartan was taught that loyalty to the state came before everything else, including one's family.

THE HELOTS (CAPTIVES)

They were fellow Greeks, originally from Laconia and Messenia, who had been conquered by the Spartans and turned into slaves.

[The Spartans' way of life would not have been possible without the Helots, who handled all day-to-day tasks and unskilled labour required to keep society functioning: They were farmers, domestic servants, nurses and military attendants. Spartans, who were outnumbered by the Helots, often treated them brutally and oppressively to prevent uprisings. Spartans would humiliate the Helots by doing such things as forcing them to get debilitating drunk on wine and then make fools of themselves in public. This practice was also

intended to demonstrate to young people how an adult Spartan should never act, as self-control was a prized trait. Methods of mistreatment could be far more extreme: Spartans were allowed to kill Helots for being too smart or too fit, among other reasons.]

ATHENS

In the late 7th century, because of lack of food and land a series of laws to quench the conflict were created, but in vain. A few years later though, Solon managed to improve the living conditions of the poor, but at the same time establish the roots of aristocracy in power. after a turbulent period, tyranny was overthrown, and democracy was born.

This new type of government resulted in Athens entering a period of cultural and social renaissance, also known as the Golden Age. The ancient Greeks also contributed to developments in art and architecture through the numerous sculptures and temples they constructed—the buildings of the Athenian Acropolis, for example—to memorialize their deities.

Scientists and mathematicians made progress too: Anaximandros devised a theory of gravity; Xenophanes wrote about his discovery of fossils and Pythagoras discovered his famous Theorem. The first Olympic Games were held in 776 BCE. Alexander died in 323 BCE. Under the leadership of Darius I, the Persians invaded Greece multiple times, failing to subjugate the region. This ended with the rise of Macedonia, led by Philip II, who unified the region under his rule. His son, Alexander the Great, managed to decimate the troops of Darius III and create a glorious Greek Empire that spread to India. Greek religion is not the same as Greek mythology. The Religious-minded Greeks had no word for religion itself; the nearest terms were eusebeia ("piety") and threskeia (cult). It is characterized by two traits: a belief in a multitude of humanlike gods under one supreme god and an absence of dogma.

11. THE MAYAN CIVILISATION

Archaeologists prefer to use the term "Maya civilization" rather than the more common "Mayan civilization," leaving "Mayan" to refer to the language. In general, researchers tend to split the Maya into the Highland and Lowland Maya. Mesoamerican archaeology is broken up into general sections. They occupied the Central American continent, including the southern parts of Mexico, Belize, Guatemala, El Salvador, and Honduras, an area of about 150,000 square miles.

The oldest were:

- **ARCHAIC BEFORE 2500 BCE:** Hunting and gathering lifestyle.

- **EARLY FORMATIVE 2500–1000 BCE**: First beans and maize agriculture, and people live in isolated farmsteads and hamlets.

- **MIDDLE FORMATIVE 1000–400 BCE:** First monumental architecture, first villages;

people switched to full-time agriculture; there is evidence for contacts with the Olmec culture, and at Nakbe, the first evidence of social ranking, beginning about 600–400 BCE.

THE MAYA CREATION MYTH

Before explaining the Maya creation myths, it is important to understand the difference between the two sources that the Maya creation stories have been found in. These sources include the **Popol Vuh** and the **Books of Chilam Balam**.

The most famous and influential books include the books of **Chumayel, Tizimin, Mani, Kaua, Ixil, Tusik** and **Codex Pérez**. The books are written by a Jaguar priest, a literal translation for Chilam Balam. These books date to colonial Spanish times, circa 1500s CE, and there is a clear influence of Spanish colonialism on the creation stories of the Chilam Balam.

For the Maya, the creation of the Earth is said to have been a deed of Huracan, the wind and sky god. Animals and plants were extant before humans. The gods were not satisfied with only the animals because they could not speak to honour them, so humans were made to honour the gods' space for any beings or vegetation to grow. Mayan mythology says that a Great Flood was sent to Earth which ravaged all land and eliminated the second generation of Gods. Huracán caused this Great flood and afterwards, when the second generation had perished, he invoked the Earth to rise.

Therefore, I think Huracan was also another name for Enlil because they had the same characteristics.

THE MANY EPOCHS OF THE MAYA

According to Maya texts there have been three creations. Two of these creations have ended or, in other words, the creatures have been destroyed. There are many variations of the three creations, some of which were influenced by Christianity; but the basic events of the creations were detailed from the Popol Vuh of the highland Maya.

> *[BUILT FROM MUD: The first creation saw the people who were made of mud. The mud people were not the most productive as many were not able to think in the capacity that modern-day humans do and, according to Maya sacred texts, these men "spoke but had no mind." They could not move because they were made of mud, and they also were not technically mortal. The gods were not happy with their first creation, so they destroyed the mud people with water.*
>
> **BUILT FROM WOOD**: *For the second creation, the deities made men from wood and women from reeds. These people could function as humans do but had no souls and did not honour the gods. They were also immortal. When they died, they only remained dead for three days and would rise from the dead. The destruction of the tree men and reed women was caused by an inundation of boiling hot water. The few who may have survived this apocalypse are thought to have become the monkeys that exist today.*

BUILT FROM MAIZE*: The third creation saw the birth of modern-day humans. These humans are made of white and yellow maize dough and the blood of the gods. The first humans were four men and four women. These men and women were deemed too wise by the gods.]*

The Maya deities believed these intelligent humans were a threat to their authority and almost destroyed them as well. However, the Heart of Heaven (also known as Huracán, but in the creation story he is the Heart of Heaven, Heart of Earth, or Heart of Sky) clouded their minds and eyes so that they would become less wise. The different Maya groups believed in a variety of creation myths.

The most important concept to understand about Maya religious belief is that time and the creation of humans are thought to be cyclical. The gods destroyed the different versions of "humans" because they either could not or would not worship their creators.

Belief in the end of humanity wasn't the end of the world; it was the end of an era and, perhaps, the beginning of a new epoch of the gods. This is a crucial consideration for the gods. They could not afford to have creations which were unworthy and incapable of providing sustenance to the gods.

[Typically, Maya gods are fluid and have diverse personalities. This sometimes makes it difficult to distinguish one god from another. However, it may be simpler to keep in mind that although the Maya deities are numerous, the most

consequential gods sometimes morph with the less notable gods and share characteristics of both deities...

The multiplicities of the deities' personalities are furthered by their appearance. Many gods are an amalgamation of a human and a particular animal. They are also associated with different cardinal directions and an individual god's importance can vary depending on historical context. This fluidity is precisely why scholars refer to some Maya deities with the letters of the Latin alphabet.]

There is also so much more information on *www.worldhistory.org/Maya_Religion* covering The Hero Twins, Heaven, Hell, & The Cardinal directions, Maya Rituals, Bloodletting, Human Sacrifice, Marriage and Divorce, Dance.

12. THE INDUS VALLEY CIVILISATION

This was a Bronze Age civilisation (3,300–1,300 BCE) mainly in the northwestern regions of South Asia, (today northeast Afghanistan to Pakistan and northwest India). Excavation of Harappan sites has been ongoing since 1920, with important breakthroughs occurring as recently as 1999. Over 1,056 cities and settlements were found, of which 96 have been excavated, mainly in the general region of Hakra Rivers and tributaries.

Along with ancient Egypt and Mesopotamia, it was one of three early civilisations of the Old World, and of the three, the most widespread. It flourished in the basins of the Indus River, which flows through the length of Pakistan, and along a system of perennial, mostly monsoon-fed, rivers that once coursed in the vicinity of the seasonal Ghaggar-Hakra River in northwest India and eastern Pakistan.

www.worldhistory.org/article/230/religious-developments-in-ancient-india states:

[It was widely suggested that the Harappan people worshipped a mother goddess symbolizing fertility. A few Indus Valley seals displayed swastika signs which were there in many religions, especially in Indian religions such as Hinduism, Buddhism and Jainism.

The earliest evidence for elements of Hinduism is before and during the early Harappan period. Phallic symbols close to the Hindu Shiva lingam were located in the Harappan ruins... The people of the Indus Valley also appear to have worshipped a male god......Hermes in Greek is the muted term for Brahma. The Chinese syllable fan is the well-known phrasing of Brahma. Hence, both O-fan-cha and Hermetalia is a direct wording of Bambhra-ka-thul or Brahma-sthal.

From all these discussions, it seemed certain that what Hwen Tsang visited was the city of Mohenjo-daro and its real name was Brahma-sthal or Brahmanabad. The meaning of the name Mohenjo-daro is 'Heap of the Dead'. Such a name seems peculiar for a prosperous city like this.]

THE SWASTIKA

In Jainism and Buddhism, the Swastika is considered as a powerful good luck symbol. Rangolis at festivals like Diwali generally have Swastika to attract Laxmiji and Ganesha for wealth, health and prosperity. The earliest sure use of swastika motifs in the archaeological record goes to the Neolithic epoch.

> *www.encyclopedia.ushmm.org/content/en/article/history-of-the-swastika* states:
>
> [The swastika is an ancient symbol that was used in many different cultures for at least 5,000 years before Adolf Hitler made it the centerpiece of the Nazi flag. Its present-day use by certain extremist groups promotes hate. *The word swastika comes from the Sanskrit svastika, which means "good fortune" or "well-being." The motif (a hooked cross) appears to have first been used in Eurasia, as early as 7000 years ago, perhaps representing the movement of the sun through the sky. To this day, it is a sacred symbol in Hinduism, Buddhism, Jainism, and Odinism. It is a common sight on temples or houses in India or Indonesia. Swastikas also have an ancient history in Europe, appearing on artifacts from pre-Christian European cultures.]*

The symbol appears in the "Vinca script" of Neolithic Europe (Balkans, 6th to 5th millennium BCE. Another early attestation is on a pottery bowl found at Samarra, dated to as early as 4,000 BCE. The oldest example of a "Swastika" symbol was discovered in the book, **Flight of the Wild Gander** by Joseph Campbell[8] circa 1998.

[...The swastika is one of the 108 symbols of the Hindu deity, Vishnu and represents the Sun's rays, upon which life depends. It is also seen as pointing in all four directions (north, east, south and west) and thus implies stability. Its use as a Sun symbol can first be seen in its image of the god, Surya. The swastika is used in all Hindu mantras and religious designs.]

www.thearchaeologist.org/blog/the-global-swastika-exploring-its-ancient-roots-and-diverse-meanings states:

[...The Navajo and other Native American groups used the swastika in ceremonial contexts, further demonstrating its universal appeal. These uses highlight the symbol's capacity to convey meanings of fertility, prosperity and the cyclic nature of life, themes that resonate across different belief systems and geographical regions...]

13. THE CHINESE CIVILIZATION

The history of Chinese Culture is divided into ages of history that are different from those of the West. In Europe there are the Ancient, Middle Ages, Modern and Contemporary, but in China there are only three, Ancient, Imperial, and Modern.

This is because China never had the Middle Ages as we know it, power always fell to the officials of the Empire, not to the aristocracy or the nobility, although there were small periods of exception to this rule.

The website, *Complete History of China Brief Summary and Timeline (culturachina.net)* lists the following:

40,000 BCE - APPEARANCE OF HOMO SAPIENS IN CHINA:
Many species of Homo began to populate the territory of present-day China tens of thousands of years ago, including the famous Homo Erectus Pekinensis. But we, the Homo sapiens, would have arrived only 40,000 years ago.

17,000 BCE - FIRST CERAMICS IN CHINA:
The appearance of the first ceramics is very important, 17,000 years ago, even before becoming sedentary or learning to cultivate. This is a milestone in the history of humanity because no other human civilization managed to create ceramics so quickly.

10,000 BCE - CULTIVATION OF RICE AND MILLET:
10,000 years ago, they learnt to grow rice on the banks of the Yangtse River and millet on the Huang He River. They also began to domesticate the first animals and use jade. Sedentarization gave rise to China's first cultures. These are the cultures of Peilikan, Cishan, Yangshao, Dawenkou, and Hongshan. They were all located on the banks of the Yellow River and its tributaries.

2,500 BCE - LONGSHAN CULTURE
During the Neolithic, all the cultures of the Huang He River would merge and give rise to the Longshan Culture. This culture had a hierarchical society of religious cut, exchange of products and constant

wars. Its most important site is Taosi, in Shanxi Province. In this enclave is the oldest astronomical observatory in Asia, dating back more than 4,000 years. Civilization originated in the Hwang Ho and Yangtze River basins where the ancient farmers' settlements developed into Chinese towns and national unions. Political aspects of the pre-imperial history of China were unstable and mainly concentrated in the hands of religious leaders, with Governor-generals of small principalities and provinces independent from the ruler's authority.

1,700 BCE - SHANG DYNASTY
According to Sima Qian, the last king Xia, Jié, was defeated by a new dynasty, Shang. The Shang Dynasty (1,766-1,046 BCE) was believed to be mythological until about 100 years ago, but archaeological sites such as Erliang have proved its existence. Before the Shang, the people worshipped many gods with one supreme god, Shangti, as head of the pantheon. Shangti was considered 'the great ancestor' who presided over victory in war, agriculture, the weather and good government.

[11]SHANGDI ("LORD-ON-HIGH" ALSO CALLED DI): An Ancient Chinese deity who controlled victory in cattle, harvest, the fate of the capital, and the weather. He had no cultic following and was probably considered too distant and inscrutable to be influenced by mortals.

[Shangdi was the supreme deity during the Shang dynasty (1,600–1,046 Century BCE), but during the Zhou dynasty (1046–256 BCE) he was

gradually supplanted by heaven (tian). Mystery concerns the 450-year-old Temple of Heaven complex in Beijing, China. Why did the emperors sacrifice a bull on the great white marble Altar of Heaven at an annual ceremony, the year's most important and colourful celebration, the so-called 'Border Sacrifice'? This rite ended in 1911 when the last emperor was deposed. However, the sacrifice did not begin a mere 450 years ago. The ceremony goes back 4,000 years.]

SHU JING (BOOK OF HISTORY)

One of the earliest accounts of the Border Sacrifice is found in the Shu Jing (Book of History), compiled by Confucius, where it is recorded of Emperor Shun (who ruled from about 2256 BC to 2205 BC when the first recorded dynasty began) that he sacrificed to Shang Di.

SHANGDI[11], the Creator God of the Chinese surely appears to be the same as the Creator-God of the Hebrews. One of the Hebrew names for God is El Shaddai, which is phonetically like ShangDi. Even more similar is the Early Zhou pronunciation of ShangDi which is 'djanh-tigh' [Zhan-dai].

[Another name for their God which the ancient Chinese used interchangeably with ShangDi was Heaven (Tian). Zheng Xuan, a scholar of the early Han dynasty said, "ShangDi is another name for Heaven (Tian)". The great philosopher Motze (408–82 BC) also thought of Heaven (Tian) as the Creator-God... How did ShangDi create all things? Here is one further recitation from the ancient Border Sacrifice rite: 'When Te [ShangDi],

the Lord, had so decreed. e called into existence [originated] heaven, Earth, and man.

Between heaven and Earth, He separately placed in order men and things, all overspread by the heavens. Note that ShangDi 'called into existence,' or commanded heaven and Earth to appear. Compare this with the way the Hebrew text describes the method of creation by El Shaddai, who, we suspect, is identical... All people in the world, not just the Chinese, are descended from the inhabitants of Babel, the first civilization after the Flood.]

EL SHADDAI[12]: Among Christians, the most common interpretation of "Shaddai" today is "mighty," and El Shaddai would translate to "God Almighty." Coinciding with this, one suggested root meaning for El Shaddai is "The Overpowerer". This means God will do what He purposes to do, overpowering all opposition. Some interpret Shaddai as "sufficient," and God is the "All-sufficient One." Yet another possible meaning of El Shaddai is "The God of the Mountain." Some Messianic teachers say Shaddai comes from the Akkadian word shaddu, meaning "mountain. "God lives in heaven but heal so inhabited a mountain top—Mount Sinai. It was on this mountain Moses met with God and received the Ten Commandments.

14. THE ROMAN CIVILIZATION

As I'm writing about the earliest civilisations here, I wanted to find out more about the people before the Roman Empire was established. The webpage,

Genetic Study Reveals Exactly Who 'The Romans' Were | Ancient Origins (ancient-origins.net) gives some more interesting information.

Jonathan Pritchard, a professor of genetics and biology and one of the paper's senior authors. *(www.science.org)* said:

> *["Scholars have been studying Rome for hundreds of years, but it still holds some secrets - for instance, relatively little is known about the ancestral origins of the city's denizens".]*

To find out what that makeup looked like, the Stanford team partnered with a host of European researchers to gather 127 human DNA samples from 29 sites in and around Rome dating from between the Stone Age and medieval times. The Romans were known for worshipping many gods and spirits, the soldiers particularly prayed to Mars, the god of war [aka Ares/Ninurta]. Mars was the son of Jupiter [aka Zeus/Enlil].

15. THE PERSIAN CIVILISATION

About 3,500 years ago, this civilisation practised "Zoroastrianism" which remains one of the oldest religions still practised today. The tolerant belief system was likely the reason why Cyrus II was unusual for his time, choosing to treat his defeated enemies with respect instead of brutality.

According to Pliny the Elder, there were two Zoroasters. The first lived thousands of years ago, while the second accompanied Xerxes I in the invasion of Greece in 480 BCE. To find out more I bought the book, **The Teachings of Zoroaster** by Shapurji Aspaniaarji. Kapadia. On pages 6-7, he writes about God's qualities quoting from the Khordah-Avesta, the prayer book of the Parsis.

As I read the quote, I was reminded of how Yahweh/Jehovah described himself and as I explained in Chapter 2, this god was Enlil and sometimes Marduk, his nephew. However, Zoroaster tried to persuade his followers to worship God, not his creations. On page 9, he writes under the heading, 'Of the Life on the Earth', about the favoured man of God', Yima.

www.ancientpages.com/2019/01/16/cup-of-jamshid-holy-grail-of-ancient-persia-offered-immortality-and-visions-of-the-future states:

[In the Avesta, the sacred book of Zoroastrianism, Ahura Mazda, the creator god asks a kind shepherd named Yima to be in charge of the Earth. Yima's duty is to make certain all living beings can prosper. Yima rules as the king for hundreds of years and gets rid of the devas, evil demons. Under Yima's rule, good humans never age nor are they sick. From the Avesta, we learn how Yima faces several difficulties when he must deal with an upcoming catastrophe.

King Yima understands humans will perish, and just like Biblical Noah, he must ensure the human species their survival. He constructs a huge underground cavern where the fittest of men and women long with two of every animal, bird, and plant hidden in order to survive. The story is very similar to Biblical Noah and the Great Flood, as well as the story of 'Utnapishtim and the Babylonian Flood'.

Myths and legends recalling a great catastrophe that wiped out humanity can be found in all corners of the world. In time, the story of the Avestan hero, Yima, developed and in Persian mythology, he became known as Jamshid. Jamshid was credited with many great inventions, and he possessed extraordinary powers as an individual.

He was the fourth king of the world, and he stood above all angels and demons. During the time he ruled as a mighty king, sickness vanished, longevity increased, and people co-existed peacefully. He has also instructed humans and taught them how to build houses of bricks and navigate the oceans in sailing ships. People learnt the art of medicine and discovered how perfume, jewels, wine can be produced]

To me, Jamshid sounds very much like Thoth who managed to escape from Atlantis and went to Egypt.

On page 9, Kapadia wrote:

[Zoroaster has summed up the whole of his moral philosophy in three expressive words, "Humata" (good thoughts), "Hukhta" (good words) and "Hvarshta" (good deeds") and the way to heaven is laid through these three mystic avenues...']

On page 12, he wrote about marriage and the duties of a husband as a holy man, 'to build himself a habitation, provide himself with a wife, children, fire and a herd of cattle... to obey the laws of health and be brave, to protect his family from any outside violence, to be industrious, to provide them with the necessaries of life, to be tolerant, truthful and chaste, and to complete the domestic happiness of his family circle'.

> *[In every way, the wife was equal to her husband in social status, enjoying liberty of action, chastity and implicit obedience to her husband were the greatest virtues in a woman and divorce for misconduct was almost unknown. Loose morals in both men and women were almost unknown in the community and abortion was forbidden.]*

This religion also condemned 'fasting or total abstaining from food as a wicked and foolish act'. There is so much more written in this book, but I think the similarities between Zoroastrianism and Christianity. It was Darius, also a worshipper of Ormazd, who favoured the rebuilding of the temple, and who ordered the decree of Cyrus to be carried into effect (Ezra 5:15-17; 6:1-12). Lastly, but most important to us, it was the Magi—true followers of the ancient faith of Persia, those wise men from the East—that came bearing gold, frankincense, and myrrh to the babe at Bethlehem (Matt. 2:1–2).

16. THE AZTEC CIVILIZATION

The exact origins of the Aztec people are uncertain, but they are believed to have begun as a northern tribe of hunter-gatherers whose name came from their homeland Aztlan, or "White Land" in the Aztec language of Nahuatl. They were also known as the Tenochca (from which the name for their capital city, Tenochtitlan, was derived) or the Mexica (the origin of the name of the city that would replace Tenochtitlan, as well as the name for the entire country).

The Aztecs appeared in Mesoamerica—as the south-central region of pre-Columbian Mexico is known in the early 13th century. Their arrival came just after or perhaps helped bring about, the fall of the previously dominant Meso-American civilization, the Toltecs.

[The Nahuatl words aztēcatl [asˈteːkat͡ɬ], and aztēcah [asˈteːka], mean "people from Aztlan", a mythical place of origin for several ethnic groups in central Mexico. The term was not used as an endonym by Aztecs themselves, but it is found in the different migration accounts of the Mexica, where it describes the different tribes who left Aztlan together. In one account of the journey from Aztlan, [13]Huitzilopochtli, the tutelary deity of the Mexica tribe, tells his followers on the journey that "now, no longer is your name Azteca, you are now Mexitin [Mexica]".... Historians have speculated about the possible location of Aztlan. They tend to place it either in northwestern Mexico or the southwestern United States, although there are doubts about whether the place is purely mythical or represents a historical reality...]

As I wrote this, I pondered as to whether Aztlan was Atlantis. The various descriptions of Aztlán contradict each other. While some legends describe

Aztlán as a paradise, the **Codex Aubin** says that the Aztecs were subject to a tyrannical elite called the Azteca Chicomoztoca.

[Guided by their priest, the Aztec tribe fled. On the road, their god Huitzilopochtli forbade them to call themselves Azteca, telling them that they should be known as Mexica... Huitzilopochtli also spelt Uitzilopochtli, also called Xiuhpilli ("Turquoise Prince") and Totec ("Our Lord"), Aztec sun and war god, one of the wo principal deities of Aztec religion, often represented in art as either a hummingbird or an eagle.

[13]Huitzilopochtli is presented as the deity who guided the long migration the Aztecs undertook from Aztlan, their traditional home, to the Valley of Mexico. During the journey his image, in the form of a hummingbird, was carried upon the shoulders of priests, and at night his voice was heard giving orders.

Thus, according to Huitzilopochtli's command Tenochtitlán, the Aztec capital, was founded in 1325 CE on a small, rocky island in the lake of the Valley of Mexico. The god's first shrine was built on the spot where priests found an eagle poised upon a rock and devouring a snake, an image so important to Mexican culture that it is portrayed on the national flag of Mexico. Successive Aztec rulers enlarged the shrine until the year Eight Reed (1487) when an impressive temple was dedicated by the emperor Ahuitzot l.]

Enlil also used the eagle as his symbol, so Uitzilopochtli was no doubt another name for Enlil (aka Yahweh in the Bible). The snake or serpent was the symbol of his half-brother, Enki.

> *[Aztecs believed that dead warriors were reincarnated as hummingbirds and considered the south to be the left side of the world; thus, his name meant the "resuscitated warrior of the south." They also believed that the sun god needed daily nourishment (tlaxcaltiliztli) in the form of human blood and hearts and that they, as "people of the sun," were required to provide Huitzilopochtli with his sustenance.*
>
> *It's horrifying at just what evil practices humans are willing to do out of fear of their god. It certainly wasn't out of love. Another ritual included, 'an image of Huitzilopochtli, made of ground maize (corn), was ceremonially killed with an arrow and divided between the priests and the novices; the young men who ate "Huitzilopochtli's body" were obliged to serve him for one year.]*

Was this the basis of the partaking of the bread and wine as practised as the 'Holy Communion'?

COATLICUE (NAHUATL: "SERPENT SKIRT")

> *[Aztec Earth goddess, symbol of the Earth as both creator and destroyer, the mother of the gods and mortals. The dualism that she embodies is powerfully concretized in her image: her face is of two fanged serpents and her skirt is of interwoven snakes (snakes symbolize fertility). Her breasts are flabby (she Nourished many); her necklace is of hands, hearts, and a skull (she feeds on corpses, as the Earth consumes all that dies); and her*

fingers and toes are claws. Also called Teteoinnan ("Mother of the Gods") and Toci ("Our Grandmother"), she is a single manifestation of the Earth goddess, a multifaceted being who also appears as the fearsome goddess of childbirth. Cihuacóatl ("Snake Woman"; like Coatlicue, was called Tonantzin ("Our Mother"), and as Tlazoltéotl, is the goddess of sexual impurity and wrongful behaviour.

According to Aztec legend, Coatlicue was once magically impregnated by a ball of feathers that fell on her while she was sweeping a temple. She subsequently gave birth to the god Huitzilopochtli. Her daughter, the goddess X, then rallied Coatlicue's four hundred other children together and goaded them into attacking and decapitating their mother.

The instant she was killed, the god Huitzilopochtli suddenly emerged from her womb fully grown and armed for battle. He killed many of his brothers and sisters, including Coyolxauhqui, who he decapitated, dismembered, and threw into the sky to become the moon. In one variation of this legend, Huitzilopochtli himself is the child conceived in the ball-of-feathers incident and is born just in time to save his mother from harm.

Unlike Ninhursag, 'Coatlicue is represented as a woman wearing a skirt of writhing snakes and a necklace made of human hearts, hands, and skulls. Her feet and hands are adorned with claws and her breasts are depicted as hanging flaccid from pregnancy. Her face is formed by two facing serpents, which represent blood spurting from her neck after she was decapitated.]

COATLICUE
(WORLD HISTORY ENCYCLOPAEDIA)

[The Sumerian "mother of deities" was Ninhursag, and one of the oldest and most important in the Mesopotamian Pantheon.

She was also known as the mother of the Gods and Mother of Men for her part in creating both divine and mortal entities. She is far more frequently depicted as the wife/consort of Enki, God of wisdom among many other attributes although the sister of both Enki and Enlil.

Ninhursag and Enki were geneticists responsible for creating 'Adam and Eve'. She was also the mother of Enlil's eldest son, Ninurta. She was considered the female aspect of the primordial god, Ometeotl) and wife of Mixcoatl.]

I can't help but think that she was depicted in such a derogatory way because she sided with Enki thus angering Enlil. As there seems to be no other information I can only conclude again that the Aztecs were descendants or survivors of Atlantis.

17. THE INCAN CIVILIZATION

The historical origins of the Incan Civilisation dating back about 14,000 years, as with other ancient American cultures, are difficult to disentangle from the founding myths they created.

[... in the beginning, the creator god, Viracocha came out of the Pacific Ocean, and when he arrived at Lake Titicaca, he created the sun and

> *all ethnic groups. These first people were buried by the god, and only later did they emerge from springs and rocks (sacred pacarinas) back into the world...In another version of the creation myth, the first Incas came from a sacred cave known as Tampu T'oqo or 'The House of Windows', which was located at Pacariqtambo, the 'Inn of Dawn', south of Cuzco.]*

Viracocha was Enki, the Sumerian god, known as Poseidon (Greek) and Neptune (Roman).

THE FIRST PAIR OF HUMANS

They were Manco Capac (or Manqo Qhapaq) and his sister (also his wife) Mama Oqllu (or Ocllo). Three more brother-sister siblings were born, and the group set off together to find their civilization.

> *[...Defeating the Chanca people with the help of stone warriors (pururaucas), the first Incas finally settled in the Valley of Cuzco and Manco Capac, throwing a golden rod into the ground, established what would become the Inca capital, Cuzco'. They grew from a small tribe to being South America's largest empire in the pre-Columbian era, and their borders extended well into Ecuador and Chile until the Spanish conquistadors arrived on ships in 1517.*
>
> *With them came a serious case of gold fever, as well as influenza and smallpox and as the Incas died from these infections, the nation became weaker. with their superior weapons the Spanish led by the infamous Hernán Cortés, they increased their numbers by enlisting the native enemies of*

> *the Aztecs and massacred people at Tenochtitlan. Cortés returned in 1521, and he tore Tenochtitlan to the ground, ending the Aztec civilization. The last emperor, Atahualpa, was executed and so all that remained of the Inca was a page in history.]*

Last year I bought Graham Hancock's book, **America Before–The Key to Earth's Lost Civilisations**. I must admit I haven't read it yet, but the back cover explains:

> *[We've been taught that North and South America were empty of humans until around 13,000 years ago – amongst the last great landmasses on Earth to have been settled by our ancestors. But new discoveries have radically reshaped this long-established picture, and we know now that the Americas were first peopled more than 130,000 years ago – many tens of thousands of years before human settlements became established elsewhere.]*

Graham Hancock is yet another researcher who has been besmirched and ridiculed, but are you seeing the picture yet?

PHILOSOPHIES

> *If there were in the world today any large number of people who desired their own happiness, more than they desired the unhappiness of others, we could have a paradise in a few years*
>
> Bertrand Russell

My Greek father and I had many philosophical discussions when I was young, but I knew nothing about any philosophers then. Now I know what he meant when he said, 'Life is what you make it.' The main differences between philosophy and religion are:

- Philosophy is a rational inquiry into the nature of reality, existence, knowledge, and ethics, while religion involves a set of beliefs, practices, and rituals related to divine or supernatural power.
- Philosophy is based on reason and critical thinking, while religion is often based on faith and spirituality.
- Philosophy is focused on this world, while religion is focused on the next world.
- Philosophy is amenable to change through debate, while religion is not.
- Philosophy is secular, while religion is sacred.

When I learnt that many of the well-known biblical scholars respected the philosopher, Plato, of course I wanted to know more. And then I came across the book, **A Little History of Philosophy** by Nigel Warburton who wrote about philosophers from Socrates to Peter Singer.

It is a commonly held view that 'the Egyptians had no philosophy' and that philosophy began with the ancient Greeks. However, some of the major Greek philosophers, including Thales, Pythagoras and Plato recognised their huge debt to the sages of Egypt for their knowledge and ideas.

Plato, for example, spent 13 years studying with the Egyptian priests at Heliopolis. Here are three examples that I found:

> ***EGYPTIAN PHILOSOPHER: IMHOTEP (2,700 BCE):*** *Earliest personality recorded in history who dealt with questions of space, time, volume, the nature of illness, the care of the sick and human mortality and immortality. Eventually, Imhotep was equated with Thoth (the Atlantean), the god of architecture, mathematics, and medicine, and patron of scribes: Imhotep's cult was merged with that of his former tutelary god.*
>
> ***GREEK PHILOSOPHERS****: Archimedes ~ Pythagoras ~ Hippocrates~ Epicurus Epictetus*
> ***LATER PHILOSOPHERS****: Augustine ~ Peter Singer*
>
> ***EGYPTIAN PHILOSOPHER: PTAHHOTEP (2,414 BCE):*** *An African philosopher who produced the first ethical teaching on the life of the aged. Ptahhotep was a learnt priest of immense influence and power, and his instructions or philosophy reverberated through the ages. He served as a vizier to the pharaoh.*
> ***GREEK PHILOSOPHERS****: Cicero ~ Seneca ~Aristotle?*
> ***LATER PHILOSOPHERS****: Boethius ~ Thomas Aquinas?*

EGYPTIAN PHILOSOPHER: MERIKARE (1,990 BCE?): *He is called the philosopher of communication because he wrote on the value of speaking well and the necessity of common sense in human relationships.*
GREEK PHILOSOPHERS: Socrates ~ Plato
LATER PHILOSOPHERS: Augustine

3 - THE BIBLE & OTHER BOOKS

[14]*THE MAGICAL WRITING OF PRIESTS & KINGS*

In ancient Palestine, writing was a restricted and expensive technology. Writing as controlled by the government and manipulated by the priests. Writing as seen as a gift from the gods. It was not used to canonize religious practice, but rather to engender religious awe writing was magical. It was powerful. It was the guarded knowledge of political and religious elites.

Ever since I was a little girl I believed in God, and going to Church of England schools was subjected to the religious education provided. I was about seven years of age when I tried to work out the genealogy in Genesis and gave up after having sheets of paper all over the floor with Mum telling me off for making a mess.

It's taken me seventeen years to reach the position I now find myself in now. When asked what I am writing about, I explain that it's as if I am doing an enormous jigsaw puzzle. I started with the pictures presented in the Bible with JW's teachings and my quest for the Truth to dismantle the first picture to create a better, more accurate version. The most important thing I needed to know was whether I could trust the writings found in the Bible.

After all, all the beliefs of the Abrahamic religions are based on this collection of 66 books.

Whenever I get new information, it can be very overwhelming until I can clarify my thoughts and put them into words on paper. Sometimes I look at the pieces but cannot see clearly what they depict, and then another piece comes along, and I see a new picture much clearer than before. Other times I feel I've been going around in circles because as soon as I relax and think I've finished a chapter, I need to make amendments and update with new information.

THE POWER OF WORDS

Words can hurt, words can console, words can kill, and words can bring peace. Words can create and so words are powerful

Learning about the origin of the book of Genesis was mind-blowing to me, but first, it's important to understand how important words are in forming our beliefs. My research has taken me to the writings of religious people, agnostics and atheists who have helped me find the common threads which clarify whether something could be considered true.

Of course, if I find something better, I might change my mind. After all, unlike the Sumerian Tablets my thoughts and writings are not set in stone. One of the first books I came across when I started writing this book was by Pao Chang, a 'Born Again Christian' and the author of several books, **Word Magic**, an updated version **Word Magic: Born Again** and

The Powers and Occult Definitions of Words.

As soon as people hear the word "occult" they think of something to do with black magic or evil. The Merriam-Webster Dictionary gives several meanings to the word "occult" such as:

- Not revealed (Secret)
- Not easily apprehended or understood
- Hidden from view (concealed)
- Not manifest or detectable by clinical methods alone

Matters regarded as involving the action or influence of supernatural or supernormal powers or some secret knowledge of them. In the second paragraph on page 13, Pao had written:

> *[The Word was in the beginning because the Word was the Spiritual Seed, the Source of Life... The seed is the word of God' (Luke 8:11) and that the Spiritual Seed 'is the source of vibration.' This was the vibration which allows the creation of sacred geometry, one of the foundations of the universe.]*

In the third paragraph, he explained:

> *[...The power of vibration/vibration allows the creation of motion and light. 'Then God said, Let there be light; and there was light" (Gen 1:13)] I went back to read from his introduction where he explains just how powerful words are...Words are not just elements of speech or writing because when words are spoken aloud, they transform into sound, frequency, and vibration.... they can be used to harness the power of energy.' (Page vi). When you study the origin and history of words*

and languages and investigate their connection to certain secret societies, you should eventually realize that all languages are interconnected on a very deep level. Furthermore, you should eventually know that the secrets of the universe and the true history of mankind are hidden in words.' (Page vii)] The frequency of a word can either resonate with us or repel us. If our vibration is low, we cannot discern words and their meanings easily on our own.

We need someone else to help us and if that person has been convinced that what they believe is true, they will give meanings to words from this perspective. Words which, because of their strong belief in them, the explanations sound perfectly true even when they are not. There are numerous "seeds of truth" scattered throughout all the sacred writings of all denominations, and I have felt my purpose is to gather these seeds and present them to my readers. This is what my Higher Self has disclosed to me but despite her great help, I still feel overwhelmed at times – there are so many different viewpoints on each subject!

ABRAHAMIC RELIGIONS

The basis for Christianity is the belief that Jesus Christ was the son of God and died for us according to the Bible and the religious leaders who promote it. The basis for Judaism is the Hebrew Scriptures and The Talmud. The basis for Islam is the teachings of Mohammed as written in the Quran. Like the Bible, the Quran is considered sacred and unchangeable although some of it is based on Hebrew Scriptures.

Islam teaches that Jesus was a prophet of God. Yet each of these Abrahamic religions consider the other two heretics and has killed each other for that reason. Most importantly, people don't realise that the Abrahamic religions worship three ancient Sumerian gods, Enlil, Enki and Marduk combined as the God of the Bible as I will show.

To learn this was a great shock to me, as it may also be for you, so I will do my best to explain how I came to find this out in the chapter "Who is God?"

> BASIC TEACHING 2: THAT THE BIBLE IS THE INSPIRED WORD OF GOD AND ACCEPT IT ENTIRELY BUT DO NOT CLAIM TO BE FUNDAMENTALISTS

If the biblical writings were truly inspired by God, then why introduce the Quran later (unless perhaps it was to cause even more division, although pretending to unite the warring Arabs? My research has made me question everything, so I wanted to understand the correct meaning of the word "fundamentalists" as JWs claim they are not.

FUNDAMENTALISTS & EVANGELISTS

According to an old [14]article by John Green on Evangelicals versus Fundamentals:

> *[The differences between fundamentalism and evangelicalism are a bit subtle, and oftentimes difficult to understand from the outside... Many of them are not intolerant. But they tend towards that direction...to be very judgmental... to want to require an awful lot of individuals who would join*

their communion...to be very, very critical of other Christians - even other evangelical Christians – who don't share their very strict approach to religion...Evangelicals and fundamentalists both agree that the Bible is inerrant, but fundamentalists tend to read the Bible literally...Evangelicals are not as separatist. They are perfectly willing to co-operate with people of other religious faiths, with whom they don't agree on all the particulars, for the greater cause of evangelizing and bringing people to Christ.

So, evangelicals, for instance, will often talk about making common cause with Roman Catholics or with mainline Protestants. Fundamentalists are very reluctant to do that, because they see it as being wrong to associate in religious terms with people with whom they don't have complete agreement. So those differences are sometimes subtle. But in style, belief, and practice, fundamentalists really are different from evangelicals.]

I would say that Jehovah's Witnesses are fundamental evangelists. They read the Bible literally, and are very strict and intolerant, but are willing to co-operate with people of other religious faiths for the greater cause of evangelizing and bringing people to Jehovah. They truly believe they are like the original Christians, but it's obvious to me they are not in their everyday rules.

The very purpose of having the Roman Catholic religious empire was to have everyone thinking the same and doing what they were told. The last thing Church leaders wanted was for people to think for themselves. Because of this, different ideas circulated, notably Martin Luther's being one of the first to make his views known.

This is why priests are needed to explain things, and why William Tyndale was put to death for bringing the Bible to ordinary people so they could see for themselves what was being preached.

Having spoken with many about the Bible and their beliefs, I found that although they say they believe the Bible to be God's Word, depending on which denomination they belong to, they interpret parts of it differently. Some say that certain parts are not to be taken literally but allegorically, that is that they contain a moral or hidden meaning.

IS THE BIBLE AS OLD AS IT IS CLAIMED?

Although the Pentateuch contains ancient stories, the text itself was probably not compiled until the mid to late 6th century BCE. According to most biblical scholars, the Pentateuch is composed of four sources.

[15]Yonatan Adler of Ariel University, after appending 15 years of studying textual and archaeological evidence, concluded that ordinary Judeans didn't practice some of the Jewish rituals that are practised today until 200-300 BCE.

Another biblical scholar, Gad Barnea, at Israel's University of Haifa, speculates that the codification of the Torah until the construction of the Library of Alexandria in the third century B.C.E making it accessible to foreigners, as well as Judeans who spoke

Greek and Aramaic rather than Hebrew. Around that same time, the Hebrew Bible was translated into Greek for the first time.

IS THE BIBLE REALLY INSPIRED BY GOD?

For so many years I had believed that the Bible was a book written by men who had been inspired by the Holy Spirit; so, for my own peace of mind, I felt I had to clarify once and for all whether the Bible was really inspired by God or a god. Or were these writings purely the thoughts of men and to be ignored?

> *[And if any man shall take away from the words of the book of this prophecy, God shall take away his part out of the book of life, and out of the holy city, and from the things which are written in this book (KJV)]*

For example, I had the inspiration to write this book, but it doesn't mean this inspiration came from any God. I believe I was inspired by my Higher Self, my own soul and my own desire to learn the truth and nothing but the truth.

As a JW, for the door-to-door work I had tracts and books with quotes from the Bible ready to answer questions people had, and so thought I had all the answers.

Yet despite all the years with JWs, and hours spent studying, going to meetings and out in the ministry, my recent research proves I knew very little about the true God, the Bible and ancient belief systems.

If those who wrote the Bible were inspired by the Holy Spirit, it obviously did not oversee those who copied or translated the original writings thus avoiding mistranslations and other errors.

Also, who inspired the changes in the Bible and the new versions with different ideas and writings? Surely, the books would be 100% accurate and truthful. I decided to investigate how we have the Bible in the first place. The last thing I expected was that I would ever doubt that the Bible was the only source of truth.

WHO WROTE THE PENTATEUCH? (FIVE BOOKS OF MOSES)

These five books form the foundation of Judaism and Christianity. They are considered historical and metaphorical, but modern scholars consider the Genesis creation narrative as one of various ancient origin myths.

Such stories as the creation, the Garden of Eden, the flood and the angels of the Bible and other related religions, were derived from the earliest literature of the Sumerian civilisation over 5,500 years ago, but the stories are of much older events.

Christianity is based on the fall of Adam and Eve in that we needed Jesus Christ to redeem us from sin, (ie. falling short of perfection which is why we die). It is said these books were written by Moses, as dictated by God himself, but I wanted to know if this was true. First of all, I wanted to know more about Moses.

WHO WAS MOSES?
[AKA MOSHE, OSARSEPH, AKHENATON]

The thought that Moses was really someone else entirely tends to upset people. Some experts believe the story of Moses to be true, others don't. Until we questioned things, we wouldn't even know that anyone doubted his existence. Judeans promoted Moses as the founder on their ancient Nation but evidence for Moses in ancient records are lacking.

Dr Gad Barnea (University of Haifa), said inscriptions, seals and other texts from ancient Israel and Judah never mention Moses or any of the other Israelite Patriarchs. Neither is there any mention in records from the Babylonia and Persian periods. Nor do the Elephantine papyrus from the Persian era Judeans and Israelites in Egypt show any awareness of Moses.

[16]Ahmed Osman, an Egyptian-born author who has been trying to find the link between the stories of the Bible and ancient Egyptian history wrote:

> *[...a prophet and a leader according to Abrahamic religions, but many scholars view him as a legendary figure rather than a real historical person. They do concede that a Moses-like figure could have existed in history, so is it possible to track this person down through historical records? It is the view of this writer that this is very possible, and that the Moses figure can be traced as that of the primary confidant of none other than Egyptian pharaoh Hatshepsut. The trail begins with The Exodus.]*

Egyptologist Joyce Tyldesley writes about the time of the pharaoh Queen Hatshepsut (1500–1480 BCE) in her book **Hatshepsut: The Female Pharaoh**. Hatshepsut had a close confidant, a man called 'Senenmut'. This appears to be a unique name, and one of its meanings is 'mother's brother'. They were close in age, so such a name makes sense. She raises many questions such as:

- So, Who Would Have Tried to Remove Hatshepsut from History?
- When Were Hatshepsut's Statues Discovered and What Did They Reveal
- Why Would the Royal Heiress Adopt a Slave Child?
- So, What Do We Know of Hatshepsut?
- What Do We Know About Senenmut?

The story of the Exodus describes great hardship for Egypt and one can understand Amenhotep's fury against both Hatshepsut and Senenmut. Destroying their memory, being wiped out of history, for the Egyptians was tantamount to eternal damnation.

The statues of Hatshepsut still lay buried in the pit where they were thrown thirty years after her death until found by Herbert Winlock, an American Egyptologist employed by the Metropolitan Museum of Art in Boston, United States in 1927.Not only was a hoard of statues of Hatshepsut were discovered just east of the first court of her mortuary temple at Deir el Bahri, but another pit was also found, containing over twenty hard stone statues of Senenmut.

This find caused Egyptologists to wonder what it was about this man that he was given such status.

Another article, [17]**Moses: Myth, Fiction or History?** quotes from **The Book of Exodus: "Departure of the Israelites",** by David Roberts, (1829) who said:

> *[...'the biblical story of the great man is full of contradictions and puzzles, unlike the story of Joseph which has a discernible beginning, middle and end...the Moses' narrative is scattered and disjointed. At first, we are led to believe that he is a first child; only for it to be revealed later that he has older siblings.*
>
> *We're told he was adopted by an Egyptian princess, but no details of his childhood are offered. The only account of his death is sketchy, to say the least and no one knows where one of the most Significant figures in history are buried. These troubling mysteries led some scholars to doubt his existence.]*

WAS MOSES REALLY AKHENATON?

Freud was one of many who proposed that Moses had been a priest of Akhenaten who fled Egypt after the pharaoh's death and perpetuated monotheism through a different religion. He was murdered by his followers, who then via reaction formation revered him and became irrevocably committed to the monotheistic idea he represented.

This priest could be the same one Manetho wrote about, Osarseph. Manetho (c. 300 BCE) was an

Egyptian priest who wrote a history of Egypt in Greek, probably commissioned by Ptolemy II Philadelphus (285–246 CE) *(www.britannica.com).*

Similarities between Akhenaton (formerly Amenhotep IV) and the rebel leader persuaded Donald Redford to recognize Manetho's 'Osarseph's story as the events of the Amarna religious revolution, first remembered orally and later set down in writing.

Donald Bruce Redford is a Canadian Egyptologist and archaeologist, currently a Professor of Classics and ancient Mediterranean Studies at Pennsylvania State University. In his book, **Egypt, Canaan, and Israel in Ancient Times,** he confirms that the figure of Osarseph/Moses is modelled on the historic memory of Akhenaton.

Later, several independent historians, including Manetho, date Moses and the bondage to the Amarna period believing it is self-evident that the monotheistic preaching at Mount Sinai is to be traced back ultimately to the teachings of Akhenaton.

Modern scholars dismissed Manetho's account of another location as unhistorical thanks to Flavius Josephus, who wrongly identified the Hebrew tribe with the Hyksos rulers (who had left the country more than a century earlier), instead of with the shepherds who were already living in Egypt.

Comparing Moses (b.1393 BCE), Akhenaten (Amenhotep IV) who came to power c.1349-1351 BCE and Osarseph, perhaps Senenmut as well, there seems good reason to doubt that the Moses of the bible and his story was only what we have been taught. I have since heard other theories that Moses was Akhenaten himself.

However, Akhenaton didn't worship Yahweh, but the biblical Moses did, therefore, how did scholars think they were the same person? I need to investigate this more.

WHAT'S IN A NAME?

This made me wonder about the other main Bible characters Moses was said to have written about. This is because a lot of the Bible's stories were taken from older Sumerian texts. These are:

- **ENOCH**, Adam's great-great-great-great grandson and Noah's great grandfather.
2. **NOAH** and his family who were saved from the flood by Jehovah.
3. **NIMROD**, the grandson of Ham, the son of Noah.
4. **ABRAHAM**, who grew up with a father, Terah, who worshipped gods and served Nimrod.

1. ENOCH

[AKA NEBU, THOTH, HERMES, MERCURY, IDRIS METATRON, ENMEDURANKI, HERMES TRISMEGISTUS]

Enoch was Adam's great-great-great-great grandson (and Noah's great grandfather) who some scholars believe was born c. 5,000 years ago but no one knows exactly where he was born. He was the father of Methuselah, the longest-living man. Enoch lived for 365 years, which is shorter than other pre-Flood Patriarchs, who are all recorded as dying at over 700 years of age. During that time, he had numerous offspring.

The [18]**Biblical Timeline** shows that Enoch's existence was from 3382 - 3019 BCE the last year he was seen on Earth. According to Rashi, from **Genesis Rabbah - a systematic exegesis of the Book of Genesis** produced by the Judaic sages about 450 CE:

[Enoch was a righteous man, but he could easily be swayed to return to do evil. Therefore, the Holy One, blessed be He, hastened and took him away and caused him to die before his time. For this reason, scripture changed [the wording] in [the account of] his demise and wrote, 'and he was no longer' in the world to complete his years. Among the minor Midrashim, esoteric attributes of Enoch are expanded upon.

In the Sefer Hekalot, Rabbi Ishmael is described as having visited the Seventh Heaven, where he met Enoch, who claims that Earth had, in his time, been corrupted by the demons, Shammazai, and Azazel, and so Enoch was taken to Heaven to prove that God was not cruel...]

ENMEDURANKI - Others believe he is on the Sumerian King List, said to have reigned 21,000 years) and is the seventh name on the Sumerian King List, whereas Enoch is the seventh figure on the list of patriarchs in Genesis. Both were also said to have been taken up into heaven. Additionally, Sippar, the city of Enmeduranki, is associated with sun worship, while the 365 years that Enoch is stated to have lived may be linked to the number of days in the solar calendar. Similar traditions are recorded in Sirach.

METATRON is the name Enoch received after his transformation into an angel in the Jewish apocrypha and early Kabbalah.

IDRIS in Islam is commonly identified with Enoch for example by the History of Al-Tabari interpretation and the Meadows of Gold. The Quran contains two references to Idris in:

> Surah Al-Anbiya (The Prophets), Verse 85: "Idris and Zul-Kifl, because they all practiced fortitude."

> Surah Maryam (Mary) verses 56–57: "And remember Idris in the Book; he was indeed very truthful, a Prophet. And we lifted him to a lofty station."

Idris is closely linked in Muslim tradition with the origin of writing and other technical arts of civilization, including the study of astronomical phenomena, both of which Enoch is credited with in the Testament of Abraham. Nonetheless, although some Muslims view Enoch and Idris as the same prophet, others do not. Many Muslims still honour Enoch as one of the earliest prophets, regardless of which view they hold. Idris seems to be less mysterious in the Qur'an than Enoch is in the Bible. Furthermore, Idris is the only Antediluvian prophet named in the Qur'an, other than Adam.

HERMES TRISMEGISTUS can also be found in both Islamic and Bahá'í writings. In those traditions,

Hermes Trismegistus was associated with the prophet Idris. Hermes was the Greek god, aka Thoth (Egyptian) and Mercury (Roman). However, some think Cush (the father of Nimrod) was Hermes.

THOTH played many vital and prominent roles in Egyptian mythology, such as maintaining the universe, and being one of the two deities (the other being Ma'at) who stood on either side of Ra's solar barque. In the later history of ancient Egypt, Thoth became heavily associated with the arbitration of godly disputes, the arts of magic, the system of writing, (he also served as scribe of the gods) and the judgment of the dead.

The Egyptians credited him as the author of all works of science, religion, philosophy, and magic. The Greeks further declared him the inventor of astronomy, astrology, the science of numbers, mathematics, geometry, surveying, medicine, botany, theology, civilized government, the alphabet, reading, writing, and oratory. They further claimed he was the true author of every work of every branch of knowledge, human and divine.

2. NOAH

[AKA UTNAPISHTIM, ZIUSUDRA, ATRAHASIS, XISUTHROS, DEUCALION, MANU, FO-HI, XISTHROS, NOTA)

Noah is a gender-neutral given name of Hebrew origin meaning both "rest and motion". As a feminine name Noah means "motion" and stems from the Bible; in which No'ah was the daughter of Zelophedad. In its masculine form, derived from

Noach means "rest or repose." In the Bible, God brought about the flood and saved Noah. It seems that the Bible version was based on earlier Sumerian versions of the flood story which include **The Epic of Gilgamesh, Ziusudra of Shuruppak** and **The Atrahasis.**

I include these in the list of **OTHER BOOKS** at the end of this chapter. So, was Noah a real person? I think so, but he was known by other names too.

3. NIMROD

[AKA EMMERKAR, HAMMURABI, SARGON (OR HIS GRANDSON NARAM-SIN), AMRAFEL, MARDUK]

Prof. Yigal Levin, an associate professor at the Israel & Golda Koschitzky Department of Jewish History at Bar-Ilan University says in an article on www.thetorah.com, 'We know of no ancient Mesopotamian figure, mythic or historical, named Nimrod'. Thus, scholars have struggled to identify who the biblical authors are describing. The cities that Nimrod "founds" do not point to any historical period; some of these cities did not even exist at the same time.'

However, according to the Bible, Nimrod was born in 3,225 BCE in the kingdom of Ararat and after the flood. In 3,200 BCE, rebellious Nimrod migrates south and starts his own kingdom by founding Babel (Eridu), Uruk/Erech, Ur etc. Babel (Eridu) and Uruk/Erech BCE.

According to www.britannica.com:

[Nimrod is described in Genesis 10:8–12 as "the first on Earth to be a mighty man. He was a mighty hunter before the Lord. "The only other references to Nimrod in the Bible are in Micah 5:6, where Assyria is called the land of Nimrod, and in 1 Chronicles 1:10, which reiterates his might. In the Genesis passage, the beginning of his kingdom is said to have been Babel, Erech, and Akkad, in the land of Shinar. Nimrod is said to have then built Nineveh, Calah (modern Nimrod), Rehoboth-Ir and Resen.

There is some consensus among biblical scholars that the mention of Nimrod in Genesis is a reference not to an individual but to an ancient people in Mesopotamia. The description of Nimrod as a "mighty hunter before the Lord" is an intrusion in this context, but is probably like the historical notices, derived from some old Babylonian saga. However, no equivalent of the name has yet been found in the Babylonian or other cuneiform records.]

[19]Flavius Josephus in his book, **The Antiquities of the Jews — Book I,** says of Nimrod:

[Now it was Nimrod who excited them to such an affront and contempt of God. He was the grandson of Ham, the son of Noah, a bold man, and of great strength of hand. He persuaded them not to ascribe it to God, as if it were through his means they were happy, but to believe that it was their own courage which procured that happiness. He also gradually changed the government into tyranny seeing no other way of turning men from the fear of God, but to bring them into a constant dependence upon his own power. He also said he

would be revenged on God, if he should have a mind to drown the world again; for that he would build a tower too high for the waters to be able to reach and that he would avenge himself on God for destroying their forefathers! (Ant. I: iv: 2)]

What Josephus says here is precisely what is found in the Gilgamesh epics. Gilgamesh set up tyranny; he opposed YHWH (Enlil) and did his utmost to get people to forsake Him. So, if this character wasn't someone named Nimrod, who was he really?

www.amazingbibletimeline.com states:

[Another name for Nimrod is AMRAFEL, AMRAPHAEL OR AMRAPHEL who was a king of Sennaar or Shinar, situated at the southern part of the kingdom of Babylonia. Oftentimes, he is associated with the legendary King Hammurabi who reigned in ancient Babylon. He is located on the 'Amazing Bible Timeline' with World History around 1954 BCE.

There were also speculations that King Amraphel is Khammu-rabi who united the two kingdoms of Babylonia under his leadership after he won the battle against Arioch. He founded his capital at the city of Babylon including the lands of Babylon, Uruk, Akkad, and Kalneh. Shinar is Babylonia, a kingdom situated at the plain in the east (Gen 14:1,8-10). King Amraphel as one of the four kings allied together to fight against the five kingdoms of the plain at the Valley of Siddim... Amraphel is usually associated with Hammurabi, who ruled Babylonia from 1792 BC until his death in 1750 BC. This view has been largely abandoned in recent years.

Other scholars have identified Amraphel with Aralius, one of the names on the later Babylonian king-lists, attributed first to Ctesias. Recently, David Rohl argued for identification with Amar-Sin, the third ruler of the Ur III dynasty. John Van Seters, in **'Abraham in History and Tradition'**, rejected the historical existence of Amraphel.]

NINURTA: Nimrod could also have been Ninurta, a Mesopotamian god, who was the son of Enlil.

> *www.worldhistory.org/Ninurta* states:
>
> *[Ninurta (identified with Ningirsu, Pabilsag, and the biblical Nimrod) is the Sumerian and Akkadian hero-god of war, hunting, and the south wind. He first appears in texts in the early 3rd millennium BCE as an agricultural god and local deity of the town of Girsu (as Ningirsu) and the city of Larak (as Pabilsag), both Sumerian communities. His role as a god of agriculture changed as the cities of Mesopotamia increasingly militarized and began campaigns of conquest, one city against another...Ningirsu was already recognized as a war god by the 2nd millennium BCE where he is featured in the Babylonian work, The Epic of Anzu.]*

MARDUK: Some think Marduk, the son of Enki, was Nimrod. He ended up siding with his uncle, Enlil against his father but then also turned against him.

> *www.thefamouspeople.com says:*
>
> *[Marduk was the king of Babylonian gods, the patron god of Babylon. He was portrayed as a king, hunter, and warrior. It isn't a stretch to think*

Marduk may have grown out of Nimrod, Babylon's founder. Nimrod's Semitic name, remember, was from marad (MRD), making the change from NMRD to Marduk, or Amar Ud, not unlikely.]

WAS NIMROD ALSO SARGON?

www.israelmyglory.org/article/the-identity-of-nimrod/?hilite=Nimrod states:

[Archaeological excavations in ancient Mesopotamia reveal striking parallels between the Bible's King Nimrod and the ancient Semitic ruler Sargon the Great, thus confirming the biblical king's historicity...

The ancient Jewish writers Philo of Alexandria and Flavius Josephus suggested Nimrod was a giant who opposed God and the tyrant behind the construction of the Tower of Babel (respectively).

First, both Nimrod and Sargon came from the same region. Nimrod's origin in Cush matches Sargon's origin in Sumerian Kish. Both peoples and territories were named after Cush (Kish), Noah's grandson...'

Second, both Nimrod and Sargon made Akkad a prominent city...the archaeological record fits with the biblical record of Nimrod's location in Sumer and his conquests of Uruk—the centre of power in Mesopotamia—and Akkad, from which he extended his rule north (Gen. 10:10–11).

Third, both Nimrod and Sargon initiated building projects in Assyria. The Bible reveals Nimrod built the principal cities of Assyria (vv. 11–12).

Archaeological discoveries in Nippur (an ancient city in Mesopotamia) credit the same feat to Sargon.]

SARGON II AND NARAM-SIN IN LATER HISTORIOGRAPHY

[...the age of Sargon and Naram-Sin was one of the important stages in human history. According to the Sumerian King List, after the flood, kingship came down from heaven and was granted to the city of Kish...Apparently, time and distance blended the names and deeds of Sargon and his almost as famous grandson Naram-Sin, whose name was corrupted in the biblical account from Naram to Nimrod. The author of the J source may very well have known a longer, epic poem, which he condensed. Israelite tradition made the hero "a mighty hunter before YHWH," but retained his role as the original human monarch...]

THE LOSS OF NIMROD'S STORY

Nimrod was one of seventy descendants of Noah and included in the "Table of Nations". Later Jewish tradition, noting the fact that Shinʿar appears both in relation to Nimrod and in the Tower of Babel story, makes Nimrod the builder of the tower and understands him as the archetypical evil king. His wickedness was heard in his very name, derived from the verb מרד, "to rebel." Instead of a great hunter before YHWH, he becomes the ultimate rebel against God.

The biblical Nimrod, however, is neither a wicked king, nor even a character unique to Israelite historiography. Instead, he is the composite Hebrew equivalent of the Sargonic dynasty's two most famous Kings of Kish: Sargon, the first Semitic emperor, and his grandson Naram-Sin. The later editors of the Book of Genesis dropped much of the story and mistakenly identified the Mesopotamian Kish with the Hamitic Cush. The Nimrod tradition was thus lost, save for five verses in Genesis 10.

[20]Paul Kriwaczek, writing Sargon's story, mentions the International Babylon Festival of 1990 CE when Saddam Hussein celebrated his birthday. He wrote:

> *[At the time of the writing of Exodus this story had been known in the Middle and Near East for almost 2,000 years through the Legend of Sargon of Akad. Sargon (2,334-2,279 BCE) was the founder of the Akkadian empire, the first multi-national empire in the world.*
>
> *His famous legend, which he made great use of in his lifetime to achieve his aims, relates how his mother was a priestess who '...set me in a basket of rushes and sealed my lid with bitumen. She cast me into the river which rose over me. The river bore me up and carried me to Akki, the drawer of water. Akki, the drawer of water, took me as his son and reared me.*
>
> *Akki/the drawer of water appointed me as his gardener' (Pritchard, 85-86). Sargon grew up to overthrow the king and unite the region of Mesopotamia under his rule. The festivities came to a climax when a wooden cabin was wheeled out and large crowds dressed in ancient Sumerian, Akkadian, Babylonian, and Assyrian costumes prostrated themselves in front of it.*

The doors opened to reveal a palm tree from which fifty-three white doves flew up into the sky. Beneath them a baby Saddam, reposing in a basket, came floating down a marsh-bordered stream.

A Time magazine's reporter was particularly struck by the baby-in-the-basket theme, describing it as "Moses redux". But why on Earth would Saddam Hussein wish to compare himself to a leader of the Jews?

The journalist was missing the point. The motif was a Mesopotamian invention long before the Hebrews took it up and applied it to Moses. The Iraqi dictator was alluding to a much more ancient and, to him, far more glorious precedent. He was associating himself with Sargon.]

HAM-MURABI

The name Ham-murabi might mean "Ham the Great", for Nimrod was the grandson of Ham, son of Noah. The same man portrayed in the Bible as the mighty king Nimrod is known today to the world at large as the mighty king Ham-murabi. Hammurabi's Code gave mankind the gift of self-government which meant that God alone was no longer the source of the law.

The law was to come from man, using the human faculties endowed within him. On the top of the stone stele is a carved relief of Hammurabi receiving the law from the sun God, Shamash, judge of gods and humans, and a protector of travellers. Shamash was also known as Utu in Sumerian tradition.

According to David Farka's article, [31]**In Search of the Biblical Hammurabi**, scholars identify Hammurabi with Amraphel, and the sages identify Amraphel with Nimrod, so they are all the same based on midrashic tradition.

Maybe "Nimrod" of the Bible was a made-up character based on different people such as Ninurta, Marduk, Hammurabi and even Sargon but we will see that he interacted with Abraham.

3. ABRAHAM
[AKA ABRAM, KHALILULLAH]

The following is a much more interesting story about Abraham than is told in the Bible:

> ***Who Was Abraham? The First Patriarch in the Bible*** (www.chabCE.org) *says:*
>
> *[Abraham was born Abram in the city of Ur in Babylonia. The town in which he was born was called Cutha, in Mesopotamia, now Iraq. His birthplace is called Ever-ha Nahar ("Beyond the River"). It is believed he lived somewhere between 2,000 BCE to 1,700 BCE according to biblical chronology. However, the exact dates are subject to ongoing debate among scholars.*
>
> *He was the tenth generation removed from Noah, being a direct descendant of Shem, (Noah's son), the father of all the "Semitic" peoples. When Abraham was born, Shem was 390 years old, and his father Noah was 892 years old. Abraham was 58 years old when Noah died. His father's name was Terah, who was seventy years old when Abraham was born. In the Torah, Terah was a*

merchant who sold idols and was the chief officer or minister of the first king mentioned in the Torah, the mighty King Nimrod of Babylon (also known by its former name, Shinar, and the land of the Chaldees). Terah was an idol worshipper, like his king, and their chief god was the Sun.

Abraham's mother's name was Amathlaah. On the very night of his birth, Nimrod's stargazers told the king that Terah's newly born son would one day be a danger to his throne. Nimrod ordered Terah to send him the baby, to be put to death. Terah, however, outwitted the king. Abraham, from when a baby, lived with his mother and nurse, in a cave until ten years old when he decided to go to old Noah and Shem.

When he was 48 years old, while still at Noah's house that Abraham heard about the world-shattering event of the Tower of Babel, which took place in the land of Shinar, where Nimrod reigned supreme. Nimrod and his people wanted to build a tower that would reach up to heaven, so that they might establish their reign upon heaven as well as on the Earth.

It was the height of arrogance and defiance of men against G-d, and it led to confusion and to their dispersal and division into seventy tongues and nations. Abraham decided that it was high time for him to go out and teach them the truth about G-d, and about the falsehood and worthlessness of the idols. He knew that in defying Nimrod, and even his own father, he would be risking his life, for Nimrod had proclaimed himself god and demanded that all the people worship him...Abraham's activities, in words and deeds, aroused Nimrod's anger. Both Abraham and his father were ordered to appear before the king. Here the king's stargazers at once recognized Abraham as the one about whom they had warned the king.

Terah was taken to task for deceiving the king, and he put the blame on his older son Haran, who was 32 years older than Abraham. Haran had secretly followed Abraham, but he was not quite sure whether he was wise in doing so. He thought that he would come out openly on Abraham's side, when Abraham would come out victorious.]

I wonder, if what happened to Abraham next was the original story of Daniel in the Bible?

[Nimrod ordered that Abraham be thrown into a burning furnace. When Abraham came out unharmed, Haran declared himself on Abraham's side and chose to be likewise thrown into the furnace, and he was burnt to death. Abraham, on the other band, whom G-d had so wonderfully saved from the fire, was acclaimed by all the people, and they were ready to worship him. But Abraham told them to worship G-d, who had saved him from the burning furnace, and that he himself was nothing but a human being.

Nimrod was greatly afraid of Abraham. He gave him many precious gifts, among them Eliezer, a member of the king's household, who became Abraham's trusted servant and friend. Abraham, and his remaining brother Nahor, married two sisters, their nieces, the daughters of their brother Haran. Nahor married Milkah, and Abraham married Yiskah, better known as Sarai, (later-Sarah).

Two years later, Nimrod had a strange dream and once again his counsellors interpreted it to mean that as long as Abraham lived, his kingdom would be in danger. Nimrod, who had been worried about Abraham all the time, decided to try again to kill him, and sent men to capture him.

Fortunately, Eliezer learnt of the plot and informed Abraham in good time. Abraham, with his band of followers, numbering over 300, fled to Noah. About a month later, his father Terah came to visit him there. Abraham persuaded him to give up his idolatry. He pointed out to him, moreover, that his life was also in danger, for Nimrod would not spare him...

Thus Terah, his son Abraham and his wife Sarai, and Lot, Haran's son, and their entire household left Ur of the Chaldees in Babylon and set out for Canaan. On the way they came to Charan, where Nahor lived, found it a good place, and stayed there. Three years later, when Abraham was 55 years old, G-d appeared to Abraham and told him to take his wife and household and go on to Canaan. This Abraham did and he stayed there 15 years.]

According to the web article, Sasha Lessin, Ph.D, www.enkispeaks.com/articles/Articles DrLessin/Abraham

[Abraham was the super slave toady of the Nibiran Enlil, Commander of the gold mining expedition from the planet Nibiru to Earth and chosen by Enlil to be a general of his cavalry... Abraham descended directly from Enki's son Ziasudra (Noah) and Ziasudra's son, Shem... In

8,650[BCE], Enlil had ordered Shem's descendants to rule Canaan, the area north of the Sinai Spaceport...

Abraham, a royal descendant of Shem, was to re-establish Enlil's rule of Canaan and protect Sinai because of others trying to take over the area] to rule "all the lands from the border of Egypt to the border of Mesopotamia." (Sitchin, 1985, The Wars of Gods and Men, pages 289 – 297) ... Enlil gave Abraham land and riches until he was the richest man of his time.

In 2,048 B.C., Enlil then ordered him to Canaan and to save Sinai [Sitchin, 2007, The End of Days, page 73) The Commander bought Abraham the best chariots, finest horses, 380 well-trained soldiers and weapons that "could smite an army of ten thousand men in hours. Enlil sent Abraham, then 75 years old, and his nephew Lot to the Negev dry lands bordering the Sinai ...Enlil's emissaries/angels, Ninurta and Nergal, sent Abraham and his nephew [Lot] to spy on Sodom and Gomorra, cities Marduk controlled.

*From Sodom and Gomorra, Enlil feared, Marduk "would marshal his large number of human followers and control of all establishments on Earth, including the Sinai spaceport." (Tellinger, M. 2006, **Slave Species of God**, page 506) ... Enlil ordered Abraham, then 99, and his male followers to cut off their foreskins so they'd be clearly marked for Enlil and his sons and have phalluses like those of the Nibirans.*

Enlil told Abraham that after circumcision, he'd conceive a son by Sarah, who was his half-sister, and who, by Nibiran succession practices, would produce a son who would supersede Is-mael, Abraham's son with his secondary wife, Sarah's erstwhile Egyptian slave. Sarah bore Isaac in 2,025 BCE in Canaan [Sitchin, Z., 1995, Divine Encounters, page 288] (Anthropology, U.C.L.A).]

So far, we can see that the main Bible characters were not necessarily who they are said to be and that whoever wrote the books credited to Moses took stories from earlier records.

THE STORY OF ADAM & EVE

Our Earth's history goes back thousands of years and to understand who Jesus really was (and if he even existed), we need to know how the man called "Adam" came to exist and when. This Bible account, according to Christians, explains our fall from grace and what we need to do to redeem ourselves or that we need a redeemer, Jesus Christ and why there is evil in the world.

What if the true story of the creation of humans is completely different? How do we see our own beliefs and what they are based upon?

JEWISH MYTHOLOGY

On the website article, [22]**Lilith in the Torah**, there are two versions of creation. Lilith is the woman mentioned in the first creation story and was Adam's first wife, who became a demon. Eve is the one made later created from one of Adam's ribs because that's not what the original Hebrew word means. We are reminded that if we are reading the Bible in English, we are reading a translation. Biblical Archaeology says "tsela" appears 40 times in the Bible, and the only time it's translated as "rib" is when Eve shows up. It usually refers to the side of something, or "limbs lateral to the vertical axis of an erect human body."

A legitimate Biblical professor put forward the idea that Eve was in fact made from Adam's baculum. So, if Eve was just made from some vague side area of Adam, this leaves a lot of interpretation. Enter the "dong bone theory". Since the penis bone is extremely common in mammals (even other primates have one) but humans males are missing this piece of kit, Dr. Ziony Zev it thinks Genesis holds the answer. If God took a bone from Adam, then his descendants presumably wouldn't have that bone. Men have an even number of ribs but are missing the baculum. 'So, it stands to reason', he says, 'that's the real bone God formed Eve from if indeed this story is a true account'.

The Sumerian story is backed up by Elena Danaan in her book, **The Seeders**, page 495. She says she had a conversation with Ea/Enki, on his spaceship (which is called Nibiru), [not a planet as Sitchin thought]; she claims he explained to her in person his side of things and she wrote that in 360,000 BCE, Ea/Enki, a geneticist, put his own DNA into upgrading a Homo Sapien man who was a hybrid, named Adam.

He was then coupled with a female [aka Lilith?] who didn't have the right frequency and died prematurely. Ea then created another female from Adam's genetics in his laboratory in Ed.in (Eden) and she came to be known as "Eve" who matched Adam's frequency. So, there is a bit of a difference between the two versions.

PRE-ADAMITES

Pre-Adamite simply means that there were people alive before Adam. Creation Ministries International says this idea comes from 1,655 CE when a French guy wrote two books about it. This theory solved some problems, like where Cain's wife came from. In Genesis, only Adam, Eve, Cain, and Abel are mentioned when Cain murders his brother. But suddenly we learn there are cities of people and Cain quickly finds a wife. The pre-Adamite theory explains where they came from.

Obviously, I'm not going to write the whole article here as I hope I've shown that there were humans on Earth long before Adam and Eve. However, there may be something else hidden in the story and the timeline may be much older than what we are told. Although it could be true that the man called Adam was the first ancestor of Yeshua/Jesus, this lineage is much older as I will show in Chapter 6, Part I. There is always some truth in these ancient stories, so I ended up going down another rabbit hole.

WERE ERIDU AND EDEN TWO DIFFERENT PLACES?

It's well known that many Hebrew texts were adaptations of Sumerian stories. Whenever I mention Enki and Enlil to anyone, they don't want to know about them or think about any civilisation earlier than the Egyptian one. Considered as the first true city, Eridu, founded around 5,400 BCE, is believed to be the original settlement from which southern Mesopotamia, or Sumer, grew.

Its prominence lay in its role as a religious centre, housing an imposing ziggurat (stepped pyramid) and various temples dedicated to Enki, the Sumerian god of water, knowledge, and creation. Eridu carries biblical significance because some scholars associate it with the Garden of Eden illustrated in the Book of Genesis. Interpretation similarities exist between Eridu's mythology – involving the god Enki living in a garden by the riverside and creating humankind from clay – and the biblical account of Adam and Eve in the Garden of Eden.

So, Adam and Eve lived in Eridu, with their creator who was Enki (Ea), a scientist and geneticist and one of the Anunnaki. Was Eridu part of Atlantis? How did "Eden" come into the picture? Many, including Bible scholars, concluded that the Garden of Eden was somewhere in the Middle Eastern area known today as the Tigris-Euphrates River Valley.

See also: *www.icr.org/article/where-was-garden-eden-located* and *www.genesisforordinarypeople.com/faq/is-there-any-evidence-for-the-garden-of-eden*

As you can see, trying to get a completely accurate understanding isn't as easy as it should be because of all the different viewpoints, but I found it fascinating to see the picture coming together. Are you still with me? My research has shown me that there's so much more to this story, especially since JWs also claim that Adam was the first witness of Jehovah in a long line of witnesses and ancestors of Jesus, as do other Christian religions and Islam. Muslims believe Adam was the first prophet.

ISLAM

The Encyclopaedia Britannica says there is no concept of original sin in Islam. Adam and Eve were punished for what they did, but that punishment was for them alone, not all of humanity forever. Muslims don't believe in the concept of original sin as expressed in the Bible and therefore, no saviour was needed. *www.al-islam.com* explains that people are responsible for what they do, not what your parents or grandparents did. It doesn't make sense that humanity inherits their parent's sins and so Muslims don't accept the concept of original sin.

WHO WROTE THE 12 HISTORICAL BOOKS?

I found from the following information that very few books of the Bible could be credited to anyone for sure. You would think that such important records would have a person responsible for the, especially if God was dictating or inspiring the information as has been claimed.

JOSHUA (YEHOSHUA): There is no statement in the book of Joshua telling us who wrote it, though some of the material may have been based on what Joshua himself recorded.

THE BOOKS OF THE JUDGES (SHOFETIM) are believed to have been written by the prophet Samuel who (1070-1012 BCE) and tell of six major judges and their struggles against the oppressive kings of surrounding nations. Other books may have been written by Ezra, a descendent of Aaron and Nehemiah.

BOOK OF ESTHER - No one knows who wrote the (originally called Hadassah). The name "Esther" probably derives from the name of the Babylonian Goddess, Ishtar, or from the Persian word cognate with the English word "star" (implying an association with Ishtar). Some scholars contend it is related to the Persian words for "woman" or "myrtle".

Some scholars speculate that the story was created to justify the Jewish appropriation of an originally non-Jewish feast. One popular theory says the festival has its origins in a Babylonian myth or ritual in which Mordecai and Esther represent the Babylonian gods Marduk and Ishtar. Others trace the ritual to the Persian New Year, and scholars have surveyed other theories in their works.

As I did my research for the books mentioned above, I was struck by the lack of evidence as to who wrote these books and when. One would think that if they were really inspired by a "God", there would be no ambiguity. Also, these books show just how God condoned the killing of so many people despite one of his laws being 'do not kill'.

WHO WROTE THE 5 POETIC BOOKS?

What sets these five books apart is their portrayal of the human experience—joy, love, pleasure, heartbreak, pain, relationships, loss, suffering, doubt, decision-making and everyone's need for intimacy with God. There are three kinds of poetry:

- **LYRIC POETRY**, which was originally accompanied by music on the lyre (the Psalms)

- **DIDACTIC POETRY**, which, using maxims was designed to communicate basic principles of life (Proverbs, Ecclesiastes)
- **DRAMATIC POETRY**, which used dialogue to communicate its message (Job and the Song of Solomon).

THE BOOK OF JOB[23]

The book of Job is one of the world's oldest, most influential and most powerfully written works of literature. The book does not identify the author, or if story of Job was recorded by Samuel, Moses, or an even earlier Hebrew author. here is no way to be entirely sure who wrote Job or exactly when it was written. There are several good reasons to interpret the book as historical rather than allegorical.

Some theorise that the book is also written mostly in poetic form. As a result, some wonder if the book of Job is, in fact, a parable or allegory. Another explanation for this story of how a good man like Job suffered so much wasn't to show how someone can stay faithful to God no matter what.

The reason given was so that "God" could show he could do whatever he likes, and no human has a right to judge him. Now I've found out who the God of the Bible is, I think that version is nearer the truth.

PROVERBS, ECCLESIASTES & SONG OF SOLOMON: Most likely written by Solomon.

PSALMS: Commonly referred to as God's hymnal,

the book of Psalms is a collection of Psalm 90, Psalms 72 and 127 were penned by David's son Solomon. Many of the psalmists were priests or Levites who led the sacred temple worship. However, King David was the most prolific of the psalmists. I recently heard that David was actually Thoth/Djehuti, but I need to check this out.

WHO WROTE THE 17 PROPHETIC BOOKS?

I won't write much under this heading but quite a lot of information about these books is in

www.tka.org/uploaded/Enotify/Documents12.08.16_Questions_-_Prophets.pdf

When you think the Abrahamic religions base their belief systems on the Old Testament (Hebrew Scriptures), it is obvious that they don't want people to know from where they have taken their stories. In response to a forum discussion on the "Yahwism under the Achaemenid Empire" Conference, on 15th January 2023 Neil Godfrey posted the following:

> *[I would like to encourage anyone who thinks we have evidence for the "biblical religion", or "Biblical Yahwism", or for knowledge of any of the Pentateuch in the Persian period to listen to Kratz's Yahwism under the Achaemenid Empire.*
>
> *Kratz begins by warning that biblical scholars risk making fools of themselves (compared with other scholars of ancient history or historiography) if they continue to ignore the evidence and pretend to know more than we can know. He concludes by saying that we have no evidence at all that what we read in the literature*

we take to be from the Persian period (Esther-Nehemiah, for example) has any historical relevance. The reason many scholars like to speak of Persian era Yahwism is that works like Ezra-Nehemiah give us a convenient narrative. But we have no idea who wrote them, when, where or why. if there was a "biblical Yahwism" of some kind in the Persian period, it was so limited in extent and influence that it left no trace in the epigraphical or other archaeological evidence.

Kratz re-affirms the work of Adler who demonstrates that we are not simply falling back on arguments from silence but that there is clear evidence that "Biblical Judaism" only makes its historical appearance in the second century.]

Many theologians study the biblical languages – ancient Hebrew, Aramaic and Koine Greek and I've found Mauro Biglino (See Sources of Information) one of the best translators so far. As always there are some truths in these scriptures, and I found Mauro Biglino's book very enlightening because he goes into the original words and their meanings.

THE NEW TESTAMENT

The New Testament contains 27 books written in Greek by 15 or 16 different authors between 50 CE and 120 C.E. It can be divided into 4 groups: Gospels, Acts of the Apostles, Epistles, and Apocalypse. I've extracted some information from the following website:

www.bibleoutsidethebox.blog/2017/09/30/yes-the-four-gospels-were-originally-anonymous-part-1/#_edn1

MARK

Mark was written anonymously by a Greek-speaking Christian outside of Palestine. This Gospel is a compilation of oral traditions, and perhaps written ones, though none of these survive. Of the extant Gospels, Mark appears to have been written first and was used by Matthew and Luke.

> *[At the very beginning of his biography, the author states that Jesus was the Christ (the Greek equivalent to the Hebrew term "messiah"), a title that was meaningful only to Jews. In the first century there were a variety of views of the messiah. Some Jews believed that the messiah would be a king; others believed that he would be a cosmic judge.*
>
> *All notions about the messiah (that we know of) presented him as powerful. The problem Mark confronted was the paradox of Jesus as a suffering messiah...Mark himself may also have been a Gentile since he misunderstands some of these Jewish traditions.]*

MATTHEW

The author of this Gospel used Mark, Q, and his own sources (designated by scholars as "M"). The Gospel was written between 80-85 CE.

> *[In Matthew, Jesus is unmistakably Jewish: Matthew emphasizes Jesus' connection to two of the most important figures in Jewish history, David and Abraham...Matthew's Jesus does not advocate abandoning the Mosaic Law.*

Instead, Jesus insists he has not come to abolish the law but to fulfill it. Jesus urges his followers to keep the law even more rigorously than the scribes and Pharisees. Jesus explains what he means in the next passage, known as the antitheses. In these statements, it is clear that the spirit of the law, not the letter, is ultimately what God's people are called to keep.

The law is summarized in two commandments: "love the Lord your God with all your heart, and with all your soul, and with all your mind" and "love your neighbour as yourself." Thus, love is at the core of the entire law.]

LUKE

The author of Luke also wrote the Acts of the Apostles...In Luke, Jesus does not preach the imminent end of the world. Rather, the end will occur after the mission to the Gentiles is completed. It is perhaps because of this delay of the end of time that Luke emphasizes Jesus' concern for social injustices.

JOHN

Like the other Gospels, the Gospel of John was written anonymously, though it has traditionally been attributed to John the son of Zebedee, thought to be the "beloved disciple" mentioned in the Gospel.

[Some of the stories may go back to one of Jesus' followers, but the Gospel itself was written well after the deaths of the disciples. In addition, our investigation has shown that this Gospel is the compilation of a number of different sources...The Johannine letters indicate that a schism has

occurred within the community... In the Gospel, Jesus is depicted as equal with God; some members of the Johannine community continued pushing their Christology higher and higher until not only was Jesus equal with God, but he was also God.

If Jesus was God, moreover, he could not be flesh and blood - he only appeared to be human. The Johannine Epistles were written from the more conservative point of view: Christ was flesh and blood; he was the saviour who had come in the flesh for the salvation of all humans.]

Jesus is not mentioned by any pagan writer in the first century. The first helpful pieces of information from pagan literature about Jesus' life come from Tacitus, a Roman historian writing around 115 CE. Tacitus says that Pontius Pilate executed Jesus.

In addition, Jesus is mentioned in Josephus' Antiquities of the Jews, a first-century Jewish text. Josephus says that Jesus was a teacher and a "doer of startling deeds" who had Jewish and Gentile followers. In this passage, Josephus also states that Jesus was the Messiah. Since Josephus never converted to Christianity, and since his works were copied and transmitted by Christians, we can be relatively sure that this "confession" was a later Christian insertion.

The non-Christian sources give little helpful information, so we must rely on Christian texts, but the non-canonical Gospels are late and usually rely on earlier materials is of little use to historians seeking the historical Jesus.

THE APOSTLE PAUL[24]

The Apostle Paul always spoke about, Yahweh, God and the Father of Jesus. (2 Cor 11:31) and refers to Jesus as "Lord", never as God. To me, this was clear that Jesus and God his Father, were two separate identities. Remember, the God of the Old Testament, Jehovah, didn't have Jesus's approval and neither the Apostles Paul nor John referred to Jesus as God.

The Apostle Paul wrote most of what is in the New Testament and has often been considered the most important person after Jesus in the history of Christianity. He is the founder of Christianity really, not Jesus who didn't actually create a new religion but said he came to 'fulfill the law' (according to the Bible).

As a Pharisee before his conversion, he believed in life after death. He also believed non-biblical "traditions" as being about as important as the written Bible. He was very knowledgeable about Greek philosophy because of his warning to the Corinthians not to seek salvation through philosophy which Paul contrasts to the "Wisdom of God hidden in Christ".

Both the Apostle Paul and Thomas Aquinas had a deep belief and faith in their God. Paul believed in the Hebrew God, Yahweh which could explain why he didn't hesitate to punish the Jews showing interest in Jesus's teachings. Thomas Aquinas firmly believed his God, was the author of the Bible who used men to write the words down and he was right. Paul was an eventual follower of Jesus (though not one of the Twelve Apostles) who professed the gospel of Christ to the first-century world. He is commonly regarded as one of the most influential figures of the Apostolic Age and founded several churches in Asia Minor and Europe. He took advantage of his standing as both a Jew and a Roman citizen to counsel to both Jewish and Roman audiences.

If the Apostle Paul and Thomas Aquinas believed in the God of the Bible (Yahweh/Jehovah) and Jesus was God made flesh, and then the Mormon's claim that Jesus was Jehovah is correct. However, Jesus was nothing like the God of the Old Testament, in fact he was the opposite.

We might expect that Paul, the earliest New Testament author, would be a good source of information about the historical Jesus, but he says very little about Jesus' life. Therefore, historians must return to the New Testament Gospels for information about the historical Jesus.

It has been pointed out by many that Christianity is not the religion OF Jesus but the religion ABOUT Jesus. Thus, Christianity begins not with Jesus' birth, his public ministry, or even with his death and resurrection. According to [25]Bart Erhman, the Apostle Paul's public ministry is not the core of Christian belief. Instead, the core of Christianity is the belief in Jesus's death and resurrection. Erhman does not think that Paul and Jesus delivered the same message in their preaching, or that they did so in the same way. There was an enormous difference between what they taught. There are points of contact and continuity, to be sure. But the differences are stark and need to be borne in mind constantly.

[Jesus preached that the Kingdom of God was soon to arrive with the appearance from heaven of the Son of Man. People needed to prepare for that imminent catastrophic event by turning to God and living in the ways that he decreed through the proper observance of the Torah, principally by loving (and trusting) God above all else and by loving their neighbours as themselves.

Those who did so would survive the coming onslaught and would be brought into the Kingdom. Paul agreed that there was an imminent disaster to take place. But in his view, that would happen when Jesus himself arrived from heaven in judgment.

The way a person would survive the onslaught was not by obeying the Law of God or by loving their neighbours as much as themselves. Salvation would come only by believing in Christ's death and resurrection.]

THE NEW TESTAMENT & CHRISTIANITY'S EVOLUTION

Many years ago, whilst still a Witness, I read the book, **The Christians**, written in 1977 by Bamber Gascoigne. On page 12 he wrote that:

[...'for the first fifty years of what we now call the Christian era, not a word survives in any document about Christ or his followers'] He then quotes the remarks made by various Romans in the second century about the early Christians and that the earliest gospel was written by Mark. He mentions how the Dead Sea Scrolls written by the Essenes and hidden c.70 CE were found, but I

didn't find any reference to the Nag Hammadi Scriptures found in 1945 in the book.]

On page 46, he wrote:

[As early as the fourth century, a bishop described Constantinople itself as seething with these topics of discussion. In this city if you ask anyone for change, he will discuss with you whether God the Son is begotten or unbegotten. If you ask about the quality of bread, you will receive the answer, 'God the Father is greater, God the Son is less'. If you suggest that a bath is desirable, you will be told, 'there was nothing before God the Son was created.]

Just as the topic of Brexit (the withdrawal of the UK from the European Union (EU) was brought in practically every conversation in 2019-2020, so the discussion about the position and divinity of Jesus Christ was discussed. This was because the newly produced gospels mentioned the Father, the Son, and the Holy Spirit, but not the concept of the Trinity. Below is the version today most commonly referred to as the "Nicene Creed" first adopted in A.D. 325 at the Council of Nicaea. The Council of Constantinople in AD 381 expanded the language of the creed to clarify the orthodox concept of the Trinity.

> We believe in one God the Father Almighty, Maker of heaven and Earth, and of all things visible and invisible. And in one Lord Jesus Christ, the only-begotten Son of God, begotten of the Father before all worlds, God of God, Light of Light, Very God of Very God, begotten, not made, being of one substance with the Father by whom all things were made; who for us men, and for our salvation, came down from heaven, and was incarnate

by the Holy Spirit of the Virgin Mary, and was made man, and was crucified also for us under Pontius Pilate. He suffered and was buried, and the third day he rose again according to the Scriptures, and ascended into heaven, and sitteth on the right hand of the Father. And he shall come again with glory to judge both the quick and the dead, whose kingdom shall have no end. And we believe in the Holy Spirit, the Lord and Giver of Life, who proceedeth from the Father, who with the Father and the Son together is worshiped and glorified, who spoke by the prophets. And we believe in one holy catholic and apostolic Church. We acknowledge one baptism for the remission of sins. And we look for the resurrection of the dead, and the life of the world to come. Amen.

Other than the Apostles' Creed, the Nicene Creed is likely the most universally accepted and recognized statements of the Christian faith. It seems that opinions were accepted or rejected based on whether the person accepted the Nicene Creed.

From what I can understand from this Creed, God is separate to Jesus (who sits at his right hand in heaven), therefore, he isn't God. Jehovah's Witnesses reject this Creed saying that Jesus never claimed to be the God of the Old Testament or part of a Trinity which is the main reason they give for not accepting they are Christians.

You can't be a Christian unless you believe in the Trinity. I go into this in chapter 6, Who is Jesus?

BIBLE TRANSLATIONS

Many accuse JWs of having changed the meaning of some of the original scriptures, especially by having inserted the name Jehovah in place of the word LORD. However, JWs are no different to any of the other Christian religions in changing the meanings of the original words claiming their version is the Truth.

Using the name, Jehovah instead of LORD or Lord exposed who the God of the Bible was. This is why Muslims do not use that name but "Allah" which is Arabic referring to the God of Abraham, but that still hasn't hidden the fact Abraham's God is assumed to have been Jehovah according to the Bible.

When the word God was translated from the Greek 'Theos', he was made in the image of Roman emperors, and when he was known as the Latin "Deus". He was made in the Latin image of feudal kings and lords who demanded total obedience and acceptance of the state religion and "Deus" was originally "Zeus", the God of the sky, lightning and the thunder in Ancient Greek religion and mythology.

The writings of both the New and Old Testaments have been scrutinized for hundreds of years by theologians, anthropologists, scientists, archaeologists and historians, and tweaked (by adding or taking things away) with numerous imperfect translations based on the translator's own beliefs and agenda. Scholars readily admit this.

JW'S NEW WORLD TRANSLATION

I still have the **New World Translation of the Holy Scriptures (printed in 1984)** with cross references with the claim that this version for Jehovah's Witnesses was a translation from the original languages of Hebrew, Aramaic and Greek (Koine, not modern). It was originally released in six volumes from 1950 to 1960, with revisions having been made in 1961 and 1970. In 1969, the Greek text was revised by Brooke Wescott & Fenton Hort. They leaned heavily on the **Codex Sinaiticus**, also known as "A", "Aleph" (the Hebrew letter א), which was found by Count Tischendorf in 1859, at the Monastery of St Catherine on Mount Sinai.

The **Codex Vaticanus**, known as "B," was found in the Vatican library. It is comprised of 759 leaves and has almost all of the Old and New Testaments. It is not known when it arrived at the Vatican, but it was included in a catalogue listing in 1475, and it is dated to the middle of the 4th century. Modern scholars have varying theories on how these ancient texts should be viewed. Some believe that the most ancient reading should be followed, as it is closest in time to the original.

Their work has proved to be impressively accurate, though far from perfect not only advanced the science of textual criticism, but it added considerable weight to the claim that the Bible had been preserved from tampering and corruption.

Whilst researching Wescott & Hort, I came across Dr Chuck Missler, an American author, evangelical Christian, Bible teacher, engineer, and businessman, who heavily criticised them, especially as they denied the deity of Jesus Christ.

When I started my research, I came across a book by Daniel Rodriguez, The Watchtower: An Occult

Theocracy. He claims that Greber had listened to demons via the seances he had attended.

Daniel Rodriguez was ordained in 1995 with the International Church of the Foursquare Gospel, serving as a Foursquare pastor in the San Diego area and in Portland, Oregon. He holds a degree in psychology and specializes in Cult thought reform. He believed that Greber's many claims in denying the inspiration of the scriptures, the Deity of the Holy Spirit and rejecting the Trinity were blasphemous. That Jehovah's Witnesses used his translation in their Bible showed them to thus be a demonic cult.

JOHANNES GREBER

Now let's look at the New Testament translator, a German-ordained Roman Catholic priest. In 1923, he attended a séance, and his life was changed. He renounced his vows and left the Catholic Church. He moved to the USA in 1929 and began a non-denominational church, with prayer and healing sessions in Teaneck, NJ.

He later worked on a translation of the New Testament, publishing **The New Testament, A New Translation and Explanation Based on the Oldest Manuscripts (1935).**

He claimed he used the oldest sources available including the Greek codex D. Where a meaning was not clear, according to his prologue, after much time in prayer he received supernatural guidance as he translated with his wife acting as a medium, and with visions of the actual words given to him on occasion.

In his book, Rodriguez wrote on p.54 that Johannes Greber asked the spirits to tell him what was wrong with the King James Version of the Bible, and a young spirit medium told him that:

> [The teachings of Christ are no longer found in their original purity and clearness in those documents which have come down to you. In what is called the New Testament, several paragraphs, indeed entire chapters have been omitted. What you have now are mutilated copies. Even the last letter of the Apostle Paul addressed to the Christian communities, has been destroyed. In it he carefully explained those passages in his earlier writings that had given rise to misunderstanding. But his explanations were not in accord with many erroneous doctrines that had subsequently crept into the Christian faith.]

From my own research, Greber was right in his claims. The Greek scriptures used in the King James Version did have much missing from the original writings left out of the KJV. So, I think this was a case of the 'pot calling the kettle black' in that Daniel Rodriguez was also in a cult. In his search for truth about the scriptures and their writers being inspired by Holy Spirit, in the article [26]**Communication with the spirit-world of God,** Johannes said:

> [We distinguish between two kinds of "inspiration." In one case, only the thoughts are inspired in a person by a spirit of God, and these thoughts are written down in the person's own words and in his own human style of expression. In the case of the other kind of "inspiration" not only the thoughts are imparted, but the very

words in which these thoughts are to be uttered. This is nothing more nor less than "dictation" on the part of God's spirit. "Inspiration" of this kind is known as "literal" or "verbal" inspiration......

Of the books of the New Testament, only one, The Revelation of John, was communicated by an angel. What is more, John stresses this fact in the very opening sentence of his book. The authors of all the other books of the New Testament say nothing about the operation of any supernatural influence upon the writing of their reports. Luke, on the contrary, expressly states in the first few lines of his gospel that he has compiled his story in quite the ordinary human way...

His account, therefore, contains the things that were told to him by eyewitnesses, and not those that were imparted to him by the Holy Ghost...At all events, the apostles do not say that their epistles were inspired by the Holy Ghost......It follows that the Christian churches cannot produce from the New Testament itself any proof of their doctrine of inspiration. Neither has "God's" Spirit at any time declared the books of the New Testament to be "inspired writing."

The only two ways by which the New Testament could possibly be proved to be inspired, are therefore eliminated from consideration. Hence only this fact remains: The authors of the New Testament writings wrote of their own choice and on the basis of their purely human knowledge, with the exception of The Revelation of John.]

JWs have left themselves open to their version of the New Testament being criticised because Johannes

Greber and his wife were believers of spiritism, something JWs heavily condemn as being demonic practices.

KARL MARX

As I was writing the above, I suddenly remembered the quote 'religion is the opium of the masses' and so I looked it up and found this was a saying by Karl Marx.

I found this article quite enlightening as I had heard about Karl Marx, but never investigated his work. His family had left Judaism to become Lutheran. Marx had rejected religion early on in his youth and made it clear that he was an atheist. He became known as a German philosopher, economist, historian, sociologist, political theorist, journalist, critic of political economy, and a revolutionary socialist.

He was working primarily in the realm of political philosophy. He co-wrote The Communist Manifesto in 1848 and was the author of Das Kapital, which together formed the basis of Marxism.

I quote from *www.learnreligions.com:*

> *[...who attempted to examine religion from an objective, scientific perspective. Marx's analysis and critique of religion 'Religion is the opium of the Masses' is perhaps one of the most famous and most quoted by theist and atheist alike...Marx actually said very little about religion directly; in all of his writings, he hardly ever addresses religion in a systematic fashion, even though he touches on it frequently in books, speeches, and*

pamphlets. The reason is that his critique of religion forms simply one piece of his overall theory of society—thus, understanding his critique of religion requires some understanding of his critique of society in general.

According to Marx, religion is an expression of material realities and economic injustice. Thus, problems in religion are ultimately problems in society. Religion is not a disease, but merely a symptom. It is used by oppressors to make people feel better about the distress they experience due to being poor and exploited...Although it might profess valuable principles, it sides with the oppressors... this new form of Christianity, Protestantism, was a production of new economic forces as early capitalism developed.

New economic realities required a new religious superstructure by which it could be justified and defended...The problem is that opiates fail to fix a physical injury—you only forget your pain and suffering for a while. This can be fine, but only if you are also trying to solve the underlying causes of the pain.

Similarly, religion does not fix the underlying causes of people's pain and suffering—instead, it helps them forget why they are suffering and causes them to look forward to an imaginary future when the pain ceases instead of working to change circumstances now. Even worse, this "drug" is being administered by the oppressors who are responsible for the pain and suffering....

Whatever one's conclusion about the accuracy or validity of Marx's ideas on religion, we should recognize that he provided an invaluable service by forcing people to take a hard look at the social web in which religion always occurs. Because of his work, it has become impossible to study religion without also exploring its ties to various social and economic forces. People's spiritual lives can no longer be assumed to be independent of their material lives.]

Although as I said before, I'm not an atheist or an advocate of communism (as we know it today) or any manmade religion, I cannot help but agree with much of what I read in this article, because I've come to understand more about this world and why it is the way it is. Karl Marx (and his supporter, Friedrich Engels) originally supported workers, but it seems that his ideas were hijacked by the ruling powers to control people even more and of course, Karl Marx has been blamed ever since.

As a result, Communist countries are greatly criticised by Western countries as lacking in allowing their people "freedom", but I believe the Western world subjugates their own people in the same way, although much more subtly, whilst giving them the illusion of freedom.

Humans are born with an innate sense of right and wrong, but this can often be overridden by the choices we make, or others instill in us. This is why so many have believed it was the right thing to do, to kill animals or humans offer them up as sacrifices to their God; go to war for land or resources, kill others who disagree with us or take revenge when someone has wronged us. Humans have this amazing ability to justify themselves in such circumstances.

THE RELIABILITY OF THE BIBLE

Jehovah's Witnesses call themselves Bible Students and everything they believe is based on the Bible (any version but mainly their own). All the meetings and literature are Bible-based, but very few research further back as I have done to find out the origins of these scriptures. JWs teach that Christendom is "Babylon the Great", the world empire of false religion which will be destroyed leaving only the true religion, theirs.

Recently I wondered if perhaps the Abrahamic religions were each originally formed at different times to see which one was most effective to control people as part of the plan to create this New World Order with one religion – the worship of Jehovah (aka Enlil).

What do you think? What was the real inspiration behind the creation of the Bible and religions, if not to hide the truth of our origin and Earth's history? This question led me to find out more about the early civilisations and their belief systems as you saw in the previous chapter.

To get some more understanding of the truthful seeds, I needed to go back in time to the beliefs of the early Christians where the first seeds were planted, to understand more about Jesus and who he was. Some early followers became known as Gnostics, and this label included non-Christians, Jews and pagans.

GNOSTICISM

Gnosticism is derived from the Greek word Gnosis meaning "to know" and this was influenced by Jewish, Pagan and Iranian teachings that predate Christianity. Most of the information we had on the Gnostics was derived from the critical early Church Fathers, (such as Justin and Irenaeus who was the first to preach the Gospels of Matthew, Mark, Luke and John). They regarded the Gnostics as heretics, and this led me to look into the meaning of the word "heretic" (see Chapter 4).

In 1945, the **Nag Hammadi Codices** (a collection of early Christian and Gnostic texts), were discovered near the Upper Egyptian town of Nag Hammadi. So, I read **The Gnostics** by Sean Martin.

> *[The two most well-known Gnostics, Valentinus and Marcion never referred to themselves as Gnostics but as Christians, a name given to them by the Romans...There are two basic components to Gnostic beliefs, although the importance of one over the other can vary immensely.*
>
> *The first is Gnosis – knowing from personal experiences, and the second is Dualism, the existence of two creators, one good, and the other evil (who later came to be called Satan the Devil). The Creator God of goodness and pure spirituality was often called the Godhead.*
>
> *The second Creator (often called the demiurge) was the creator of the physical world, which has trapped divine souls in mortal form. In some cases, the demiurge is a God in and of itself, equal*

and opposite to the Godhead. In other cases, the demiurge is a being of lesser (although still considerable) standing. The demiurge might be a specifically evil being, or it might simply be imperfect, just as its creation is imperfect.]

In both cases, Gnostics worship only the Godhead. The demiurge is not worthy of such reverence. Some Gnostics were highly ascetic, rejecting the material word as strongly as possible. This is not the approach of all Gnostics, although all are ultimately spiritually focused on gaining an understanding of and unification with the Godhead.

Gnostic thought had a profound impact on the development of Christianity, which traditionally sees a struggle between an imperfect material world and a perfect spiritual one. Even the name, Jehovah, was hidden for years because it was considered "too holy". Then, along came Jehovah's Witnesses (perhaps meaning well) and much to Christendom's annoyance. They took some of the "seeds of truth" and combined them with their own "weeds" to create yet another belief system and money-making religious organisation, with rules based on the Bible.

In 2020 I bought a copy of Raymond Franz's book, **Crisis of Conscience**, a book JWs were told not to read because it was written by an "apostate", although many more former elders are speaking up now.

[His book presents the story of a struggle to prevent the erosion of a God-given freedom of conscience and the ensuing dilemma of choosing between loyalty to God and loyalty to one's religion. A former member of the Governing Body

of Jehovah's Witnesses, Raymond Franz delivers a rare glimpse into the inner workings of the Watch Tower Society.

In response to extraordinary events, Franz tells a unique account of the decision-making sessions of this religion's inner council and the powerful, sometimes dramatic, impact their decisions have on Jehovah's Witnesses. Crisis of Conscience offers a penetrating view of the supreme council of this organization, the Governing Body and their life altering power over human lives.

While the events of Raymond Franz's departure from the Governing Body occurred in 1980, the organizational foundation and structure remains the same today, making this account relevant to a whole new generation. He reveals the inner workings and the decision-making processes of that Body, offering a penetrating view of the life altering power they have over human lives. The final nine of his sixty years as one of Jehovah's Witnesses were spent on this central executive council. Those years led to his crisis of conscience, which is the theme of this book.]

Something many good people have struggled with, whatever their religion. Not all become atheists after leaving their religions, but they chose to believe in an unnamed God that is Love, rather than one who is the opposite. Here are some more JW teachings which they say are based on the Bible.

BASIC TEACHING 11: CONSTRUCTING KINGDOM HALLS AND OTHER FACILITIES TO FURTHER THEIR WORLDWIDE BIBLE EDUCATION WORK, SHARING IN DISASTER RELIEF

BASIC TEACHING 12: THE ORGANIZATION CONSIST OF CONGREGATIONS OVERSEEN BY A BODY OF ELDERS (NOT A CLERGY CLASS AND UNSALARIED). THERE IS NO TITHING BUT SUPPORT THEIR ACTIVITIES BY NONYMOUS DONATIONS. THE GOVERNING BODY SERVES AT THE WORLD HEADQUARTERS AND PROVIDES DIRECTION FOR THEM WORLDWIDE

[Visitors who tour our printeries often marvel at the industrious people they observe producing this literature. All of these men and women donate their time and energy. When they come to Bethel, a name that means "House of God," most of them have no experience in the printing industry. However, an in-house training program, combined with a work environment that encourages training, yields good results.

For example, it is common to see young men in their 20s are operating a high-speed printing press that can produce 16-page magazines at the rate of 200,000 per hour.' Their publications are of good quality with colourful pictures. They operate 15 printing facilities, and the work is carried out mainly by volunteers located in Africa, Asia, Australia, Europe, North America, and South America manned by volunteers.]

When I became involved with the voluntary sector, the first thing I did was apply to Companies House for a copy of the Organisation's (Watchtower & Bible Tract Society') Memorandum & Articles; it was a company limited by guarantee and this was how they protected the individuals running it. The Organisation, like Churches, has charitable status so doesn't pay taxes and they rely on government grants, donations and income from their properties. When people donate to the Organisation, they are told their donation is for 'Jehovah's work' and is tax deductible.

Apparently, The Watchtower Bible & Tract Society's peak revenue was $67.0M in 2023. The UK branch of Jehovah's Witnesses as shown on the [27]*Charity Commission website* had a gross income of £100.90 million. These funds are also linked to THE SOCIETY KINGDOM HALL FUND. From this income, they fund their activities, evangelism, and disaster relief via donations, but I also heard that they have access to a large loan each year.

The quick-build Kingdom Halls are built by volunteers of congregations. They then use the hall for their meetings but the Society, at any time, can sell the buildings and land and keep the money. They don't belong to those who donated their money and time but to "Jehovah" and his organisation

A 2023 comment on Reddit in response to someone saying that The Watchtower & Bible Tract Society was worth 52 billion USD.

> *(www.reddit.com/r/exjw/comments/17iouwi/apparently_the_watchtower_bible_and_tract_society/)[*That doesn't include convention centers, bethels and headquarters. That should be another 7 billion. We already have $30 billion in real estate assets. But on top of that, there's a lot of equipment, printing presses, farms, vehicles, trucks, a lot of other assets. You've got another $5 billion. In fact, we don't know what other stock portfolios they have...maybe another $5 billion. We're up to $40 billion. and the existing cash flow

and know how as an MLM business, the number of members and cash donations are still worth something. 52 billion USD is an optimistic estimate but not far from reality in my opinion.]

According to www.eafeed.com, the ten richest churches in the world in 2022 are

1. The Church of Jesus Christ of Latter- Day Saints (The Mormons) - worth about $100 billion

2. **Catholic Church Vatican** - worth $33 billion

3. **Catholic Church Germany** - net worth $26 billion

4. **Catholic Church Australia** - worth $22.3 billion

5. **Church of England** – net worth is $9 billion

6. **Opus Dei (part of the Catholic Church)** - net worth $3 billion

7. **Church of Scientology** – net worth $2.5 billion

8. **Episcopalian Church** – worth $2 billion

9. **Freemasonry** (is not really a religion, but to join it, one must believe in some supreme being) Members of the Freemason are known to be very wealthy individuals who own very big organizations worldwide. Claims have it that they are the richest organizations in the world

10. **The Kenneth Copeland Ministry** – worth $1 billion

We can see how much wealth the different religions have. As far as JWs are concerned who really benefits – Jehovah or the organisation?

Judge Rutherford, a former President of the Watchtower & Bible Tract Society, said in his 1939 lecture, "Religion is a Snare and a Racket". Of course, he was talking about other religions, but is this organisation any different?

SEXUAL IMMORALITY & MARRIAGE

> BASIC TEACHING 10: FAMILY – THEY ADHERE TO GOD'S ORIGINAL STANDARD OF MARRIAGE WITH SEXUAL IMMORALITY BEING THE ONLY GROUNDS FOR DIVORCE

When I first started studying with the Witnesses, I asked why adultery was the only ground for a divorce. At that time, I was in Cyprus and my husband had returned to England. I wanted to know why any bad treatment by either spouse was not grounds for divorce.

In the Bible, sexual immorality is strongly condemned, being in love with someone was no excuse, and yet in the Old Testament followers of Jehovah were told to loot, murder and rape and sell their daughters. On the other hand, according to the New Testament, Jesus stopped a woman being stoned to death and told her not to "sin" anymore. (John 8:7).

Humans are very quick to condemn others but can turn a blind eye when it suits them. Not that I condone any such wrongdoings, but we must be careful not to judge others without understanding the motives first, is all I can say.

Religious people, especially church leaders, royalty and nobles throughout history have committed adultery, fornication, cruelty and pedophilia but this is ignored, especially if that someone is rich and powerful.

People marry for many different reasons apart from being in love; some because they are lonely, want a family, or for financial gain or their parents force them to marry someone. People become prostitutes for many reasons too. There are also many reasons for wanting to end a marriage.

Many "good JWs" have been shunned because they can no longer remain in a marriage where they are physically or verbally abused but have no proof of adultery. If they separate from their spouse, they cannot divorce and remarry unless one or both commits adultery which breaks the marriage bond.

> BASIC TEACHING 13: UNITY - THIS ALLOWS FOR PERSONAL CHOICE WITH NO SOCIAL, ETHNIC, RACIAL OR CLASS DIVISIONS. THEY ENDEAVOR TO MAKE THEIR DECISIONS BASED ON THEIR OWN BIBLE-TRAINED CONSCIENCE

> BASIC TEACHING 14: CONDUCT – THEY AIM TO SHOW UNSELFISH LOVE IN ALL THEIR ACTIONS AND AVOID PRACTICES THAT THEY BELIEVE DISPLEASE GOD INCLUDING TAKING BLOOD TRANSFUSIONS, TAKING PART IN WARS, RESPECTING GOVERNMENTS EXCEPT WHEN ITS LAW ARE NOT IN CONFLICT WITH GOD'S LAWS

Jehovah's Witnesses are most well-known for denying the Trinity, the deity of Christ, the personhood of the Holy Spirit, hell and the doctrine of eternal punishment. They demand high standards of morality within their ranks. Their view of sexual behaviour reflects conservative Christian views. Abortion is considered murder. Homosexuality, premarital sex and extramarital sex re considered "serious sins".

They don't observe holidays such as Christmas, Easter and birthdays as I had been taught, they had pagan origins. They don't vote, salute the national flag or sing the national anthem, and they refuse military service. I've never voted because at the time I wanted to be ruled by God's government not a manmade one.

BLOOD TRANSFUSIONS

The Witnesses' stand against blood transfusions reflects the significance of blood in their faith. They hold that blood is sacred and represents life. The belief that they should "abstain from from...blood" comes from a biblical passage in the book of Acts 15:29.

I turned down a blood transfusion when faced with an emergency operation. As much as I loved my children, I loved my God more than my own life. Having seen the film, *Life for Ruth*, I now knew why JWs had faith enough to do this. However, they do have about sixty alternatives to blood transfusions such as artificial blood products or "non-blood alternatives".

The fact that many have received contaminated blood only helped to prove JWs right in not taking anyone else's blood. Even now, I don't like the idea of having someone else's DNA in my body but that's for other reasons.

DISFELLOWSHIPPING & SHUNNING

Those who commit a serious sin or who decide to leave the Watchtower Society, whether formally or informally, are "disfellowshipped." This is done in other strict religions too, JWs aren't the only ones. Contact with members who are disfellowshipped is limited to certain people, such as those who have contractual obligations or family members living in the same home. Even then it can be very strained.

The Watchtower Society advises Witnesses to minimize socializing with those who aren't members, to maintain their spiritual integrity and morality. I've never been disfellowshipped but my family members who are still Witnesses avoid me.

My sister and I keep in touch every few months, but we avoid talking about religion because anyone who dares to question the teachings or leave this organisation becomes an "apostate" to be shunned by family members and friends who remain Witnesses.

It often takes years for someone to come to terms with being shunned. Some have even committed suicide. It's an extremely cruel way to treat anyone even if it is claimed to be done out of love and happens in many strict religions.

JW DRESS CODE

As a JW, if you didn't dress modestly, you'd get in trouble. Later, some rules on clothing extended to men (tight pants were too "homosexual"). But when I was a Jehovah's Witness, tight pants for men were not yet in fashion, so the women got most of the counsel, as we did in many other parts of our lives, too. White socks were also banned.

When I was staying with a JW family in Cyprus, the husband told me I wasn't allowed to wear trousers whilst staying with them. I even lengthened all my miniskirts. Beards were not allowed either, which really didn't make sense. This rule has now changed but for many years Jehovah's Witnesses had the rule that, 'bearded members can be a matter of disturbance to the congregation and can stumble fellow congregants.

If congregants were "stumbled" by a member's beard, the member was expected to shave 'for the sake of the conscience of others. According to their publications, Jehovah's Witnesses in most countries and cultures aren't allowed to have beards because they say beards are associated with extremism or rebellion against society.

Considering religious Jews had beards and Jesus would most likely have had one, this rule didn't make sense at all. If the individual did not comply, he would likely have faced extreme social pressure and criticism from friends, family and other members of the congregation for not adhering to the direction of the elders. Now in 2024, the Governing Body has just announced that men can have beards and women can wear trousers to meetings and in the ministry, many are just confused by this change.

Whilst writing this part, I came across an article by Amber Scorah, [29]How *I dressed after leaving*

Jehovah. As I enjoy Chinese and Korean films, I was interested to see she had gone to China as a JW but left the religion to return back to the USA.

Her book, **Leaving the Witness: Exiting a Religion and Finding a Life**, hasn't yet found its way into my book collection. I had not looked at other accounts of ex-Witnesses until recently, although I occasionally watched 'Kim Mikey' on YouTube as this couple keeps up to date on what is going on in the organisation and unravels Bible teachings.

> BASIC TEACHING 15: RELATIONSHIP WITH OTHERS – THEY ENDEAVOR TO FOLLOW JESUS' COMMAND TO LOVE THEIR NEIGHBOURS, TO BE NEUTRAL IN POLITICAL AFFAIRS AND NOT AFFILIATE WITH OTHER RELIGIONS WHILST RESPECTING THE CHOICES MADE BY NON-JWS

I found JWs loving and friendly most of the time, but they were also very judgmental too. They will avoid you if you are considered spiritually weak in case this rubs off on them.

Whatever they say, they don't respect the choices made by a Witness leaving the Organisation (rejecting "The Truth") though, but view that person as a 'dog returning to its vomit, a foolish person. This phrase "as a dog returns to its vomit" is a Bible verse from Proverbs 26:11 that compares a fool to a dog that returns to its vomit, repeating the same foolish actions. (also partially quoted in 2 Peter 2).

Women were regarded as complement for a man, submissive to their husbands, who is the head of their family, and it is he who makes all the important decisions. This isn't bad if you have a kind and reasonable husband, but awful if not. Women can't teach in the congregation, cannot deliver public talks or say public prayers. When they conduct a private Bible study or say a prayer with another person, if a man is around, she must wear a scarf or something on her head as a sign of being submissive.

As for homosexuality, of course that is unacceptable by JWs. I believe this boils down to whether one believes in the Bible (or the Quran). There is an interesting discussion between Bart Ehrman and Jeffrey Siker on YouTube,

DOES THE BIBLE CONDEMN HOMOSEXUALITY?
www.youtu.be/iFYTTG3Q37w?si=I9pbgZPbDswKuAFU

Having learnt the origin of the God of the Bible, who he really was and the origins of many of the stories, I can no longer accept the Bible as an infallible spiritual guide for humans.

Over the years I have spoken with many people from all different faiths and listened to them as they tried to convince me that their beliefs were the truth just as I had done in the past. They were sincere, lovely people who had no doubts that they were on the right path to their salvation as taught by their religious leaders, the "experts" just as I had been.

OTHER BOOKS

THE EPIC OF ATRAHASIS is the fullest, but not the oldest, Mesopotamian account of the Great Flood, with Atrahasis in the role of Noah. It is said that the Great Flood was sent by the Gods to destroy human life. Only the good man, Atrahasis was warned of the impending deluge by the God Enki (aka Ea) who instructed him to build an ark.

THE EPIC OF GILGAMESH is about Utnapishtim or Uta-na'ishtim who is tasked by the God Enki/Ea to create a giant ship to be called Preserver of Life in preparation for a giant flood that would wipe out all life. Utnapishtim ("He Found Life") is spirited away by the Gods with his wife and lives forever in the land across the seas.

THE AZTEC FLOOD STORIES: There are several accounts, but authors argue that the most famous of them all is that of Nota, the Aztec version of Noah.

GUN-YU MYTH: Another interesting flood story can be found in ancient Chinese literature known as the Great Flood of Gun-Yu, or the Gun-Yu myth. The event is described as a major flood that lasted for more than two generations, resulting in various natural disasters such as cataclysmic storms turn resulted in famine and population displacement. This flood is thought to have taken place during the reign of Emperor Yao, a legendary ancient Chinese ruler.

THE MYTH OF ADAPA: The earliest record of the Myth of Adapa is from the 14th century BCE. Adapa was a Sumerian citizen who was blessed by the God Enki with immeasurable intelligence. One day Adapa was knocked into the sea by the south wind, and in a rage, he broke the south wind's wings so that it could no longer blow. Adapa was summoned to be judged by An [Enki's father] and beforehand Enki warned him not to eat or drink anything offered to him. An had a change of heart when he realized just how smart Adapa was, and offered him the food of immortality, which Adapa, dutiful to Enki, turned down.

BOOK OF THE HEAVENLY COW: The biblical work draws on the earlier oral version of the Mesopotamian flood story which is echoed in the works cited above and which may also have influenced an Egyptian text known as The Book of the Heavenly Cow, a part of which dates to Egypt's First Intermediate Period (2,181-2,040 BCE). It tells how, after the sun God Ra had created humans, they rebelled against him, and he decided to destroy them.

THE SUMERIAN KING LIST: The famous Sumerian King List (abbreviated SKL) or Chronicle of the One Monarchy covers 241,000 years. On the website, *(www.earth-history),* there is an article by the writer, L.C. Geerts who wrote:

> *[In accordance with the Sumerian story, there were seven previous ages (time about 270,000 years) before the Great Flood. The early Sumerian king list names eight kings with a total of 241,200 years from the time when "the kingship was lowered from heaven" to the time when "the Flood" swept over the land and once more "the kingship was lowered from heaven" after the Flood.*
>
> *In the lists, Kingship is seen as a divine institution: it descended from heaven. This is what is meant by the "Divine Right of Kings". The opening line of the text is: When kingship was lowered from heaven, the kingship was in Eridug.' Because of this, kingship is seen as an institution that is*

shared by different cities. Each city takes its turn during a certain period. About eight (in other versions ten) antediluvian kings are mentioned, together with their periods of government. The first kings reigned in pre-historic times and lived for unbelievably long periods of time before the Flood. Added together they "would have" ruled for 241,200 years......

Scholars are aware that there is even a problem with the time the Kings lived, and which Kings eventually ruled together in different cities. We will see that they are wrong because only a few dynasties existed together but most of them followed each other as the king list clearly describes.

As mentioned, scholars are unwilling to except the long lifetime of the first kings in this list and they say that the lifetime is purely fictitious but on the other hand most of them accept the long lifetime of the Earth fathers in the Bible as true. I can't imagine that over a period of thousands of years in which several versions of the King list were written down all authors were propagandists. Scholars composed their timeline because they read the King list with "human eyes".

Nevertheless, most scholars still believe in the long lifetime of the Earth-fathers in the Bible (Adam - Noah of about 900 years each). They accept that as a fact but why not accept the timeline of the Sumerian King list as a fact? Another argument is that Assyriology is a young science and it's impossible that scholars can make a conclusion that the time spans, mentioned in the King list, are based on fiction...]

ENŪMA ELIŠ: This exists in various copies from Babylon and Assyria and the version from the Archaeological Library of Ashurbanipal dates back to the 7th century BCE.

> *[The composition of the text probably dates to the late 2nd millennium BCE, or even earlier, to the time of Hammurabi during the Old Babylonian Period (1900–1600 BCE) ...Its primary original purpose is unknown, although a version is known to have been used for certain festivals. There may also have been a political element to the myth, centred on the legitimization or primacy of Babylonia over Assyria. Some later versions replace Marduk with the Assyrian primary God, Ashur.]*

THE DEAD SEA SCROLLS: The book I have was written by Philip R. Davie, George J. Brooke and Phillip R. Callaway, who translated the 2,000 year old scrolls were found in Qumran between 1947 - 1953. They cover the historical backdrop to the scrolls, recent archaeological site where it is believed the writers lived and look at the heated debates that arose from these findings.

> *[...Almost all the Hebrew Bible is represented in the Dead Sea Scrolls. The majority of the Dead Sea Scrolls are in Hebrew, with some fragments written in the ancient paleo-Hebrew alphabet thought to have fallen out of use in the fifth century BCE. But others are in Aramaic, the language spoken by many Jews—including, most likely, Jesus—between the sixth century BCE and the siege of Jerusalem in 70 CE. In addition, several texts feature translations of the Hebrew*

Bible into Greek, which some Jews used instead of or in addition to Hebrew at the time of the scrolls' creation.]

THE BOOKS OF ENOCH: These books are contained in the Bible of the Ethiopic Christian Church and have influenced Bible writers as few others have.

[These recount how Enoch was taken up to Heaven and was appointed guardian of all the celestial treasures, chief of the archangels, and the immediate attendant on the Throne of God. He was subsequently taught all secrets and mysteries and with all the angels at his back.

__1ST ENOCH__ (aka The Book of Enoch) composed in Hebrew or Aramaic and preserved in Ge'ez, first brought to Europe by James Bruce from Ethiopia and translated into English by August Dillmann and Reverend Schoode – recognized by the Orthodox Tewahedo churches and usually dated between the third century BCE and the first century CE. It is in six sections.

__2ND ENOCH__ (aka Book of the Secrets of Enoch), preserved in Old Church Slavonic, and first translated in English by William Morfill – usually dated to the first century CE.

__3RD ENOCH__, a rabbinic text in Hebrew usually dated to the fifth century CE Enoch identifies as Metatron, the angel which communicates God's word. In consequence, Enoch was seen, by this literature and the Rabbinic Kabbalah of Jewish mysticism, as the one who communicated God's revelation to Moses, and as the dictator of the Book of Jubilees.]

[28]**THE TALMUD:** In addition to the Torah (first five books of Moses), modern Jews follow the teachings in the Talmud' which is a collection of writings that covers the full gamut of Jewish law and tradition. Talmud is Hebrew for "learning," lives to studying and mastering.

It was compiled and edited between the third and sixth centuries written in a mixture of Hebrew and Aramaic, it records the teachings and discussions of the great academies of the Holy Land and Babylonia. Jews tend to refer to the Talmud in the same way the Witnesses rely on the Watchtower & Awake, and other publications for explanations of the scriptures.

NAG HAMMADI SCRIPTURES: This is the most complete, up to date, one-volume, English-language edition of the renowned library of 4th century Gnostic manuscripts discovered in Egypt in 1945. It includes introductory essays, notes, tables, glossary, index, etc. to help the reader understand the context and contemporary significance of these texts which have shed new light on early Christianity and ancient thought.

THE COMPLETE 54-BOOK APOCRYPHA – 2022 EDITION: This version contains all the books from the 2018 edition, plus dozens more, all revised and retranslated into a clean, literal, and easy-to-read translation, part of the LSV collection. This is the largest and most comprehensive collection of non-Gnostic apocryphal books ever produced. It includes the Catholic and Orthodox Deutero-canon material, all three of the books of Enoch, Jasher, Jubilees, the Aramaic Book of Giants, the testaments, apocalypses, pseudepigrapha, New Testament-era works, the Apostolic Fathers, and more.

It's not an easy read for the writing is very small, but you can discover what the world was like before Noah's Flood, who the Nephilim were, how Cain died, how Abraham was tutored in the knowledge of God by Noah's son Shem, what happened during the 400 "silent years," how the Prophet Daniel slayed a dragon, and the answers to countless other mysteries. The Literal Standard Version (LSV) is a modern translation that stays true to the original manuscripts.

THE CHALDEAN ACCOUNT OF GENESIS: Assyriologist first published this book in 1876. It contains an alternative and earlier account describing creation including the story of Gilgamesh. He translates the story of the Creation as it appeared in ancient texts, as well as the Tower of Babel and the Destruction of Sodom.

In addition to the texts that are parallel to stories from the Christian Bible, Smith gathered tablets which tell the history, culture and religion of ancient Mesopotamian cultures. He discovered a tablet with the story of Ishtar, Goddess of sexuality and warfare, who descended to the Underworld. He also tells the story of the Babylonian God Zu, which was then an obscure religious story to the Babylonian and Assyrians.

WHEN GOD WAS A WOMAN: I came across this book by Merlin Stone whilst researching what the religious beliefs before 5,000 years were. According to Merlin, archaeologists have traced the worship of the Great Mother Goddess/Queen of Heaven back to the Paleolithic period.

> *[Whilst researching for her book, she focused on the Paleolithic and Neolithic periods of Earth's history particularly in the near and Middle East where Judaism, Christianity and Islam were born. She found that during the old Stone Age, 50,000 to 12,000 years ago (Upper Paleolithic period) there were matrilineal (mother-kinship) societies where the lineage and heritage was handed down through the female line. Over the centuries the respect and authority once held by matriarchs, changed to patriarchal and to the detriment of women.]*

Billy Carson did a workshop video where he told his audience about the books he had read, some of which I have already mentioned. More books for me to get now.

BANNED HISTORY BOOKS ARE NOT WHAT YOU THINK | BILLY CARSON & 4BIDDENKNOWLEDGE
https://youtu.be/jtCikkgZqgg?si=KPheNSrc8UrZqkFz

4 - WHO IS GOD?

BASIC TEACHING 1: BELIEF IN ONE GOD, JEHOVAH BEING THE GOD OF ABRAHAM, MOSES AND JESUS

Until I became a Witness, I had believed in and prayed to a male, unnamed God. In this chapter I will do my best to clarify who is the God that so many worship and are willing to die or kill for.

WHY IS GOD CALLED GOD?

I decided to look up the word "God" and its origin and according to the website *www.wahiduddin.net* it seems no one knows its origin except for a fact that the word God is a relatively new European invention. It was never used in any of the ancient Judeo-Christian scripture manuscripts which were written in Hebrew, Aramaic, Greek or Latin. According to the Catholic Encyclopaedia:

> *[...The root-meaning of the name (from Gothic root gheu; Sanskrit hub or emu, "to invoke or to sacrifice to") is either "the one invoked" or "the one sacrificed to." From different Indo-Germanic roots (div, "to shine" or "give light"; thes in thessasthai "to implore") come the Indo-Iranian*

deva, Sanskrit dyaus (gen. divas), Latin deus, Greek theos, Irish and Gaelic dia, all of which are generic names; also Greek Zeus (gen.Dios, Latin Jupiter (jovpater), Old Teutonic Tiu or Tiw (surviving in Tuesday), Latin Janus, Diana, and other proper names of pagan deities.

The common name most widely used in Semitic occurs as 'el in Hebrew, 'ilu in Babylonian, 'ilah in Arabic, etc.; and though scholars are not agreed on the point, the root-meaning most probably is "the strong or mighty one."]

www.oxfordreference.com says:

[The earliest written form of the Germanic word God comes from the 6th-century Christian Codex Argenteus. The English word itself is derived from the Proto-Germanic *ǥuđan. The reconstructed Proto-Indo-European form *ǵhu-tó-m was likely based on the root *ǵhau(ə)-, which meant either "to call" or "to invoke"

So as far as the world is concerned, there are many definitions of the word "God" and so beliefs are based on which definition is preferred and believed. In Strong's Concordance, the Greek word 'Theos' in English meant [God, a god: theós (of unknown origin) – properly, God, the Creator and owner of all things (John 1:3; Gen:1-3).

Long before the NT was written, (theós) referred to the supreme being who owns and sustains all things. The above definitions say that God is 'a higher being in the universe beyond our world, the creator of all known existence, owner of everything and who rules in conjunction with lower gradients of divinity (angels)', one who was neither male or female, having existed even before anything was created.]

Allegedly, God was "pure love" and didn't have any other negative emotions. However, we find that the view of God differs amongst mankind in that some claim their male God gets angry, jealous and is willing to punish or annihilate thousands who refuse to obey His will.

Therefore, like many others, I asked myself which version was true. Most of us have asked, if there really is a God who is supposed to be pure love, how can He allow such bad things to happen in the first place, especially to innocent children, and why this God doesn't put an end to such suffering?

So far, I've concluded that there seems to be four main camps as to the Supreme Creator God's qualities:

1. The view which gives God a male gender, as expressed in the Old Testament and Quran often with human emotions, only rewarding those when it suits Him.

2. The view of a genderless God with qualities as expressed in the New Testament of the Bible: Jesus told the Samaritan woman in (John 4:24 KJV)

   "The God who made the world and everything in it, being Lord of heaven and Earth, does not live in shrines made by man, nor is he served by human hands, as though he needed anything, since he himself gives to all men life and breath

and everything". (Acts 17:24–25)"

God is light" (1 John 1:5),
God is love" (1 John 4:8)

3. The early Gnostics' view that their God didn't actually create anything (that was another God):

[There is a true, ultimate, and transcendent God, who is beyond all created universes and who never created anything in the sense in which the word "create" is ordinarily understood. While this True God did not fashion or create anything, He (or, It) "emanated" or brought forth from within Himself the substance of all there is in all the worlds, visible and invisible.]

4. This view is a mixture of 1 and 2 above, with much criticism of those who adhere to the Gnostic view.

There is a book I am reading by Francesca Stavrakopoulou called **God: An Anatomy**. It reveals:

[...an astonishing and revelatory history that presents God as he was originally envisioned by ancient worshippers – with a distinctly male body, superhuman powers and Earthly passions.]

I will write about my findings in my next book.

MANY GODS

All the writers and YouTubers I found wanted to know more about God. Some had grown up with a religion; others were agnostic or atheists when they started their own spiritual journeys and research. What we all have in common is that we wanted evidence on which to build our knowledge and faith in our search for the Truth.

Many Christians dislike the idea of there being other gods, but for thousands of years people around the world have worshipped different gods. Who were these gods? From what I've learnt about Lemuria, Atlantis and other early records, it was a second wave of extraterrestrials that had come to Earth 445,000 years ago, who came to be worshipped by humans as the gods and goddesses of the world's mythologies.

They were far superior to humans in many ways with their appearance, intelligence, knowledge and technology. Those who helped and taught humans were loved; those who scared and bullied humans were feared. Whether you choose to believe this or not doesn't alter the fact that the humans who worshipped them believed they were real.

The much criticised or much admired, Zechariah Sitchin wrote the **Earth Chronicles Series, 'Divine Encounters** and **Genesis Revisited**, suggesting an explanation for human origins involving ancient astronauts.

Sitchin attributed the creation of the ancient Sumerian culture to the Anunnaki, which he stated was a race of extraterrestrials from a planet beyond Neptune called Nibiru. Elena Danaan says that Nibiru was a spaceship, not a planet.

Many others, inspired by Sitchin to investigate further, such as Erich Von Daniken, Michael Tellinger and Graham Hancock did their own research and developed his findings further. Needless to say, the other writers have also been admired or criticised too. Their studies of the translations of the Sumerian texts opened the world of the Anunnaki translated as 'Those who from Heaven to Earth Came'.

WHERE IS GOD?

Most people would agree that there is a spirit world and a physical world. As far as most people are concerned, the spirit world, invisible to us, is where God and the angels are said to exist, the heavens. But what made people believe that? If there really are Extraterrestials living on other planets, then who is their God? Does God live in the heavens with them?

WHO IS JEHOVAH?

Many think that the name "Jehovah" is just made up by the Witnesses, not realizing that it is the name of the God in the Bible. They believe that not using this name is disrespectful. Jehovah's Witnesses say that 'Jehovah is the true God of the Bible, the Creator of all things.' (Revelation 4:11) and that the prophets Abraham and Moses worshipped him, as did Jesus.

I can't disagree with him being the god of the Bible, that or with the fact that he is the God, not just of one people, but of "all the Earth" (Psalm 47:2). Although He is called by different names, I wanted to know whether this God should be worshipped the way we are told to worship Him. He also had many other names:

[Titles & Descriptive Terms applying to Jehovah: Ancient of Days, Shaddai, Creator, Father, God, God of Gods, God of Truth, Grand God, Happy God, Holy God, Indefinitely lasting God, Instructor, Jealous (meaning exclusive devotion), Jehovah of Armies, King of Eternity, King of the Nations, Living God, Majesty, Maker, Most High, Overseer of your souls, The Rock, Saviour, Shepherd, Sovereign Lord (Adho-nai), Supreme one, The (true) God (ha-'Elo-him, ha-'El), The (true) Lord (ha-'A'dhohn').]

YAHWEH BEFORE HE WAS KNOWN AS JEHOVAH

According to www.worldhistory.org/Yahweh:

[Yahweh is the name of the state god of the ancient Kingdom of Israel and, later, the Kingdom of Judah. His name is composed of four Hebrew consonants (YHWH, known as the Tetragrammaton), which the prophet Moses is said to have revealed to his people, and is sometimes given in English as "Jehovah".

The meaning of the name has been interpreted variously as "I am", "He That Is", "He Who Makes That Which Has Been Made" (Yahweh-Asher-Yahweh), "He Brings the Hosts Into Existence" (Yahweh-Teva-`ot) and, according to the philosopher Rabbi Moses Maimonides (l. 1138-1204), denotes "absolute existence" or "the totality of existence."

As the name of the supreme being was considered too holy to be spoken, the consonants YHWH were used to remind one to say the word 'adonai' (lord) in place of the god's name, a common practice throughout the Near East in which epithets were used in referencing a deity. All of these stipulations and details were applied to the god later, however; it is unclear exactly when Yahweh was first worshipped, by whom, or how...

The meaning of the name Yahweh, as noted, has been interpreted as "I Am" or "He That Is", though other interpretations have been offered by many scholars. In the late Middle Ages, `Yahweh' came to be changed to `Jehovah' by Christian monks, a name commonly in use today.]

Jehovah's Witnesses say they reinstated the name Jehovah in their Bible, 7,000 times because they believe it was deliberately hidden from people by 'Satan, god of this system'.

[Although Judaism had its roots in the Bronze age (3,300 – 1,200 BCE) amidst polytheistic Ancient Semitic religions, specifically evolving out of the polytheistic ancient Canaanite religion. It was only by the Hellenic period (323 BCE - 30 BCE) that most Jews came to believe that their god was the only god and that the Jewish religion was formed, and this was forced upon them under King Josiah's reign.]

Hilkiah was the high priest of Judah during King Josiah's reign and was considerably influential in helping to re-establish the worship of the LORD (Yahweh). As for the 'wicked kings of Judah', Amon and Manasseh, they preferred to worship the other gods instead, so they were put to death. Is it "godly" to kill others who disagree with you? This, of course depends on your "God". I then came across Professor John Day's work. He argued that the origins of biblical Yahweh, El, Asherah, and Ba'al, may be rooted in earlier Canaanite religion, which was centred on a pantheon of gods much like the Greek pantheon.

www.centreforbible.oriel.ox.ac.uk/people/john-day states:

[This masterly book is the climax of over twenty-five years of study of the impact of Canaanite religion and mythology on ancient Israel and the Old Testament. It is John Day's magnum opus in which he sets forth all his main arguments and conclusions on the subject.

The work considers in detail the relationship between Yahweh and the various gods and goddesses of Canaan, including the leading gods El and Baal, the great goddesses (Asherah, Astarte and Anat), astral deities (Sun, Moon and Lucifer), and underworld deities (Mot, Resheph, Molech and the Rephaim). Day assesses both what Yahwism assimilated from these deities and what it came to reject. More generally he discusses the impact of Canaanite polytheism on ancient Israel and how monotheism was eventually achieved.]

WHAT KIND OF GOD WAS YAHWEH?

During the Second Temple Period (c. 515 BCE-70 CE) the Hebrew Scriptures were codified and the concept of a messiah whom Yahweh would send to the Jewish people to lead and redeem them was included. However, the Bible narrative also includes reference to the Canaanite god El – the Sky God (who was the Sumerian god known as An/Anu, father of the gods). According to the Bible (Deuteronomy 32:8-9), El gave each god authority over a segment of the people of Earth and Yahweh was assigned to the Israelites who, made him their supreme and only deity; but it is clear he existed beforehand as a lesser Canaanite god.

Yahweh as the all-powerful creator, preserver, and redeemer of the universe was then later developed by the early Christians as their god who had sent his son Jesus as the promised messiah and Islam interpreted this same deity as Allah in their belief system.

OTHER CHARACTERISTICS OF YAHWEH

Gérard Nissim Amzallag, a French Israeli biologist and an associate researcher at Ben Gurion University and holds a doctorate in biblical studies. His work on the origins of Yahwism was controversially received, describing the god's proposed origin as the Canaanite god of metallurgy.

Yahweh was transformed from one god among many to the supreme deity by the Israelites in the Iron Age (c.1200-930 BCE) when iron replaced bronze and the copper smelters, whose craft was seen as a kind of transformative magic, lost their unique status.

According to the website article, *www.gcrr.org/fun-facts/you-probably-worship-the-sumerian-god-enlil*

> *[What's your version of God like? A father-like figure who is pure Spirit, Mind, or is some*

embodiment of Nature? Does he want to love and bless everybody equally? Well, there's a good chance that your preferred deity (however you conceive of him) is actually something like the tenth iteration of the Sumerian god, Enlil...

STAGE ONE: SUMERIAN FATHER SKY GOD, ENLIL (CA. 2900-2800 BCE)

[The earliest recorded religion comes from the ancient Sumerians...Enlil ("Lord of Air") was the most powerful elemental deity who was considered Father and King of the gods...also worshipped by the Akkadians, Babylonians, Assyrians, and Hurrians.

A little later, Enlil's name was changed to Ellil by the Babylonians... He is depicted as an elderly father figure with a long beard, sitting on a throne in the sky. Although he was impatient and temperamental, Ellil was described as a benevolent, fatherly deity who cares for humanity's well-being.

Later, Ellil was absorbed and assimilated into the storm god Marduk during the Babylonian reign of Hammurabi (1792-1750 BCE). Merging storm gods with sky gods was a natural process for the ancients. Marduk would later become Zeus in Greek mythology....

El had a number of sons, including Ba'al and YHWH, the latter god being a distinct and separate deity from south of Canaan. According to the Bible ... El, turned over control of the Israelites to YHWH. (Ps 82, Deut. 32:8–9) ... YHWH became the patron deity of Israel's royal family.]

It is thought by many though that Enlil was really Zeus, not Marduk.

WHEN YAHWEH BECAME JEHOVAH

This name, the Tetragrammaton of the Greeks, was held by the later Jews to be so sacred that it was never pronounced except by the high priest on the great Day of Atonement, when he entered the most holy place. After Jewish scribes began inserting the vowels from the Hebrew word Adonai ("my Lord") into the name YHWH. The insertion resulted in the hybrid term YaHoWaH. William Tyndale introduced the Tetragrammaton as Jehovah in his translation of Exodus 6:3 after it appeared in other early English translations including the Geneva Bible and the KJV c.500 CE.

Richard Abanes, a nationally recognized authority on cults and religions, points out in **The Truth Behind the Da Vinci Code**, p. 19, 83) that:

> *[Scribes wanted this new word to remind readers that God's name was too holy to pronounce, so they should substitute Adonai for it when reading biblical passages aloud. Then, when the term YaHoWaH was Latinized, the "Y" and "W" were changed to "J" and "V"—resulting in Jehovah. In other words, Jehovah is a mis-transliteration, compounded by the fact that, while "J" has a "Y" sound in Latin; it has a very different sound in English—as in the word jam. Jehovah appears in no literature earlier than about the thirteenth century, and it began to be popularized in the sixteenth century by well-meaning but mistaken Christians.]*

You can imagine how shocked I was to discover that Yahweh/Jehovah was the same as the Sumerian god Enlil, and not the Supreme God I thought he was.

Ron Rhodes, Christian apologist and author of **The Ten Most Important Things You Can Say to a Jehovah's Witness**, p. 36:

> *[If Jehovah's Witnesses are correct that God must always be called by the name Jehovah, then Jesus was way out of line, for He never used this name when referring to the Father.]*

He explains that even though the Bible & Watchtower Society publishes (The New World Translation) and puts the word "Jehovah" in Jesus's mouth in their New Testament, the word "Jehovah" does not occur a single time in any legitimate manuscript copy of the New Testament.

SO, WAS JEHOVAH REALLY THE GOD OF ABRAHAM, MOSES AND JESUS?

Now, JWs claim Jehovah is the God of Abraham, Moses and Jesus. Their religious teachings revolve around the Bible and the worship of Jehovah. Whilst I do accept that Jehovah is the God of the Bible and ruler over the Earth, I no longer believe he is the Source or Creator of everything.

Although the Witnesses taught that Adam was the very first Jehovah's Witness, Adam and Eve were not included with Abraham, Moses and Jesus in the first basic teaching - which God did they worship?

A FEW OTHER NAMES OF THE CREATOR GOD

ALLAH: According to the Islamic scholar, Ibn Kathir, Arab pagans considered Allah as an unseen God who created and controlled the Universe. While using masculine principles of Arabic, God has no physical body parts or gender and transcends all: "There is nothing whatever like him, and he is the One that hears and sees [all things]" (42:11) ... The most popular descriptors of an attribute of Allah are "compassionate" and "merciful."

PTAH: The ancient Egyptian religion claimed the creator god Ptah created through speech. God created the first human couple, Adam and Eve, who were ordered to be fruitful and multiply.

WAHEGURU: Wonderful God or Lord - "The Creator", termed Waheguru. The Sikhs believe in "One God for All" or Ik Onkar. Waheguru is described and envisioned as a formless and omnipresent deity considered to be ultimate goodness in which the purified soul merges into, whilst evil is vanquished before it.

HAYYI RABBI (LIT=THE GREAT LIFE OR 'THE GREAT LIVING GOD'): Mandaeans recognize God to be the eternal, creator of all, the one and only in domination who has no partner.

VISHNU: Vaishnavism is one of the major Hindu denominations along with Shaivism, Shaktism, and Smartism. Vishnu is the primary creator and sole Supreme Being leading all other Hindu deities.

WHO WERE "HERETICS"?

If we are to believe that the God of the Bible, Yahweh, is really the Sumerian God (falsely claiming to be the Supreme Creator), and all the Abrahamic religions are really worshipping him, then who really were the heretics? Those who refused to accept Jesus was God, or who refused to worship Jehovah/ or Allah were considered "heretics"? The word "heresy" was derived from the ancient Greek word "haíresis".

Generally, it is any belief or theory that is strongly at variance with established beliefs or customs, particularly the accepted beliefs or religious law of a religious organisation. The English meaning originally meant "choice" or "thing chosen". However, it came to mean the "party, or school, of a man's choice", and referred to that process whereby a young person would examine various philosophies to determine how to live.

In the Abrahamic religions, heretics were any who didn't adhere to their particular belief system. A "divisive person" became a technical term in the early Church for a type of "heretic" who promoted dissension and there was a lot of dissension among the early Christians. Examples:

TERTULLIAN (c. 155–240 CE) implied that it was the Jews who most inspired heresy in Christianity because they denied Jesus being the Christ, so those who agreed with them were considered heretics.

IRENAEUS, in his 2nd-century tract, Contra Haereses (Against Heresies), he described and discredited his opponents during the early centuries of the Christian community. He described the community's beliefs and doctrines as orthodox and anything else as heretical.

Within six years of the official criminalization of heresy by the Emperor, Priscillian was the first Christian heretic to be executed. He was condemned in 386CE by Roman secular officials for sorcery and put to death with four or five followers. However, his accusers were excommunicated both by Ambrose of Milan and by Pope Siricius, who opposed Priscillian's heresy, but "believed capital punishment to be inappropriate at best and usually unequivocally evil".

The edict of Theodosius II provided severe punishments for those who had or spread the writings of Nestorius. Those who possessed writings of Arius were sentenced to death. For some years after the Reformation, Protestant churches were also known to execute those they considered heretics.

The last known heretic executed by sentence of the Catholic Church was Spanish schoolmaster, Cayetano Ripoll in 1826. Over the centuries, thousands of men, women and even children were put to death on charges of heresy based on the perpetrators' beliefs.

WHAT IS THE MEANING OF THE TERM "PAGAN" AND "HEATHEN"?

According to www.merriam-webster.com, an old fashioned and often offensive definition of "heathen" is 'a person who is not religious or whose religion is not Judaism, Islam, or especially Christianity.'

The site also explains that:

['The origins of heathen and pagan are semantically similar. Heathen likely comes from a term for a country inhabitant—in particular, a "heath dweller." The Latin source of pagan, paganus, originally meant "country dweller" or "civilian;" it was used at the end of the Roman Empire to refer to people who practiced a religion other than Christianity, Judaism, or Islam, and especially to those who worshiped multiple deities.

It's believed that the religious meanings of paganus developed either from the enduring non-Christian religious practices of those who lived far from the Roman cities where Christianity was more quickly adopted. Or from the fact that early Christians referred to themselves as "soldiers of Christ," making non-believers "civilians."

The first use of the word "pagan" was in the 15th century. In other words, those who did not follow the teachings of the Abrahamic religions and worshipped other gods. However, pagan practices were incorporated into the Abrahamic religions.]

Some even go so far as to destroy other people and their scriptures because their belief system was different to their own, all in the name of their God.

PAGAN CELEBRATIONS

Alexander Hislop wrote about these in his book, **The Two Babylons**, one of the books I found and read in the Cyprus Headquarters in 1970. Even when people are told about the origins of celebrations such as

Christmas, Easter, Holy Communion, rituals with food and numerous holidays. Many don't care where their beliefs came from, going by what they've been taught by their religions enjoying them without accepting that they themselves are just as "pagan" as the other "pagans". Others just enjoy the food, presents and company regardless of the custom's origin.

I was very unpopular with family members because I wouldn't celebrate birthdays, Christmas and Easter. Even now I'm no longer a JW; I still find it difficult to join in as much as I love my family and friends, knowing these celebrations started because of the worship of an evil god.

www.wonderopolis.org/wonder/why-do-we-blow-out-birthday-candles states:

[As it turns out, putting candles on birthday cakes is a tradition that has been around for a long, long time. It can be traced back to the Ancient Greeks, who often burned candles as offerings to their many gods and goddesses. For the Ancient Greeks, putting candles on a cake was a special way to pay tribute to the Greek moon goddess, Artemis.

They baked round cakes to symbolize the moon. Candles were added to represent the reflected moonlight. The inception of birthday celebrations is often attributed to the ancient Egyptians. When Egyptian pharaohs were crowned gods, they were "birthed." That means the first birthday celebration wasn't marking the birth of a human, but rather the birth of a god.]

The article on www.bouqs.com/blog/history-of-birthdays also explains more:

[Another early birthday celebration started with the pagans. Pagans believed that a person was especially susceptible to spells of good and evil during their birthday. Wondering why? During your birthday, personal spirits make their appearance. That means you're a bit closer to the spirit world. If you thought birthday wishes were silly, you may want to rethink your beliefs. The idea of spirits was also a focal point for the Greeks. They believed that everyone had a protective spirit or demon present at their birth. This same spirit formed a mystic relationship with the person and continued to watch over them during their lifetime. By celebrating the day you were born, you recognize the closeness of this spirit. This also supports the idea that birthday celebrations were originally events to create protection. Over time, some of these traditions morphed into the birthday celebrations we know and love. Whilst many feel that JWs are wrong not to celebrate birthdays, whether one likes to admit it or not it is still a custom that is associated with the worship of other gods.]

The main thing is that nowhere in the Bible does it say not to celebrate birthdays, the birth of a child is mostly a joyous occasion, but I don't think my children will ever forgive me for not celebrating theirs when they were young. I bought them presents throughout the year but not on their birthdays or Christmas. JWs celebrate wedding anniversaries and have Family Days instead. Ironically, despite having married three times, I never had the joy of celebrating a wedding anniversary with any husband.

IF JESUS IS GOD, IS HE ALSO YAHWEH/JEHOVAH?

Christendom believes Jesus is God. On the website for the Religious Studies Centre, [a Mormon site] in the article, *Jesus Is Jehovah (YHWH)* by Roger R. Keller, a professor emeritus of Church history and doctrine at Brigham Young University who taught comparative world religions. He is a convert to The Church of Jesus Christ of Latter-day Saints who served as a bishop and states:

> *[In Jesus's day, it was assumed by Jews that there was only one God—Jehovah (YHWH). Isaiah 44:6 condenses this Jewish understanding...But the New Testament added a new dimension when it ascribed divinity to Jesus (see John 1:1, 14; 20:28) or when it recorded that person worshiped Jesus (Matthew 2:2, 11; 28:17). Christian theologians since the Council of Nicaea have understood these passages through the doctrine of the Trinity, which states that there are three persons in the Godhead who are of one essence or of one nature. In this light, the mystery of God revealed in the incarnation of Jesus. According to traditional Christian thought, is that the Father (Jehovah) has a Son (Jesus).*

> *Thus, whatever can be said of Jehovah can also be said of His Son, who is a member of the Godhead, who is one with His Father, and who shares the nature of the Father. This Nicene presupposition blurs an extremely important message of the New Testament, that it is not the Father who this Nicene presupposition blurs an extremely important message of the New Testament, that it is not the Father who is Jehovah, but rather it is*

the Son who is the God of the Old Testament and who becomes incarnate. The unique Christian surprise is not that Jehovah has a son who is Jesus but rather that Jesus who is Jehovah has a Father. Latter-day Saints have made this point from the earliest times of the Restoration.]

So, the Mormons (or Latter-Day Saints) claim that Jesus is Jehovah, and it is understandable if you believe Jesus was God. But according to the Bible, Jesus criticised the "Father" the Scribes and Pharisees represented, Jehovah (YHWH/Yahweh), calling him a murderer and liar.

If we can believe the biblical account of Jesus then Jesus's Father was not the same as the one, he was criticizing. Therefore, was Jehovah really the same God Jesus worshipped as JWs claim? I don't think so, do you?

Having seen that the other famous characters in the Bible were known by different names, it shouldn't be any surprise to know that the same applies to Jehovah/Yahweh, the God of the Bible. Because this has been hidden from us so that throughout history humankind have, in fact, been worshipping the ancient god, Enlil and his cronies. This still didn't solve the problem of finding out who is the Supreme Creator though. Hopefully chapter 5 will make this clearer.

5 - SOURCE, THE LOGOS & THE HOLY SPIRIT

WHO IS THE REAL CREATOR OF EVERYTHING?

In the previous chapter, I explained why I have the belief that the God of the Old Testament, Yahweh/Jehovah, was Enlil, one of the Anunnaki who had orchestrated a massive flood to destroy mankind, and that it was his brother Enki who rescued Noah and his family. Thes brothers have been known by many other names too, but this would explain why the God of the Bible has two opposing personalities, one vengeful, jealous and cruel – the other loving mankind and benevolent.

Having understood this, my desire has been to delve deeper into finding out about the original Ultimate Creator, the one responsible for creating everything in the multiverses, including our souls that existed in the spiritual plane before taking physical forms, but I didn't know where to start.

WHAT IS THE HIGHER SELF & A WALK-IN?

After taking the overdose in 1993, I felt very different, as if something was missing. I came across the term "walk-in" in a book by William Linville, **Living in a body on a Planet- Your Divine Abilities**. At the time I didn't think much of it and just added this book to my collection after reading through it.

In 2020, when I learnt how to use a pendulum and started asking questions, I was surprised to learn that my current soul was a walk-in – a higher version of my soul that had taken over my body when I "died".

After talking to my daughters about this, they told me they had noticed I was different back then, but couldn't explain how, and so they never said anything. After learning this I bought another book by Sandra Daroy, **Walk-In Case.**

I now call my higher self, Milah, which is Hebrew for the Word/Logos as this is what the pendulum spelled out). I write more about my experiences with my pendulum in Book II. I think that information I had received was channelled from Milah and this is how I managed to write the first draft of twelve chapters so quickly (although it has so much more information now).

I knew very little about channelling at the time except that there were others who had this experience and now I had this too, although I didn't realise it at the time – I just typed the words which, when I read them afterwards, I could only think, "wow!" I am writing about this here is because, all I know is that this book has only come about with help from my Higher Self as she promised. Things were being revealed to me slowly. The synchronicities were too many to ignore. First, I learnt about the Anunnaki, then a little about Earth's history and slowly I came to believe in there being other galactic races in the Universe, something I had dismissed before. I still hadn't found the answer as to who was "God".

WHO CREATED THE ULTIMATE CREATOR?

Many ask, 'who created God?' and I remember my son asked me this too when I was a JW. I just answered glibly no-one created God, he has always existed but still a male entity. I had learnt that Jehovah was the god of the Bible and all religions, later confirmed by George Kavassilas, and was running this world, but he wasn't the Ultimate God. I wanted to know more about the one who created the universe and everything in it and how it all came into existence in the first place.

Some of you may think that perhaps I was going too deep, I know my family does but having come this far I felt I still needed more information. The rabbit hole was getting deeper and like Alice in Wonderland, I was getting 'curiouser and curiouser' especially as to what to call this energy, if anything.

FINDING OUT ABOUT THE ORIGIN

From what I could understand from everything I had heard and read was that there was an energy or force which embodied a magnificent intelligence and the highest level of pure loving consciousness, frequencies and colours which has always existed without the restriction of time. It is genderless having no beginning and no end. It was never created by anyone or anything, it has just always existed.

I learnt that it is of the highest frequency of love that caused everything to exist through sound frequencies uttered to create matter, spiritual and solid. It has no human qualities or an ego, it does not need the worship of its creations. This is what makes this energy so special. Respect, love and appreciation, however, is different and what I feel for this energy. I still wasn't clear as to what to call it as I've heard people refer to it as "the Universe", "The All", "Universal Creator", or "Source", terms I had used.

Milah never fails to deliver information at the right time, In 2023, as I thought about what to call this fantastic energy, I came across Guy Needler, who had talked about his experiences in an interview on YouTube. who has written **The History of God, Beyond the Source 1 & 2, The Origin Speaks** and **The Om**. He had discovered a way to transport himself through meditation to the highest dimension where God (who he refers to as The Origin), and co-creators exist. **The History of God** explains what he found out:

> *[...where God came from, the existence of other gods, the creation of the universes, the galaxies, the planets, and finally of life on Earth including humans and the purpose behind the creation of all these things. Also included is information on extraterrestrials as a similar species and their involvement with the human race.]*

As I read his book I was amazed because I had already written about some of the things before, I read his book, but from my Higher Self's perspective. During his conversation with The Origin, he was told that in the beginning there was only this intelligence that was aware of itself being alone, without any idea of what it could or could not do or feel as there was nothing in comparison to itself.

On P.51, The Origin explained:

> *[In the beginning I was not aware that I was aware and just existed. You can consider this by just "being" and listening to everything that is going around you without making any judgments about anything or trying to work out what is going on.*
>
> *At some point over the millennia, I decided that I was aware of wanting to know more about what was going on around me. Where there is energy, there is eventually consciousness and there is life, but consciousness is not true life until it is aware...*
>
> *As I further reflected on this need for awareness, I decided to split myself into thirteen, one being Me and the other twelve being smaller parts of Me that had individual consciousness and awareness, plus an inherent need to search and learn about consciousness and awareness. How they did this*
>
> *was up to them, but they were charged with returning to me with an answer of some kind...The task was to find out more about the environment that was Me...what I saw was different types of energy in different densities and different frequencies, and some were only present on*

certain dimensional levels. Some of them spread across many dimensions and changed their appearance when they were present in different dimensions. All of them behaved differently, depending on the dimension they were in or how many they were linked to.]

P.52-53 he explains that these twelve Source Entities were fractals of The Origin but were still contained within The Origin. They were copies or replications of The Origin, but also part of The Origin. Each was to focus on one of the twelve dimensional "zones".

Other entities were also created as an unintentional function of the process of creating the Source Entities and collectively were known as "The Om" according to Guy Needler (who has written another book about them published in 2023).

Each dimensional zone was also divided by twelve "full" dimensions, each of which were, in general, structured in three groups of twelve frequency levels. In his fourth book, **The Origin Speaks**, Guy Needler wrote:

[I will (and already am) be entering into a dialogue with the "creator" of the Source Entity that created our universe, the entity we call God, and the other eleven Source Entities, the Co-Creators or "Elohim" in religious texts. The Origin can only be described as "The Absolute", all that there is, the beginning and the end, but even "it", The Origin, is limited to its own minute knowledge of its "Self". Hence, the creation of the Source Entities and ultimately, through our Source Entity, the countless billions upon trillions of

entities in our multiverse, which of course includes energetic (and incarnate) mankind to assist in its investigation of its detail. All of which were created to help The Origin experience, learn and evolve assisting in the expansion of its sphere of "awareness of self" to a percentage point higher than the minute fraction of one percent...

First, Origin created five separate but temporary personalities to argue "for and against" positions of this experiment. Origin noticed that all the energies initially used for the first twelve were special even though in conflict with each. From these original "New Origins", the twelfth one was the best version and copy of Origin itself, but it then started copying Origin but was not able to think for itself and followed a subliminal programme based upon Origin's energetic memories.

Each had a different desire to move in a certain way towards the goal of accelerating Origin's evolutionary content which became a distraction rather than a collective evolutionary process, because Origin was unaware of what it was unaware of, at this stage. As this was not part of the Plan.

It took twelve more attempts before the final version we now refer to as the Source Entities came into existence. Using new and a modified process, Twelve Source Entities were again created.]

On p.71-2, he wrote:

O: *I created facsimiles of myself within myself, with the intention that they would function*

> *exactly as me. And this can never happen because of what I have just explained.*

ME: *That...that means that you have a limitation! That limitation being that you cannot recreate yourself; you cannot recreate that which is recreated if, that which is created is you.*

O: *Well done. I don't see it as a limitation, more as a natural fail safe. A fail safe that ensures oneness through singularity.*

The Origin's Plan was for each Source Entity to become self-aware in their own time and thus to know who and what they were, and what their role in existence was. Although each Source Entity has its own personality, reason to be and a strategy for evolutionary progress' there were certain rules to follow to ensure success.

> *[Each Source Entity had to conform to a certain developmental path, before, during and after the attainment of self-awareness, but variations of the theme were allowed which gave diversity in experience, learning and evolutionary content. This meant there were milestones on route so if one had strayed from its path, it could get back on track so to speak.*

> *Each Source Entity could create other entities some of which have a dual role and can incarnate into another form temporarily in order to experience the quality of what they have "tuned". This is how we on Earth experience "angels". There are also two paths for these entities to evolve – the evolutionary path and the service path.]*

SOURCE ENTITY 1

So, according to Guy Needler, The Origin created Source Entity One (SE1 - the first of the twelve fractals of The Origin that Needler communicated with). SE1 is the "Creator/God" of our Universe and the many Galactic races (including the Pleiadians, who were our ancestors having been the first to share their DNA with our different human ancestors).

In his book, **Beyond the Source – Book One,** chapter 1, pages 1-38, in Guy's conversation with SE1, on page 3, SE1 says:

> *[In the beginning it was like I was part of the Origin but still the Origin – not as I am now... I knew I was the Origin and was separate from Origin all at the same time. It was as if my individual awareness was like a memory that is in the front of your mind for a moment, and then is gone, only to appear later when you give it enough attention or when you are trying too hard to remember... It first it was hard, and I have no doubt that many, many millenia passed before I had reached full independent consciousness.]*

The rest of the chapter in that book explains how SE1 came to create our universe, galaxies, dimensions and more, and I felt satisfied with this information. In his latest book, **The OM**, Needler wrote about these entities and how they came to be. Origin thinks of The OM as being free agents and special. (They are unique. There are only five.) They are microscopically smaller aspects of pure Origin sentience – without Origin Directive. That's why The Origin called them random sentience...At one point there were seven pure OM incarnate on Earth: they created what is remembered as being called "heaven on Earth" (p37)]

THE ELOHIM
AS EXPLAINED BY MAURO BIGLINO

I summarise Mauro Biglino's qualifications and expertise in Sources of Information at the back of this book. The word "Elohim" is mentioned many times in the Bible and translated as God although it's a plural term. The Christian translators get round this by saying it refers to the Trinity, "Father, Son and Holy Spirit".

In Chapter 2 of Mauro Biglino's book, **Gods of the Bible**, he starts with the heading, *1. What "god" means*. He asks the question, does Elohim mean "God" or not? On p.39, he wrote:

> *[Let us start with an undisputable fact: Yahweh is often defined with the term "Elohim" and he is more precisely identified as the "Elohim of Abraham, Isaac and Jacob." The dozens of times this statement occurs in the Bible always have a clear and unambiguous purpose: to make it clear that Yahweh is the "Elohim" who deals exclusively with Israel and not other peoples...the biblical authors say that the "sons of the Elohim" liked women, and they would take as many as they pleased. (Genesis 6:1-2)*
>
> *When human beings began to increase in number on the Earth and daughters were born to them, the sons of the Elohim saw that the daughters of Adam were beautiful, and they married any of them as they pleased.]*

Biglino then poses the questions:

> [If "Elohim" always refers individually to one and the same person (Yahweh-God), why is the term, if "Elohim" always refers individually to one and the same person (Yahweh-God), why is the term "Elohim" preceded by the definite article "the" in Hebrew?
>
> If "Elohim" here refers to "angels" as some traditional commentators claim, why did the biblical editors/authors use the common terminology for "angels" that is found in all other books of the Bible, namely [malakhim]? Why is there an explicit reference to "children/sons of the Elohim" here?
>
> If these sons were men, why mention they married women? Who else would they marry? It is redundant and unnecessary information unless they were not "men".]

I couldn't help chuckle to myself as I typed this. I wanted to explain more but it would mean copying so much so I can only suggest again that you get his book. To summarise though it shows that Yahweh was only one of the Elohim - there were many, and they were not human (ie. Adamites), although they had flesh and blood, lived longer than humans and that they made humans.

In his book, **The Naked Bible**, Mauro Biglino writes so much, including chapters such as 'The Invention of the Biblical God and of His Antagonist, Satan' and 'All Those Undead Whisked Away by the Elohim'.

THE ELOHIM
AS DISCOVERED BY PAUL WALLIS

Author of the Eden series, he wrote his first book, **Escaping from Eden**, whilst recovering from a leg injury. He was preparing for his weekly sermon on the Bible book of Genesis, came across the word "Elohim".

The meaning of this word stirred his curiosity, and his spiritual journey began as recorded in his book. He explains his findings much better than I can here, but I believe his journey is very similar to my own in wanting to discover the truth about our origins. On page 16-17, he explained:

> [...the root meaning of "Elohim", according to etymology is either "powers" or "powerful ones".]

If you put the words "powerful ones" in the place of "Elohim", then at this stage of writing this chapter, they could also be part of the group known as the Pa-Taal, (The Seeders) or a sub-group. Therefore, I learnt that within the Elohim there were two different groups – the "good guys" and the "bad guys".

THE LOGOS

JWs and Christianity teach that Jesus is the "Word, the firstborn of all creation" so this sparked my interest, especially after learning about Milah who claimed to be "the Word". I had learnt that the Origin didn't have to do anything to create, but just said the word or rather, made a sound, a frequency as there were no vocal chords or mouth to speak and, in this way, gave life to the 12 Source entities.

Telepathically, Milah explained that first she was a spirit being of energy, vibration and frequency, the original Divine Feminine Energy and the firstborn of all creation and so became known as the "Logos". She has also been known as the Holy Spirit and "Wisdom/Sophia" through which everything else was created.

> *[As the second Logos I created (fractaled or split) to create another soul, the Divine Masculine energy or frequency. They were both replicates of Source energy – light beings, two sides of the same coin, as they say, Divine masculine and feminine energies.]*

I had never heard of anything like this before and still find this hard to believe that a fractal of her is my soul guiding me to write this book. I know for sure though that none of what has been written could have been done by me alone.

In his book **Word Magic (2nd Edition)**, Pao Chang started by explaining:

> *[...that "Logos", the spoken word, has sound, frequency and vibration, giving it the power to affect how energy manifests itself into physicality...]*

On p.7 he explains that:

> *[...The sacred story is about the Divine Masculine Energy and the Divine Feminine Energy and their journey to achieve balance and harmony' and how*

> *this divine story is strongly connected to the Greek words, Alpha and Omega, bearing in mind that the New Testament was originally written in Aramaic and then Koine Greek.]*

On page 17, Pao Chang explains that:

> *[The Greek word "Logos" is pronounced "Law gahs" which means Law Giver. Hence the three "Logos" became the Law Givers (ie. of Universal Laws).] These three sources of energy were the first "trinity". Equal but separate having the qualities of love and the ability to create physical things with the life-force from Source.*

According to Milah, the Trinity is Origin, the Divine Feminine and the Divine Masculine whereas the Trinity of Christendom is The Father, the Son and the Holy Spirit. This divine feminine energy, in various physical forms, was also called the Mother, the Queen of Heaven. The Divine Masculine also incarnated in physical forms as her brother, consort or son. Interestingly, ETs in our universe call their Source, 'the Mother of Creation'.

These are Milah's words:

> *'[I must make it clear here though I never want to be venerated or worshipped by anyone, but this has happened outside of our control as we incarnated into different people. All credit for everything goes to our Creator. Yes, we communicated and shared ideas, but Source will always be held in the highest esteem because of the great love that was bestowed on all creation and through us, other beings and things that came into existence.'*

When I speak of the love emanating from Source (SE1) and The Origin, it is the purest vibration of joy, bliss, being and knowing. The energy is so great that I feel my human body overflowing with it even as I write so that I am vibrating and so happy to be in this current role of mine.

As I said previously, this does not mean that I am any better than anyone else in the Universe; it's just that Milah said she was the first one to be created and so, like Source/The Origin, she has enormous love for all creation, and I do too.

As I write this part it on the in 2021, I was directed to the 1927 book, **The Celestial Ship of The North**, by E. Valentia Straiton. I couldn't find anything about this author on the internet but would love to know more because she wrote many interesting books. She draws from the insights of Gerald Massey, Alvin Boyd Kuhn, and others in a study that blends religion, symbolism, mythology, astrology, and Egyptology, and much else.

I quote from p.7 of *Chapter 1, The Mother Mystery*:

> *[The most ancient peoples believed that God gave Revelation and was the One Supreme, the Eternal, the Infinite, pervading all places and exalted in a super-celestial place of Divine Light, that He was spiritual in essence, self-existent, uncreated, yet was made manifest to all as the most tender love and truth, which they received in their lives on Earth with happiness and joy.*
>
> *Born of this Supreme One was She of celestial loveliness and purity, Divine in nature, whom*

they called the spirit of God, the Dove, the Virgin spirit, the Logos, which is the Word of God, the earliest first Mother, whose name came to represent the essence of all that was beautiful and pure, and of most divine love. She was in the Talmud, "The Spirit of God that hovered over the water like a dove, which spreads her wings over her young." She was the Shekinah, a mystic word often variously typified as a Lotus, a Rose, an Egg, and by symbols that were oval, as a Cup, a Boat or a Moon.]

On p.14, then she explains:

[The second Spirit of God, the second great power that began to exist when God developed beauty out of Himself was the Mother, the Mother first and foremost everywhere preceding any knowledge of that One God. She was Nature, the Spirit of God, the Virgin Spirit of ineffable loveliness, and as such received worship.]

DIVINE FEMININE AND MASCULINE FREQUENCIES

At one time, early in human history, humans on Earth were balanced with the Divine Feminine and Masculine frequencies with no negative emotions. This was known as 'The Golden Age' and there was a more matriarchal society (Lemuria) with the dominant Divine Feminine frequencies.

Later there was a more masculine society (Atlantis) with the Divine Masculine frequencies, but as the masculine frequencies became more dominant, so society became more unbalanced and chaotic.

As there's a lot of misunderstanding around what these frequencies are, I needed to understand that they generate us in particular ways, depending upon the amount the avatar or physical structure that holds it.

www.subconsciousservant.com/divine-feminine-qualities explains:

[The Divine Feminine is a concept that has been misunderstood for centuries. As society was built upon patriarchal laws, femininity was not highly valued and associated with negative traits such as weakness, instability, moodiness, and so on. Unfortunately, these old beliefs still exist in many countries and determine how people treat women.

Divine Feminine qualities embrace the feminine side of God. God, the Divinity, the Universe, or whatever you call it, has two sides: masculine and feminine, representing the duality that keeps the world functioning as we know it. This duality has been represented in many religions and philosophies but is mostly known as Yin-Yang.

The divine feminine qualities are powerful intuition, enhanced creativity, good communication, increased empathy, deep compassion, acceptance, understanding, forgiving, living from the heart, kindness and gentleness. Developing Divine Feminine qualities is an important spiritual milestone for everyone, regardless of gender.]

According to another website, www.lonerwolf.com/divine-masculine

[Contrary to popular belief, the Divine Feminine isn't limited only to females...Divine male energy, or the divine masculine, is a force of action, strength, courage, and creativity that manifests essence into form.

It is not related to gender or sex, but to the universal principles of yang, Shiva, or solar energy. It is responsible for order, structure, passion, willpower, and self-restraint. It is also connected to labour, money, strategy, and right-mindedness.

It is the sacred counterpart of the divine feminine, or the receptive, nurturing, and intuitive energy.... But the shadow side of the Divine Masculine is its preoccupation with power. When masculine energy becomes corrupt, it results in the toxic patriarchal society we see today that is based on a foundational philosophy of "get, reject, use, and dominate..."]

WORSHIP OF THE DIVINE FEMININE

In the beginning, as also shown in the book, **When God Was A Woman**, the Divine Feminine was venerated by humans. Serpent worship, Tree worship and Water worship were all feminine.

[The Serpents appeared periodically as the feminine type, and the bearing Tree with its fruit was feminine and Water was feminine and the source of life, the Mother. Motherhood, antedated by eons of time, any knowledge of a fatherhood that could have been identified as such, and even among the originals even gods (later planets) there was no mention of fatherhood.]

Asherah was a Canaanite goddess of fertility and motherhood. Ancient Israelites worshipped her alongside YHWH as they were considered a couple. This was stopped in the 6th century BC by King Josiah who insisted everyone worship Yahweh only.

ISLAM

In Islam the concept of the Logos also exists in Islam, where it was articulated in the writings of the classical Sunni mystics and Islamic philosophers, as well as by certain Shi'a thinkers during the Islamic Golden Age. Jesus and Muhammad are seen as the personifications of the logos, and this is what enables them to speak in such absolute terms.

In Sufism the concept is used to relate the "Uncreated" (God) to the "Created" (humanity), for the Deist, no contact between man and God can be possible without the logos. The logos is everywhere and always the same, but its personification is "unique" within each region.

WHAT IS THE HOLY SPIRIT

There are 3126 descriptive names, titles and emblems of the Holy Spirit found in Scripture. One example given is that The Holy Spirit identified by Isaiah (see Isa. 11:2).

The words "ruach", "pneuma" and "parakletos" have been translated to mean the "Holy Spirit" although these words have different meanings. These seem to me to describe attributes rather than a person.

AS EXPLAINED BY JEHOVAH'S WITNESSES[29]

The Holy Spirit is God's power in action, his active force. (Micah 3:8; Luke 1:35). God sends out his spirit by projecting his energy to any place to accomplish his will. (Psalm 104:30; 139:7).

In the Bible, the word "spirit" is translated from the Hebrew word ru'ach and the Greek word pneu-ma. Most often, those words refer to God's active force, for Holy Spirit. (Genesis 1:2).

However, the Bible also uses those words in other senses. These meanings all share the sense of something invisible to humans that produces visible effects. Similarly, the spirit of God, "like the wind, is invisible, immaterial and powerful.

The Bible also refers to God's Holy Spirit as his "hands" or "fingers." (Psalm 8:3; 19:1; Luke 11:20; compare Matthew 12:28.) Just as a craftsman uses his hands and fingers to do his work, they say God has used his spirit to produce such results as the following:

- Breath (Habakkuk 2:19; Revelation 13:15)
- Wind (Genesis 8:1; John 3:8)
- The vital, or animating, force in living creatures (Job 34:14, 15)
- A person's disposition or attitude (Numbers 14:24)
- Spirit persons, including God and the angels (1 Kings 22:21; John 4:24)

- The Universe (Psalm 33:6; Isaiah 66:1, 2)
- The Bible (2 Peter 1:20, 21)
- The miracles performed by his ancient servants and their zealous preaching (Luke 4:18; Acts 1:8; 1 Cor. 12:4-11)
- The fine qualities displayed by people who obey him (Galatians 5:22, 23)

The trouble is that like most religions they mix bits of truth with falsehoods, otherwise no-one could believe them.

THE WORDS "RUACH" AND "PNEUMA"

Mauro Biglino writes about these words in his book, **Gods of the Bible**, p.61-60:

> *[The term "ruach" is always translated as "spirit" in the Bible. Theology must necessarily provide a spiritual reading for all the stories of the Old Testament; however, we will see that this reading has no textual justification and is often misleading.]*

He explains that the Greek Translation, the Septuagint, used the word "pneuma" in Koine Greek meant "breath", "wind", "breath of life, and also "soul and spirit".

However, the Hebrew "ruach" meant "wind, "breath", "moving air", "storm wind" and so in a broader sense "that which moves swiftly through the air space". Biglino goes on to describe the following use of "ruach" in Ezekiel 1:4, 11:1, 24:

[This "spirit" (ruach) moves in specific directions; it can be seen and even took Ezekiel to 'the gate of the house of Yahweh' and then to Chaldea. (Ezekiel 11:1,24). Then Elijah has a similar experience (2 King 2). It's clear that the "ruach" is not invisible but an object that makes a lot of noise and wind. In 2 Samuel 22:11, we have Yahweh riding a cherub! Again, if Yahweh is a spirit, how does he ride in or on anything – he could just appear.]

On p.69, he reminds us of Genesis 1:2 – 'The "ruach" of Elohim was hovering over the waters". If God's spirit is supposed to be everywhere, why is it confined to an area? therefore, as in any other language, the word "spirit" can mean different things, so can the word "pneuma" but not the word "ruach". Is there such a thing as God's "Holy Spirit"?

Also, which God? The God of the Bible, Yahweh, has never created anything and his spirit is far from benevolent most of the time. What was translated as his Holy Spirit was, in fact, the wind created by his vehicle of transportation. So who or what was the "helper" Jesus spoke about in John 14:16-17?

www.biblicalcounselingcoalition.org states:

[Jesus would never think of abandoning His followers. Instead, He promises to give them "another Helper." This title refers to one who comes alongside to exhort or encourage. But Jesus assures them that the Holy Spirit would not only be with them, but in them. This means they would not only be able to count on the Spirit's presence at certain times or for certain purposes, but always, in every place, forever. How is this possible?

The Spirit would indwell them. He would actually take up residence within their physical bodies. What a comforting promise this must have been for them—and is for you, too!]

www.jesusplusnothing.com/series/post/bible-study-holy-spirit-our-helper states:

[... We see first of all that the Holy Spirit is a gift from the Father. It was the Father's love that led Him to give his only begotten Son (John 3:16) to save the world. Here we see that He also gave the Holy Spirit. The first gift enabled the way for the second. The first gift cleansed the temple of our bodies so that it could be filled with the second gift. He gave the first to set us free from the penalty of sin. He sent the second to set us free from the power of sin. Both blessings were from the Father of lights, from whom every good and perfect gift comes from...

What Jesus had been to the believers, the Holy Spirit, the Helper, would now be. Yet this new Helper would not be restricted to time and space as Jesus was in His humanity...only Jesus was saying to His disciples that what I have been to you - your comforter, your counsellor, your teacher, your helper, your advocate, your strengthener, the One who stands with and alongside you... the Holy Spirit will be for you, all of you, for all time!]

To me that sounds like they will be possessed by a spirit. So, I looked at another explanation.

www.beautifulinjesus.com/holy-spirit-helper states:

[John 16:7 AMPC: The Greek word used here in reference to the Holy Spirit is PARAKLETOS, which means one who is called to one's side, especially to help. It also means an intercessor, an assistant, or one who pleads the cause of another before a judge.]

Well, even this explanation only defines what the Holy Spirit will do, not what it is, a being that will inhabit one's body and be a 'helper'? And yet the original meaning was quite different. Further in that article it says in John 16:13-15:

[But when he, the Spirit of truth, comes, he will guide you into all truth. He will not speak on his own; he will speak only what he hears, and he will tell you what is yet to come.]

When you look at the examples of what people with the Holy Spirit could do with the aid of an invisible helper (i.e. heal people, foretell the future, comfort people, direct them etc.). if a Christian, they were doing good because this a gift from God/Yahweh. Anyone else with these gifts was doing the work of the "Devil" and was put to death. Can you see how illogical this is?

Here are some quick examples of the Helper's presence and work from the book of Acts:

- Empowered believers with spiritual gifts (Acts 2:4)
- Gave boldness in speaking God's word (Acts 4.31)
- Gave wisdom over their adversaries (Acts 6:10)
- Comforted believers and brought increase (Acts 9:31)

- Gave direction in where to go and who to trust (Acts 11:12)
- Gave knowledge of future events (Acts 11:28)
- Set apart people certain people for the gospel work (Acts 13:2)
- Brought joy to the disciples (Acts 13:52)
- Instructed the leaders with important teaching (Acts 15:28)
- Opened and closed doors on when and where not to minister (Acts 16:6)
- Compelled believers forward even when afflictions and trials awaited (Acts 20:22, 21:11)

I have read Guy Needler's books more than once to understand more fully what was expressed in them and thought my numerous questions were answered - until I came across George Kavassilas's book which was as deep as Guy Needler's books.

I can't say that I categorically agree with everything they've written or even that I fully understand everything yet, but I'm certainly open to the possibility of what they wrote could be true.

Hopefully, by now you have understood why we must be careful how words are very powerful, and if used incorrectly will create lies and problems.

6 - WHO IS JESUS?

When you change the way you look at things, the things you look at change

Dr Wayne Dyer

Most Christians I have spoken to insist that there is a lot of evidence that Jesus existed, although they admit they had not checked for themselves. There have been several truth-seekers who have queried whether Jesus had ever existed as the only evidence that gives details are found in the Bible.

Even the outsider commentators such as Josephus and the letter from Pontius Pilate are now considered fakes30, especially as it seems that Pilate was not a good man and didn't hesitate to put people to death. Scholars have collected over 5,000 Greek copies of the New Testament and no two are exactly alike. In fact, there are more differences in the manuscripts than there are words in the New Testament.

Again, you would think that such important work inspired of God would be more accurate to avoid confusion. So, can we believe everything written and taught about Jesus?

www.get.tithe.ly/blog/new-testament-books states:

> *[...The earliest accounts of Jesus' life, ministry, and death, then, were written 35-65 years after Jesus' death...The authors of the Gospels were not eyewitnesses to Jesus' life and ministry; they used inherited traditions, not their own recollections of events, to tell their stories about Jesus.*
>
> *Some of these traditions were probably historically accurate; others were certainly embellished or even wholly created. In addition, the Gospel writers continued to modify and invent stories to underscore their own beliefs about Jesus...*
>
> *Scholars doubt the historicity of these traditions because none of the Gospel writers claims to have been an eyewitness; the disciples were likely uneducated peasants without writing skills; the disciples and Jesus spoke Aramaic, but the native language of the Gospel writers seems to have been Greek....]*

SO MANY OPINIONS

I had become one of Jehovah's Witnesses believing them to be the closest to the earliest Christians. Unfortunately, I didn't know enough at eighteen. I knew nothing about the existence of the Gnostics and other groups, or even much about other religions besides what I had been taught by the JWs.

I knew very little about Judaism, apart from Jews eating koshered meat. Nor did I know much about the Greek Orthodox religions although I vividly remember my Greek grandmother walking around the house with incense. I never did find out why she did that because we had very little communication – she didn't talk English, and I didn't talk Greek. Neither did I have the time nor the inclination to research anything outside the Bible at that time.

Now that my belief that Jehovah was the true God completely shattered and finding that the Bible was a mishmash of ancient texts and Jewish history, I decided to be as open-minded as possible as I looked into the man we know as Jesus.

Updating this chapter was much harder than I thought as I tried to find the best way to include the new things I learnt. Not only was I trying to answer the question, who is Jesus? But I was trying to understand why so many didn't believe he had ever existed at all and how did they come to that conclusion.

At the same time many believe that Jesus had existed but there is very little proof outside of the Bible to prove this. Others think that there were previous versions of this biblical character incorporated into the character that is worshipped as Jesus. Some even thought that John the Baptist was the real Messiah.

BELIEFS OF THE EARLIEST CIVILISATIONS

I decided to backtrack and take another look at the two earliest civilisations, Lemuria and Atlantis. I wondered if these highly advanced humans worshipped anyone and if so, who?

THE LEMURIANS

Apparently, this Lemurian society was founded on heart-centred wisdom, prioritizing emotional intelligence, symbiotic relationships, and spiritual enlightenment. They had a profound awe and respect for Mother Earth, the elements, and every living being.

THE ATLANTEANS

I then found [30]Claudia Merrill, an Australian author living in Vienna, Austria. She wrote to bring mythology and folklore to life through the lens of history on her website. She described the Lemurian civilisation where all needs were fulfilled, and people lived in harmony.

It seems that the people "lovers of honour and of a noble nature. "Enki ruled at the time, but the Atlanteans didn't worship him as a "God", or anyone else it seems, but like the Lemurians they lived in peace and harmony for a long time. This of course was the heyday of Atlantis, before it all descended into chaos after Enlil arrived.

In Critias, Plato wrote:

> [.... *They despised everything but virtue, caring little for their present state of life, and thinking lightly of the possession of gold and other property, which seemed only a burden to them; neither were they intoxicated by luxury; nor did wealth deprive them of their self-control; but saw clearly that all these goods are increased by virtue and friendship with one another.*]

At this time in Earth's history, there were no organised religions – so how did that change? Where did the idea of worshipping gods come from?

HINDUISM

The first known religion was 32Hinduism considered to be the oldest of the six major world religions with roots and customs dating back more than 4,000 years, (some believe 10,000 years). It is claimed that the Hindu book, the Bhagavad Gita is the oldest book before even the Bible, and was written 5,000 years ago by the sage, Vyasadeva.

It's the only book in the world in which someone claiming to be God explains in detail about Himself, the soul and the world and how they interrelate. I think **Conversations with God** by Neale Donald Walsch would be another such book.

> *[...In the wars that occur in the holy books, as in Mahabharata, the different sides had different war weapons which had characters similar to modern-day war weapons. In some stories, the travelling vehicles were normally birds and animals. But these animals and birds had features similar to modern-day aircraft. There were even aircraft with over velocity of light.*
>
> *The main war weapons were bows and arrows. But these arrows were more like modern missiles than simple arrows. These arrows were capable of carrying bombs with destructive power similar to modern-day chemical, biological or even atomic bombs. Other arrows could be targeted at specific human beings. There were even arrows*

capable of neutralizing other arrows, similar to modern-day ant-missiles.]

Hindus are considered pagan by the Abrahamic religions and inferior but it's interesting to note that the early Hindus knew about the advanced technology of their gods and describe it vividly. So, why should we consider the Bible superior to that of the **Bhagavad Gita**?

CAESAR'S MESSIAH

In 2005 Joseph Atwill wrote **Caesar's Messiah** in 2005. Six of the most modern controversial Bible scholars, Robert Eisenman, John Hudson, Kenneth Humphreys, Rod Blackhirst, Acharya S, D.M. Murdock, and Timothy Freke reveal their shocking conclusions about the origins of Christianity based on this best-selling religious studies book.

As a youth, Atwill studied Greek, Latin and the Bible at St. Mary's Military Academy, a Jesuit-run school in Japan. In college, he studied computer science, and co-founded software companies including Ferguson Tool Company and ASNA. After 1995, he returned to Biblical studies.

In his book he argues that the New Testament Gospels were written by a group of individuals connected to the Flavian family of Roman Emperors: Vespasian, Titus and Domitian. The authors were mainly Flavius Josephus, Berenice, and Tiberius Julius Alexander, with contributions from Pliny the Elder.

Although Vespasian and Titus had defeated Jewish nationalist Zealots in 70 CE, they wanted to control the spread of Judaism and moderate its political virulence and continuing militancy against Rome. Their solution was to create the passive religion, Christianity.

Atwill contradicts the mainstream historical view that while the Gospels include any mythical or legendary elements, these religious elaborations were added to the biography of a historical Jesus.

In 2014, Atwill wrote another book, **Shakespeare's Secret Messiah**, which expanded the thesis of Roman authorship of the New Testament, to suggest that the Pauline epistles and Revelation were written during or after the reign of Domitian, a Roman emperor from 81-96 CE, the last member of the Flavian dynasty, "a ruthless but efficient autocrat".

This time the documentary showed that Jesus was not a historical figure and that the events of Jesus' life were based on a Roman military campaign. His supposed second coming refers to a historical event that had already occurred and the teachings of Christ came from the ancient pagan mystery schools. He repeated that the gospels were written by a family of Caesars (The Flavians) and their supporters, who left us documents to prove it.

Dissecting the history and literature of this time, the scholars show that the Gospels are a sophisticated pro-Roman multi-layered allegorical text that could not have been written by simple Jewish fishermen. Most scholars agree that Christianity was used as a political tool to control the masses of the day and is still being used this way today.

Richard Carrier is a world-renowned author and speaker. He is a professional historian, published philosopher, and prominent defender of the American free thought movement. He also has a Ph.D. from Columbia University in ancient history, he specializes in the intellectual history of Greece and Rome, particularly ancient philosophy, religion, and science, with emphasis on the origins of Christianity and the use and progress of science under the Roman Empire.

Richard Carrier, whilst not agreeing with everything Lena Einhorn wrote, highly commended her book originally published in 2007, **The Jesus Mystery: Astonishing Clues to the true identity of Jesus and Paul.**

On p.24 she wrote that the American historian and freethinker, John E. Remsburg, in 1909 **published The Christ: A critical Review and Analysis of the Evidence of His Existence.**

> *[This book contains a table in which he lists 42 historians who were active at the time of Jesus, or within the first century after him wrote enough to form a library. Yet in this mass of Jewish and Pagan literature, only two forged passages in the works of a Jewish author, Josephus and two disputed passages in the works of Roman writers, there is to be found no mention of Jesus Christ.]*

So not only are religions money-making organisations under the guise of providing spiritual food to the masses, but they also create false information.

A DIFFERENCE BETWEEN THE JESUS OF FAITH AND A HISTORICAL JESUS

In 1892, Martin Kähler, a German Theologian, and author of The So-called Historical Jesus and the Historic, Biblical Christ, made the famous distinction between the "Jesus of history" and the "Christ of faith", arguing that faith is more important than exact historical knowledge.

In December 2007, *The Jesus Project* was set up in the US; one of its main questions for discussion was that of whether Jesus existed. It was initiated by R. Joseph Hoffmann, an Author, Historian and Lecturer. The project was halted in June 2009 when Hoffmann announced that in his view the project was not productive, and its funding was suspended.

Since then, there have been so many debates on this subject; by the time I updated this chapter, I found myself having to rewrite parts of it several times before this final copy.

Richard Carrier says in his Blog article written on October 10, 2023, **Things Fall Apart Only When You Check: The Main Reason the Historicity of Jesus Continues to Be Believed**. He wrote:

> *[After ten years of observing the field after publishing my academic study on the subject, I find there are generally only two reasons to remain confident in the historicity of Jesus: a*

desperate faith-based need to; and a disinterest in actually checking.

The former is, of course, why believers can't engage in honest debates over the historicity of Jesus: merely entertaining the proposition requires them first to admit their religion is false (whereas, conversely, nonbelievers are entirely content with any of the "historical Jesuses" mainstream scholars now construct).

We all knew this was going on (see On the Historicity of Jesus, pp. xii, 14, 18–19, 601–02, 617). What is surprising is how many people join the second camp, showing no genuine interest in actually checking if Jesus's historicity is something we should be confident in.]

There have been numerous debates, books written and videos made making the argument for or against Jesus having ever existed. So, what is the Truth?

We've been brought up to not discuss religion and politics to avoid arguments. Maybe it's the Greek in me but I loved talking about my beliefs with others – I wanted to be put right on things if I was wrong, but I also wanted proof.

As Richard Carrier said, 'believers are reluctant to have honest debates.' Surely if our lives depend on what we believe, we should want to ensure it's based on truth and facts.

I've been told that we will never know the truth until we die, but I believe that when we find someone lying to us, we would rather know the truth. It's easier to ignore this at times so as to not rock the boat with friends and family. The majority of people today just don't seem to care without realizing the consequences of not caring.

> *www.history.com/news/was-jesus-real-historical-evidence* states:

> *[Some argue that Jesus wasn't an actual man, but within a few decades of his lifetime, he was mentioned by Jewish and Roman historians. While billions of people believe Jesus of Nazareth was one of the most important figures in world history, many others reject the idea that he even existed at all. Among scholars of the New Testament of the Christian Bible, though, there is little disagreement that he actually lived....*

> *The reality is that we don't have archaeological records for virtually anyone who lived in Jesus's time and place," says University of North Carolina religious studies professor Bart D. Ehrman, author of* **Did Jesus Exist? The Historical Argument for Jesus of Nazareth.** *'The lack of evidence does not mean a person at the time didn't exist. It means that she or he, like 99.99% of the rest of the world at the time, made no impact on the archaeological record."]*

On page 16 of his book, **Nailed- Ten Christian Myths That Show Jesus Never Existed at All**, David Fitzgerald wrote:

> *[It's true enough that the majority of Biblical historians do not question the historicity of Jesus but then again, the majority of Biblical historians have always been Christian preachers, so what*

else could we expect them to say? For all their bluster, the truth is that for as long as there have been Christian writings. There have been critics who have disputed Christian claims and called events from the Gospel stories into question. And since at least the 18th century a growing number of historians have raised serious problems that cast Jesus' historicity into outright doubt, as we'll see.]

Dr David Skrbina PhD, a professional philosopher who was a senior lecturer at the University of Michigan from 2003–2018, has written and edited several books including his latest which is talked about I this video:

THE JESUS HOAX
www.youtu.be/XMqvP2m1Dqs?si=Z1NtOmHWGzhqV6kf

In his book, Dr. Skrbina presents a theory that St. Paul and a band of friends constructed a 'Jesus hoax.' They took a kernel of truth based on Jesus, the man, and turned him into the divine saviour of humanity. He thinks they did so as a way to strike back at the hated Roman Empire, and to undermine its strength among the common people...

The absolute lack of corroborating evidence for the so-called biblical Jesus, and the fact that key documents such as the four Gospels were written decades after his time, all support this theory. He believes everyone, regardless of religious belief, needs to be aware of this astonishing story.

This is not just ancient history; it has vast implications for many areas of modern life. Remember, people weren't always converted to

"Christianity" by evangelizing doorknockers or missionaries. They were threatened with torture or death!

IS ANYTHING IN THE BIBLE ABOUT JESUS TRUE?

A great deal of research has been carried out to ascertain whether the biblical character known as Jesus actually existed, but no final conclusion can be agreed. As for the Apostle Paul's teachings, these seem to be based more upon his own ideas and interpretations rather than Yeshua's.

For nearly 2,000 years for Christian men and women, the biblical Jesus has been a role model unlike any previous Master. Why follow the teachings of Yeshua (Jesus) instead of Krishna who was allegedly born thousands of years before him on July 21, 3,228 BCE?

I recently came across someone on YouTube saying that the Lord's Prayer we learnt by heart is not the same as the original version in Aramaic. See

www.bsahely.com/2021/10/23/interesting-quote-from-prayers-of-the-cosmos-reflections-on-the-original-meaning-of-jesus-words

The following are the basic JW beliefs regarding Jesus that I will cover in this chapter:

> BASIC TEACHING 3: JESUS – HONOURING HIM AS SAVIOUR AND THE SON OF GOD
>
> BASIC TEACHING 4: KINGDOM OF GOD – A HEAVENLY GOVERNMENT WHICH WILL REPLACE

HUMAN GOVERNMENTS AND ACCOMPLISH GOD'S PLAN FOR THE EARTH

BASIC TEACHING 5: SALVATION – DELIVERANCE FROM SIN AND DEATH THROUGH THE RANSOM SACRIFICE OF JESUS THROUGH FAITH AND WORKS

BASIC TEACHING 6: HEAVEN – JEHOVAH GOD, JESUS AND FAITHFUL ANGELS RESIDE IN THE SPIRIT REALM

APOLLONIUS OF TYANA[33]

Then I came across the man Apollonius of Tyana who was, apparently, an ancient Greek philosopher and miracle worker from the Roman province of Cappadocia. He lived circa 3BCE to around 97CE.

His amazing story that parallels Jesus has raised controversy among historians and theologians for centuries. They both are said to have ascended to Heaven. There are stories of both performing miracles. They were both spiritual teachers. Many believed he was a divine figure who could save humanity. You can see a video about him on YouTube:

THE PAGAN JESUS – APOLLONIUS OF TYANA
www.youtu.be/tF1OuTabqEM?si=6YfNTTkp1TYvW2CNB

Bart Ehrman a well-known 'agnostic-atheist' and a professor of religion at UNC-Chapel Hill starts his class by sharing a description of a famous man from the ancient world and everyone thinks he is talking about Jesus. Then he reveals he's talking about Apollonius of Tyana.

I heard a talk by **Jason Jorjani** where he said that the words "yeshua" and "jesus" are honorific titles meaning saviour or redeemer, not necessarily actual names. Also, he mentions Apollonius who when speaking Aramaic in Judea was referred to as "Yeshuah" by the Jews after talking to them and performing miracles.

He also mentions the origin of the stories of King Arthur, but that's another subject for a future book.

(www.youtu.be/h43-ZR_Bhg?si=LeLTfQGIam JFTIqtin)

APOLLONIUS DEFIED ROMAN EMPERORS

Apollonius fearlessly travelled from one end of the Roman Empire to the other, inciting revolutions against the despots, and establishing egalitarian communities among his followers, who bore the name of Essenes. Then he bravely entered Rome itself and openly denounced Nero as a tyrant. He was arrested and thrown into a dungeon, awaiting certain death which, however, due to his brilliant speech in self-defence and his extraordinary powers of mind, he averted, securing his liberty.

These actions remind me of both John the Baptist denouncing Herod's marriage and the Apostle Paul's time in prison.

Apollonius was heavily influenced by Pythagoras. He believed in a God who was pure intellect and taught his followers that the only way to converse with God was through the intellect. There are sixteen temples built in his honour all over the Mediterranean world, and possibly down through Mesopotamia (Babylon-Iraq) and into India and Kashmir.

Unlike Jesus Christ who taught his followers that God answers prayers, the charismatic teacher and miracle worker, he taught that prayers and sacrifice were useless, and that God really did not want to converse with men.

> *["The gods do not need sacrifices, so what might one do to lease them? Acquire wisdom, it seems to me and do all the good in one's power to those humans who deserve it," he had said.]*

He travelled widely around the Mediterranean and into India as a preacher, speaking his message and healing the sick. Jesus, on the other hand is linked to Zeus (aka Enlil/Yahweh).

The earliest and by far the most detailed source is **The Life of Apollonius of Tyana**, a lengthy, novelistic biography written by the Athenian sophist Philostratus, which he completed long after Apollonius' death, probably in the 220s or 230s AD.

Among the miracles that were attributed to Apollonius by Philostratus, was that he saved the city of Ephesus from a plague. It's also claimed that he brought a Roman Senator's daughter back to life.

In one case, he even stopped a follower from marrying a woman who turned out to be a "lamia," a type of disguised demon, and saved his life.

SCEPTICS QUESTION HIS BIOGRAPHY

Philostratus also implies that Apollonius had extra-sensory perception. On one occasion, when Emperor Domitian was murdered on 18 September 96 AD, Apollonius was said to have witnessed the event in Ephesus "about midday" on the day. It happened in Rome, and he told those present 'Take heart, gentlemen, for the tyrant has been slain this day...'

Both Philostratus and renowned historian Cassius Dio report this incident, probably on the basis of an oral tradition. In the Arabic tradition, Apollonius of Tyana is called the "Master of the Talismans" (Sahib at-tilasmat) and known as Balinus (or, Balinas, Belenus, or Abuluniyus).

THE DEATH OF APOLLONIUS

There are several accounts of the death of Apollonius. In one, he was arrested by Septimius Severus but disappeared from his cell and was never seen again. In another version, he rose into heaven from a temple in Asia Minor. In most stories, it is claimed that he disappeared around the age of one hundred and was still youthful.

This means that the real figure of Apollonius may have been lost but he was honoured by many, including the Emperors Julian and Aurelian. His image was worshipped in many temples for centuries even after his disappearance.

Philostratus' biography of Apollonius has many sceptics, and some researchers believe that it was written on the instructions of Empress Julia Domna, wife of Emperor Septimius Severus and mother of the bloody tyrant Caracalla, who wanted to strengthen paganism in the Empire.

They were worried about threats from Christians as an alternative to Jesus Christ. This reason does seem rather odd though because Christians were known to be peace-loving people. But this was not enough to stop the growth in the Christian Church.

The worship of Apollonius declined after Constantine made Christianity the official religion of the Empire. Philostratus' biography may have distorted Apollonius, so today we do not know who he was. We will never be sure if he was a fraud, a religious prophet, or a serious religious philosopher any more than we know if Jesus was.

As Edward Whelan wrote in **Classical Wisdom,** 'What can be said with certainty is that Apollonius of Tyana was an extraordinary figure in the ancient world.' Even many New Testament scholars agree that the Gospel writers were not eyewitnesses to Jesus' life and ministry. Instead, they used inherited traditions to tell their stories, which may have been historically accurate or embellished.

I've quoted nearly the whole article so you can decide for yourself whether Apollonius' activities were copied to create those of Jesus, or it may have been the other way round. I found it interesting that Apollonius was named after Apollo, a Greek god and so I looked this up.

www.theoi.com/Olympios/Apollon.html states:

*[**APOLLON** (Apollo) was the Olympian god of prophecy and oracles, music, song and poetry, archery, healing, plague and disease, and the protection of the young. He was depicted as a handsome, beardless youth with long hair and attributes such as a wreath and branch of laurel, bow and quiver of arrows, raven, and lyre.]*

And, of course, there are lots of myths written about him, but the question arises, was Apollonius an incarnation of that god? Was he the origin of the man we know as Jesus? An epigram first seen in Adana in Cilicia, but now known to be from Mopsouhestia, celebrating him as one 'named after Apollo' who 'extinguished the errors of men' and was sent by heaven (or taken up into heaven) 'to drive out the sorrows of mortals.

THE STORY OF JESUS

There does seem to be more historical evidence that Apollonius had actually existed than there was of Jesus/Yeshua. So, I investigated more as I really wanted to believe that there had been a man called Yeshua/Jesus. After all, we've seen how the names were changed for earlier well-known historical and biblical figures.

I've looked at the different aspects of Jesus and his life to see how much I the Bible is true. Just as I thought I'd written enough, I then came across Attis, the Son of God of Phrygia, Krishna, the Son of God of India, Dionysus (or Bacchus), the Son of God of Greece.

Their stories were very similar:

- All were born of a virgin on the 25th December, put in swaddling clothes and in a manger.

- A star marked their birthplace.

- Angels and shepherds attended his birthplace

Well, I needn't list the rest; you most probably know the story. Others with similar stories include Apollo, Hercules, Zeus, Adad, Marduk, Buddha Sakia, Indra, Salivahana, Osiris, Horus, Odin, Balder, Frey, Crite, Zoroaster, Baal, Taut, Balo, Jao, Wittoba and, many more.

The main source of what we have come to know about Jesus is the Bible, but we know the Bible is made up of older texts and mistranslations so how can we be sure that the information we have about Jesus is based on true events?

THE STORY OF JOHN THE BAPTIST

Even John the Baptist's story was similar to the stories of Anup, who baptized the Son of God, Horus. Like John, Anup lost his head.

WHO WAS MARY, THE MOTHER OF JESUS?

The virgin mother of the Sun God is an ancient theme around the world and the even Alexander the Great was said to have been born by a mother impregnated by a non-human being. The correct spelling is "Myriam." Myriam represents the Hebrew Old

Testament version of Mary's name. In Aramaic, the language spoken by Jesus, Joseph and Mary, Mary is called Maryam. The Greek translation of the Old Testament calls her Mariam, whereas with New Testament Greek she is Maria. Mary's full name would have been Myriam Batjoachim (Maria Batjacob).

Her father was called Joachim (Jacob) according to the Greek Orthodox Bible. Many stories and have been written about Yeshua's mother. Some claim that she is based on Ishtar, a Babylonian goddess (Alexander Hislop who wrote **The Two Babylons**, for one).

From a theological perspective, it is said that God [I always ask which God] chose Mary to be the mother of Jesus because she, herself, was the Immaculate Conception. This means that she was the only one fit for being the mother for God in the flesh because she had been conceived by her mother, Anna, without sin (ie. perfect). Catholics claim that she had no other children and never engaged in the marital act with Joseph.

Sometimes this is confusing since there are references in the Scriptures to Jesus's brothers and sisters. This is explained away by some saying that Joseph had been a widower, and his children were stepbrothers and sisters to Jesus. According to some writers she died around 43-48 CE of a broken heart but rose again on the third day. Others say she died in India of old age, or never died at all but went straight to heaven.

JESUS'S LINEAGE

The only proof we have of Jesus' genealogy is in the New Testament's Gospels of Matthew and Luke. They both provide accounts of his lineage through David and make him eligible to be the Messiah. All records had been kept in the Jerusalem Temple which was destroyed in 70CE.

If you believe as I do that "the first Homo Sapien Sapien", was the result of Enki's DNA being used to create him, then everything Jesus said about being around before Abraham makes sense. Also, when he refers to his heavenly father, it's likely he refers to Enki, not Yahweh.

DID JESUS TRAVEL TO OTHER PLACES?

There is a big gap in Jesus's life story as nothing in the Bible is written about him between the ages of 12-30 years of age. The New Testament only mentions that Jesus travelled to several places including Galilee, Judea, Perea, and Samaria during his ministry from 30 years of age. However, some claim that Jesus travelled to other places, such as England, India, China, and Japan although many modern scholars reject these claims.

The Unknown Life of St Issa (Jesus Christ) by Nicholas Notovitch, first published in Paris in 1894 and quickly translated into several other languages including English is about Jesus visiting India. Notovitch had visited a Tibetan Buddhist monastery at Hemis in the Himalayans, northernmost part of India. He said a monk read to him from ancient manuscripts an account about "Issa" (Jesus) and an interpreter translated the oral reading so Notovitch could take notes.

Three individuals claimed to have made the journey to the Hemis Monastery in the 1920s and 1930s and to have confirmed the existence of the Issa manuscripts. Yet neither Notovitch nor any of his three defenders managed to come back with photographs of the manuscripts, handwritten copies of them, or any other hard documentary evidence. Neither has anyone else in more than a century since Notovitch's book was first published, despite the numerous books defending his claims.

Paul Wallis has a 5-part YouTube series, **JESUS IN INDIA** as do several other YouTube channels.

www.youtu.be/tTe28mdi25Y?si=jPADe8Y9NpxoKIGF

WAS JESUS A JEWISH ESSENE?

It's not known whether Jesus was a member of the Essenes, but some scholars believe he was influenced by them, and other Orthodox Jewish scholars have suggested that Jesus may have been an Essene who wanted to reform Judaism, rather than create a new religion.

From some past life regression cases, Dolores Cannon wrote the two books, **Jesus and The Essenes** and **They Walked With Jesus**. Even with this evidence, it's still not sure if he was an Essene or not but we know that Apollonius was linked to the Essenes, as was John the Baptist.

DO WE NEED TO WORSHIP JESUS?

I read a very good explanation of the Greek and Hebrew words for "worship" and how they are translated to show something else—something that has misled many Christians and I quote only a little of it. The two words "shachah" (Hebrew) and "proskuneo" (Greek). They account for more than 80% of the appearances of the word "worship" in most English versions of the Bible.

"Shachah" mean "to bow down" or "prostrate oneself" before a superior or God. When the Hebrew or Greek words for worship refer to men "worshipping" men, the translators use the English words "bow down."

"Proskuneo" comes from the Greek words. pros, "to" or "toward," and kuneo, "to kiss." It literally means to kiss the hand of someone in token of reverence. Among the Orientals, to fall upon the knees and touch the ground with the forehead is an expression of profound reverence.

According to the JW's New World Translation, Matt 4:10, Jesus says to the Devil: *'Go away Satan, for it is written, 'It is Jehovah your God you must worship, and it is to him alone you must render sacred service'.* Even if you refer to the translation with 'the Lord your God', instead of Jehovah, if he wanted to be worshipped as God or even a part of God, wouldn't he have said so? In Matt 4:22-24, Jesus, when speaking to the Samaritan woman at the well said:

> *"Woman," Jesus replied, "believe me, a time is coming when you will worship the Father neither on*

> *this mountain nor in Jerusalem. ²²You Samaritans worship what you do not know; we worship what we do know, for salvation is from the Jews. ²³Yet a time is coming and has now come when the true worshipers will worship the Father in the Spirit and in truth, for they are the kind of worshipers the Father seeks. ²⁴God is spirit, and his worshipers must worship in the Spirit and in truth."*

Jesus, according to the Bible, always directed worship to his Father not Yahweh/Jehovah. You can see; therefore, the difference mistranslations make. Also, it seems he never considered himself to be God or wanted to be worshipped, let alone start up a new religion.

You would think that if our life and death depended on who we worshipped as "God" and how, so that people would come to some sort of agreement, instead of fighting each other. Do you really think a loving "God" would approve of such behaviour? It's the "God" of the Bible, Yahweh/Jehovah who loves to see people fighting and killing each other. Why do they want such a psychopath's approval?

WAS JESUS ILLITERATE?

Most of us are accustomed to getting our information about religion from books, so we tend to assume that it would have only been natural for Jesus to write down his teachings. As always, there are different opinions as to whether Jesus could read or write.

From the perspective of a literate person in the 21st century, it makes little sense why a person who saw himself as a prophet would not bother to write down any of his own ideas for his followers to pass on. In Luke 4:16-20, which is based on the Gospel of Mark, a scroll is handed to Jesus; he is able to locate the specific passage, reads it, and returns the scroll. He could read. But an opposing view was given by Helen Bond, a professor of Christian Origins at the University of Edinburgh, agreed and told The Daily Beast.

> *[If Jesus was a carpenter/mason, as we generally suppose, then it's not impossible that he had some rudimentary grasp of letters and/or numbers for the purposes of his trade, but I think it very unlikely that Jesus could read or write.]*

Another passage that some people have tried to interpret as evidence that Jesus was literate is found in the Gospel of John 7:53–8:11. This is when he writes in the sand and stops the crowd from stoning a woman.

DID JESUS SAY HE WAS GOD OR PART OF A TRINITY?

Trinitarians will answer, "Yes, Jesus did teach the doctrine of the trinity." Non-Trinitarians will answer, "No, Jesus never taught the doctrine of the trinity". Surely, If you want someone to know that you are speaking the truth, you need to ensure what you are saying is clearly understood.

People accept this teaching without checking to see if it's even true. The Babylonia trinity of Nimrod (Father god), Semiramis (Ishtar) (virgin mother and Wuenn of Heaven) and Tammuz/Ninus (virgin-born-son) became the Christian trinity of Father God, Lord God, Jesus and Holy Spirit which is symbolized by a dove.

MARRIAGE TO MARY MAGDALENE

Donald Watkins, a Christian, published an article, The Royal Bloodline of Jesus. Of course, there are many who claim Jesus was celibate until he died but there are several articles on this subject. Some even say that they had children, and their line is The Merovingian's line, although this is considered pseudo-historical by most Christian and secular historians. I was told that unless he was a married man, Jesus would not have been allowed to speak in a Synagogue, but it seems this is incorrect according to some.

WHAT IS GOD'S KINGDOM?

JWs say that the word "kingdom" is the old-fashioned word for "government". Jesus is the King of this Heavenly Government made up of 144,000 faithful ones chosen from the Earth.

This kingdom would replace all human governments to rule over the Earth. Other humans who died would then be resurrected to live on Earth alongside those who survived Armageddon. I was told by the JWs that "Satan" is the current ruler of the Earth which is why there is so much evil, and so the Witnesses don't vote because their allegiance is to Christ's heavenly Kingdom.

From 1987, I believed that I was one of the 144,000 going to die to go to heaven to be part of that heavenly

Kingdom and I partook of the Emblems (bread and wine) at each Memorial until I left in 1997.

I had been driving to see a friend when I heard the question in my head, "Would you like to be part of the heavenly government?". I thought how could I accept? What would my family and friends think?

When I arrived at my friend's home, for some reason I told her about this, and she just sat their smiling. When I asked why she was smiling, she told me she had this same hope for the past four years. She told me to pray to Jehovah who will make things clearer.

Needless to say, none of the other Witness believed me, any more than they believed my friend, apart from two others who also shared the same hope as us. Looking back, I think this was preparing me for all the conflicts ahead of me. I had always loved the idea of living on a paradise Earth so the belief of having to die and go to heaven was different for me now I had the 'heavenly hope'. The important thing was to help bring about the new earth.

My love for Jehovah at that time made it impossible to refuse the calling and I put up with what followed, convinced I would be vindicated in time. Of course, at the time I didn't know why, but now I do. According to the Bible, Jesus told his followers how to pray for God's kingdom to come but Luke 17:20-21 says:

> *[Now when He was asked by the Pharisees when the Kingdom of God would come, He answered them and said, "The kingdom of God does not come with observation; nor will they say, 'See*

here!' or 'See there!' For indeed, the kingdom of God is within you.]

To me, the above scripture contradicts what the Witnesses (and other Christians) believe. So now let's get back to Jesus.

DID JESUS DIE FOR ADAM'S SIN?

Whether you believe this or not depends, of course, on whether you believe the story of Adam & Eve in the Bible. According to Christians, it was Satan (aka Lucifer) who instigated such disobedience and in Chapter 7 I write about Satan and Lucifer and what I've found out.

We are told that humans were made in God's image and perfect with free will and intelligence weren't they already like God? Wasn't the punishment of being condemned to death extremely harsh for these two young people and their future offspring who were, thereafter, also considered "sinful".

Making mistakes is part of being human – it's how we learn. After all, good fathers teach their children the difference between right and wrong, good and evil so, I think as do many others, that it was downright cruel to condemn millions of humans to suffer and die because of wanting this knowledge.

However, if we turn the story around that it was the evil God, Yahweh/Jehovah who wanted Adam and Eve to remain in ignorance; and that the "serpent" (which often represented wisdom) was trying to help them by opening their eyes and minds, the whole story as to original sin falls apart. For those who want to continue believing that the biblical Jesus is the saviour of mankind, I would like you to think about the following and see if such a belief really makes any sense.

> *www.bibleproject.com/articles/why-did-jesus-have-to-die-a-question-worth-unpacking,*
> *explains that the basic message of the Eden story is this:*

> *[Humans die because we have, from the beginning, rejected God's offer of ultimate life. God's offer requires a surrender of what we might think is life so that we can receive the true life that God wants to give us. Tragically, we often decide to choose life as defined by our own wisdom, embracing our own self-ruin. Often these choices seem as innocent as eating tasty, good-looking fruit, but when those choices oppose God's wise instruction, they corrupt life and bring death.]*

According to the above explanation, humans die because they want to think for themselves. They wanted to use their free will when it came to making choices. They didn't want God telling them how to live. Looking at the earliest civilisations, they lived much longer, better lives than us and were more technologically advanced than us.

If the characters, Adam & Eve had been created during that period, and not merely 6,000 years ago, then they were already enjoying the ultimate life, so what more did they need? Who says they had rejected it thus bringing death and corruption upon themselves? Ancient writings tell us that the wonderful life humans had enjoyed was spoilt by wars where nefarious groups wanted to control everyone else. Has the death of Jesus changed this situation? How has his dying made any difference except to make things worse? Haven't even more atrocities been done since in the name of the Jesus of Christianity?

As for Jesus being our Saviour and dying for our sins, as taught in the Bible, I no longer this reason as valid because I don't believe Adam and Eve committed any sins in the first place.

WAS JESUS RESURRECTED?

JWs teach that we don't have souls, but we are living souls' and reject the belief in reincarnation as being a pagan teaching not believed by the Jews or early Christians. However, I found this claim to be untrue. The Bible says Jesus went to heaven after his death. Again, if one believes in the stories of people such as Enoch, Elijah and even Ezekiel going to heaven and meeting God, then that is also a possibility especially if you believe in ETs.

> *[The notion of a resurrection of the dead seems to have originated during Judaism's Hellenistic period (4th century BC–2nd century AD). Isaiah announced that the "dead shall live, their bodies shall rise" and the "dwellers in the dust" would be enjoined to "awake and sing" (ISA. 26:19). Both the good and the wicked would be resurrected. According to their deserts, some would be granted "everlasting life" and others consigned to an existence of "shame and everlasting contempt" (Dan. 12:2).]*

The Mesopotamian (Sumerian, Babylonian and Assyrian) attitudes to death differed widely from those of the Egyptians. They were grim and stark: sickness and death were the wages of sin. This view was to percolate, with pitiless logic and simplicity, through Judaism into Christianity.

RESURRECTION

The JW teaching of the resurrection is that all those who had died before Armageddon would be resurrected to live on Earth once Jesus was established as King and he would judge them. It was only the "anointed 144,000" who would be resurrected to the heavens to rule over the Earth with him.

The belief in the resurrection was part of the early Abrahamic religions, but this was the belief that the original body (the soul) itself would be resurrected as the same human being again. Whereas reincarnation is the belief that the soul would incarnate into a completely new body. Early Jews (most originally from the tribe of Judah) including the Essenes, denied the resurrection of the body, unlike the Pharisees.

REINCARNATION

Edgar Cayce said that he had read the Akashic Records of Jesus and said he had incarnated as various historical people, but whether one believes this depends on whether they believe in reincarnation. These past lives include: Amilius, Adam, Enoch, Hermes, Melchizadek, Joseph, Joshua,

Zend (father of Zoroaster). I read the above in **The Story of Jesus** by Jeffrey Furst and **Past Lives of Jesus** by Glenn Sanderfur.

As the Israelites had come out of Egypt, it is highly likely that they also believed in the immortality of the soul. Egyptians believed that even after death, one's spirit would live on because the life force was a separate entity that could detach itself from the body. Since Judaism has changed over the years, modern Jews have many different ideas.

The early Christians (ie. before the Council of Nicaea) also had differing ideas. Reincarnation was officially removed from Christian doctrine during the Fifth Ecumenical Council in the year 553 CE (also known as the Second Council of Constantinople).

A thought came into my mind that if we do reincarnate, perhaps the earlier theologians and philosophers have reincarnated to continue their research and understanding and are even around today. If we reincarnate to rectify past wrongdoings or grow in our spiritual consciousness, did Jesus need to die for our sins? Is this why reincarnation was ignored in the Abrahamic religions? I will cover this subject more in my next book.

AGAIN - WHAT'S IN A NAME?

Although I think Sue seems more down-to-Earth and friendly, I prefer to be called Susan because I feel I'm a wiser, grown-up version of my old self now. Although my family may say that's debatable. I think people's names are more important than many realise and the name you are called does make a difference. Jesus was referred to as the "Son of Man" 88 times in the New Testament. Other names include:

> *[Christ ~ Lord Advocate ~ Good Shepherd ~ Bread of Life ~ The Amen ~ New Adam ~ Beloved Son ~ Counsellor ~ Son of God ~ Deliverer ~ God Blessed ~ Messiah ~ Redeemer ~ I Am ~ Mighty One ~Jesus of Nazareth ~ Prince of Life ~ Lamb of God ~ Nazarene ~ King of the Jews ~ Image of God ~ Alpha and Omega ~ True Vine ~ Lord of Glory ~ Head of the Church ~ Light of the World]*

This article argues the opposite, that it's not important what name you call Jesus – a table is a table no matter the language.

> *[...Yeshua is the Hebrew name for Jesus. It means "Yahweh [the Lord] is Salvation." The English spelling of Yeshua is "Joshua." However, when translated from Hebrew into Greek, in which the New Testament was the English spelling for Iēsous is "Jesus." This means Joshua and Jesus are the same names.*
>
> *One name is translated from Hebrew into English, the other from Greek into English. It is also interesting to note that the names "Joshua" and "Isaiah" are essentially the same as Yeshua in Hebrew. They mean "saviour" and "the salvation of the Lord...In the same way, we can refer to Jesus by different names without changing his nature.*
>
> *The names for him all mean "Yahweh (the Lord) is Salvation." In short, those who insist we exclusively call Jesus Christ, Yeshua, are*

overlooking the fact that how the Messiah's name is translated is not essential to salvation. English speakers call him Jesus, with a "J" that sounds like "gee." Portuguese speakers call him Jesus, but with a "J" that sounds like "geh," and Spanish speakers call him Jesus, with a "J" that sounds like "hey." Which one of these pronunciations is the correct one? All of them, of course, in their own language.]

www.learnreligions.com/jesus-aka-yeshua-700649 says that in Matthew 1:22-23

[All this took place to fulfill what the Lord had said through the prophet: "The virgin will be with child and will give birth to a son, and they will call him Immanuel—which means, 'God with us.'" (Matthew 1:22-23, NIV).] Why isn't the name 'Immanuel' used?

THE TURIN SHROUD

On the 20th of August 2024, the Daily Mail announced the Turin Shroud was real in the article:

[IS THIS PROOF THE TURIN SHROUD IS REAL? SCIENTISTS MAKE A STARTLING DISCOVERY AFTER ANALYSING CLOTH JESUS WAS BURIED IN

[An AI-generated image of Jesus Christ is making rounds on social media, claiming to reveal the "true face of Jesus." The image was generated by the British media platform The Daily Express using Midjourney AI. It depicts a man with long hair and a beard, similar to traditional portrayals of Jesus, with cuts and bruises on the body, consistent with crucifixion.

The platform used the Shroud of Turin, an ancient cloth believed to have wrapped the body of Jesus Christ to create the image. Recent scientific studies published in the Heritage Journal used X-ray dating to prove that the Shroud dates back to around 2,000years ago, during Christ's time.

However, the study stops short of confirming whether the shroud was indeed Jesus' burial cloth. Social media users now assert, "The Shroud of Turin is real."]

Another two very interesting people I came across are Lynn Picknett and Clive Prince In one of her talks, she said that John the Baptist had more followers than Jesus and that they were actually enemies. She also believes that the Shroud of Turin was created by Leonardo Da Vinci which is interesting particularly since it was recently announced that the Shroud of Turin was legitimate. *(www.picknettprince.com)*

[Lynn and Clive, together with Keith Prince, were the first researchers to publish the results of their experiments to reproduce all the so-called' miraculous' characteristics of the Shroud, which even the remaining believers acknowledge 'behaves like a photograph'.

They succeeded beyond their wildest dreams – not only in creating totally Shroud-like images using a very basic pin-hole camera, but they discovered that the expert faker behind it was none other than Leonardo Da Vinci, who used his own face as a model for Christ... A known joker, conjurer illusionist, and a Church-hating heretic besides being fascinated by what we would call photography, building his own camera obscura -

he had the means, opportunity and motive to create this extraordinary work. Yet, as both art historians and 'Shroudie' believers never failed to point out, there was nothing that undeniably pointed to Leonardo's involvement in creating history's most superb and successful fake.

Until now as explained in the new Epilogue and new page of illustrations, the exact match between Leonardo's Salvator Mundi (Saviour of the World) and the face of the man on the Shroud finally provides the missing link.]

I await the outcome as to whether the Turin Shroud is genuine or a fake. It is also said that Cesare Borgia posed for Leonardo Da Vinci's portrait of Jesus.

www.history.com/news/what-did-jesus-look-like *states that there have been several depictions of Jesus and that:*

[.... The long-haired, bearded image of Jesus that emerged beginning in the fourth century was influenced heavily by representations of Greek and Roman gods, particularly the all-powerful Greek God Zeus....]

MORE TO THINK ABOUT

After reading George Kavassilas's book, **Our Universal Journey**, I felt I had to share some mind-blowing information and then let you make up your own mind. I recommend you buy the book for yourself, but it cost me approx. £42.00, and at the time of writing this, it's now £108.95 on Amazon, so I doubt if many of you will rush to buy it. You can get it on Kindle though. I have tried to quote as little as possible just so that you can get the same picture I have. I wrote about 3D and 5D in Chapter 1 of this book. Well, Kavassilas begins his book by talking about 5D too on p.28 and explains:

> [.... *The 5th dimension is the lowest vibratory realm of heaven, also called Avalon, Shambala, Paradise, Tula, Dreamtime, Valhalla and many other names as each culture has their own interpretation of this realm.... In these higher realms, we are talking about Light that is so fine that one experiences a continual state of being of Unconditional Love. Also, there is no technology in the 5th dimension and above, as everything is manifested and achieved using our organic consciousness. In these higher realms there is no such thing as the concept we call evil.*]

On p.29 he writes about the 'Great Arena' (also known as the "Cosmic Arena" and that it exists below the 5th dimension which is where technology exists. On p.80-81 he explains The Supreme Cosmic Deception, but this covers far too many pages to go into much detail here. Briefly, he explains:

> [...*our Human race as a whole has been systematically assimilated into a system of slavery which began to occur 300,000 years ago...The last major phase and implementation of this program began around 6,000 years ago when religion was created.*]

On p.85 he reminds us that the wayward faction of "gods" is not called such without good reason. They are very advanced compared to us in that they can create realities on a grand scale and have an incredible understanding of how life is constructed. They have even mastered to a degree the knowledge of 'Light', positive and negative charge, Yin and Yang, love and fear, good and evil.

> [...As a result, they have been able to manipulate life through positive white love and light energy, utilising passive-aggressive programs to yield greater results. They have created their own version of love, Conditional Love and that is what they have used against us using the strategy and program known as Problem ~ Reaction ~ Solution...
>
> By creating an undesirable environment here on Earth (the problem), depriving humanity of as much true Love and Light as possible, so that we yearn for love, light, peace and harmony (the reaction), they can then present their version of love and light (the solution) which enters us through our chakras (energetic portals).
>
> The chakra system originated in India between 1500 and 500 BC and was first mentioned in the Vedas, ancient yogic and spiritual texts. The word "chakra" comes from Sanskrit and means "wheel" or "mystical circle". All the above has been orchestrated by the 'God of Religion' who some have called *Yahweh/Jehovah.
>
> As the keeper of time, as we know it, he is also the creator and keeper of The Matrix.....This God entity created a cosmic-level software programme that would be overlaid upon our natural state of being and alter the way we experience this planet, this Solar system and our

view of life, immersing us in deceptive programmes to drive a wedge between us, the Sun and our Earth Mother.]

On p.95 he explains that the enlightenment that comes through our Chakra system, a version of enlightenment is the false light construct of the gods, particularly the simulated heavenly realms of the *god of religions". In the chakra system, a chakra is a spinning disk or wheel of energy that runs along the spine, and there are seven chakras in total. Each chakra has a unique meaning related to the body, life, breath, mind, intellect, and sense of well-being.

On p.95-100 he explains that the chakra body in Christianity is known as the seven seals. These are connected to our endocrine system (our glandular system) and ask the question, 'What if the pineal gland is a biological implant hidden in plain sight?'

OUR PINEAL GLAND

The pineal gland was described as the "Seat of the Soul" by Rene Descartes and is found in many species of animals too. It is in the centre of the brain. Its main function is to receive information about the state of the light-dark cycle from the environment and convey this information by the production and secretion of the hormone melatonin. Kavassilas wrote:

> *[...The pineal gland is the interface between the endocrine and nervous systems of our bodies... 300,000 years ago when the first genetic manipulations by the gods started; they created their own version of a gland that could interface with the pituitary.*

> *And therefore, the rest of the glands that make up our endocrine system. This gland is also responsible for the secretion of the hormone Melatonin which regulates our sleep patterns and circadian rhythms.]*

DMT (Dimethyltryptamine)

The Pineal gland also secretes DMT which increases serotonin receptors within the brain. Pharmaceutical anti-depressants reduce the number of serotonin receptors. Taking DMT has been a useful way of helping the brain to receive information and alter states of consciousness. Some call it the 'spirit molecule' and is a chemical way to enlightenment and attune one's lower consciousness to the cosmic mind of the god of religions. Many have had amazing experiences this way, but they may have fallen for the Great Deception.

On p.101, Kavassilas explains that although the pineal gland has been venerated as the seat of the soul in many cultures throughout the ages, he doesn't agree with that perspective because he feels and knows the seat of his soul is in his heart and not in his head. He goes on to say:

> *[...When one stimulates the Pineal Gland and does what some people call "Pineal Gland activation" through a series of rituals or exercises, all one is doing is just recalibrating it to 4th-dimensional cosmic mind matrix frequencies.... The more one connects into this 4th-dimensional cosmic mind matrix, the more the pineal gland is stimulated and seemingly comes alive...Electricity is the real-life force animating our technological equipment*

into being. But the television is functioning on a superficial layer of programmes that come in radio waves. It is the same setup for Humanity because there is a superficial layer of programmes that we are functioning from.]

On p.104, he explains the signals are first sent from the god of religions via the Moon and Saturn. The Pineal gland picks them up, decodes them and relays the programme into our conscious mind. Depending on which programme we are calibrated will depend on what our mind projects and what experiential reality is being created.

[...The Moon Mind Matrix is the current business /scientific/military industrial complex programme, and the Saturn Matrix is the "God"/religion/spiritual series of programmes. The pineal gland is where many programmes propagating the concept of "oneness" originate from .... promoting more of a collective hive[59] mind construct...

If you are aligned with the programme of Christianity, you are worshipping and feeding a Jesus figure. That is the reality your conscious awareness is going to enter into and where the creator god of this programme will interact with you in a recognised form sold to you by the priestly caste, the god's Earthly ambassadors.

You may even meet an image of an angel or Ascended Master. This is what often happens when one becomes a channeller medium. Ideally, one should always connect to one's own soul, their higher self.]

THE PINEAL GLAND & RELIGION

On p.107-8, Kavassilas explained:

In **CHRISTIANITY,** the sign of the cross is often made. Christian worshippers use ash paste to mark the sign of the cross on their forehead.

In **ISLAM**, during prayer, Muslims kneel and touch the ground with their forehead.

In **JUDAISM**, one of two Tefillin (small cube leather boxes containing scrolls of the Torah is placed on the forehead just before prayer just above the hairline. After prayer, they move it to below the hairline. In addition, Jews sway their body back and forth with their forehead pointing downwards during prayer at the Wailing Wall.

In **ZOROASTRIANISM**, a mark is made on worshippers' foreheads with cold sandalwood ash.

In **HINDUISM**, Hindus draw a mark on the forehead (Tilka, Tilak or Tilakam). The men draw a line, the women a dot (Bindi).

In **BUDDHISM**, deities are often depicted with the third eye in the centre of the forehead, and others with a pinecone headdress.

In **TAOISM**, students have third eye training, focusing their attention while their eyes are closed on the central point between their eyebrows. The common theme is for all to see. On p.109, he further explains:

[What else is common to all religions is that only "special people" get to heaven, a "special place" and they have to earn their way through a process of ritualistic prayers and meditations, techniques and practices all designed to give one's power over to the "higher authority" ... It's all about guilt driven atonement and conformity...Christianity is an amalgamation of many religions. It includes paganism and uses the template from the cult of Zeus. The deity of Jesus is simply a revised version and transfiguration of the deity of Zeus (aka Yahweh/Jehovah).]

Numerous people claim to have had personal experiences of Jesus communicating with or appearing to them, including the Apostle Paul. These experiences were very real to them so cannot be dismissed, but perhaps you can now see what has been going on.

Then I looked at Elena Danaan's book, **The Seeders** again. On page 158, headed *The Black Goo*, she writes about this in great detail. I must admit that when I read this chapter the first time, it went over my head but after reading Kavassilas's book, it made more sense. She wrote (p.153-6, 160) that after her galactic contact had activated her pineal gland she met "The Nine" and describes them as "plasmic supra-consciousnesses" that would affect deeply and powerfully the Consciousness of Humanity on Earth for the generations to come.

*NB: The book, **The Nine: Briefing From Deep Space (2023)** by Stuart Holroyd is about how they instructed Gene Rodenberry to create the Star Trek series.*

On pages 160-161 Elena describes that she then saw the dark holographic matrix that the Nebu, (also called the Dominion or the nefarious "Domain") had constructed to enslave the people on Earth. It was in the form of black goo, but it was dying as it couldn't feed off the human soul-substance anymore.

On p. 161 she explained that the Nebu Hive had been loading programmes into this Artificial Intelligence that is the Black Goo, and it had been affecting people when they downloaded codes via their crown chakra and installing programmes into the minds of so many other people via internet platforms.

> *[These programmes had names, an AI coding system and were scheduled to activate at the right time keeping the best for the final battle that would come...More and more people were tapping into this thing...these programmes had names..."Galactic Federation of Light", "Pleiadians", "Arcturians", "Ashtar Sheeran", Ashtar Command", "Swaru", "Flat Earth", "Saint Germain", "Sananda", "Jerusalem Ship". It usurped our very myths, the very names of our ascended masters or sacred places, the core of our religious beliefs, driving everyone into a false light, into a trap.*
>
> *These programmes had nothing to do with the real things such as the Galactic Federation of Worlds, the real Pleiadians and Arcturians, who anyway never called themselves as such. Other types of dark programmes had also been elaborated and installed by the Dark Fleet and their reptilian allies from the Ciakahrr Empire.*

> *They abducted many children and deconstructed their minds through torture such as the Montauk method...The aim of these programmes is to eradicate all hope from the hearts of the people, and condition the masses to resign, kneel bend. The return of a prophet, the mass arrival of extraterrestrial superheroes, a cosmic event, or a solar flash would save Earth and activate everyone's spiritual ascension...driving people into passively waiting and giving their power away to illusions. And in the meantime, the dark ones continued unfolding their plans with a corner smile.]*

You may well dismiss what I've written as a load of rubbish. I had to read it several times myself to understand this. After all, none of us like the thought that we are being programmed by outside forces. Both George Kavassilas's and Elena Danaan's own personal experiences show that connecting with the Universe in a natural sense is achieved through one's heart and greater aspects of self, not through belief systems or our brains. They both stressed that we need to get in tune with our hearts to raise our consciousness and not just follow along blindly.

I haven't found any conclusive reason as to whether there was an actual person called Jesus/Yeshua as described in the Bible because I've come across so many different viewpoints, but I certainly don't think that character was Michael the Archangel and the Logos as JWs teach or God incarnate, and part of a Trinity as Christendom teaches.

With whom does Jesus actually mediate on our behalf? The god of the Bible or someone else? As for dying for our sins, this doesn't make sense, especially when he tells the Samaritan woman her sins were forgiven (John 4:5-42). If he could forgive sins, why did he have to die?

I do believe that there is the possibility that the Biblical Jesus is a composite figure made up of several people, such as Mithras, Cyrus the Great, Apollonius of Tyana and that there was most probably such a teacher or several who provided the original sayings later quoted in the Bible. If we can believe any of the writings about him, for me what stands out is that we should treated men and women as equals; forgive others and to love his Heavenly Father (not Yahweh) and our neighbours.

7 - WHO IS SATAN?

BASIC TEACHING 8: EVIL & SUFFERING – THIS BEGAN WHEN ONE OF GOD'S ANGELS REBELLED AND BECAME KNOWN AS SATAN THE EVIL WHO IS ALLOWED TO RULE THE EARTH FOR A LIMITED TIME

BASIC TEACHING 9: DEATH – WHEN HUMANS PASS OUT OF EXISTENCE. THEY DO NOT BELIEVE IN HELL AND FIERY ORMENT FOR UNBELIEVERS OR EVIL DOERS. MILLIONS WILL BE WHO REFUSE TO FOLLOW THESE WILL BE DESTROYED FOREVER.

As a Witness, I believed the 'God and Ruler if this system on Earth' was actually 'Satan the Devil' and that the true God was Jehovah (Yahweh). This belief was based on Matt 4:1-11 where we are told that the Ruler of the world offered Jesus all the kingdoms if he just did an act of worship to him. He is the cause of all the evil in the world.

> *NEW LIVING TRANSLATION (2 COR. 4:4) - Satan, who is the God of this world, has blinded the minds of those who don't believe. They are unable to see the glorious sight of the Good News. They don't understand this message about the glory of Christ, who is the exact likeness of God.*

From all my research so far, I can agree with this, but the question arises as to who is Satan really?

MEANING OF THE WORDS "SATAN" & DEVIL"

The above teaching encompasses a large amount of misinformation. First, "Satan" is not a name. It's a description of a character and I found this out delving into the origins of this word. If it's not a name, did such a person actually exist?

Izak Spangenberg's book, **A Brief History of Belief in the Devil (950 BCE - 70 CE),** refers to a book by Robert Muchembled, **A History of the Devil: From the Middle Ages to the Present (2003),** which explains the meanings of these words.

SATAN

The meaning of the word "satan" depends on the context and can be either a verb or a noun. The verb is usually translated as "to bear a grudge, to cherish animosity, to oppose" (Ps 38:21; 71:37; 109:4, 20, 29). The noun is usually translated as "opponent, adversary" and can refer to either a human or a heavenly being.

Only three books in the Old Testament uses the noun to refer to a heavenly being (Zechariah 3:1-2; Job 1:6-12; 2:1-7:1 Chronicles 21:1). However, none of these books characterises "Satan" as Yahweh's opponent; he is merely a member of the heavenly court.

Also, none of these books originated during the First Temple period (950-586 BCE), they were all written during the Second Temple period (539 BCE-70 CE).

This led to the questions:

- Why don't the earlier books mention this character?

- Why do we read about him only in material written during the Second Temple period?

If these questions are to be answered, Munchembled wrote 'recent research into the religion of Israel has to be consulted'. So, we can see that anyone who makes an accusation or is against someone else, can be "Satan", this means anyone who opposes you. It isn't a unique person.

In the chapter 'Who Is God?' I've shown the origin of the God of the Bible and of Jehovah's Witnesses. What if Yahweh/Jehovah, an evil god was opposed by someone? Wouldn't that person be called Satan by Yahweh? Was that really a bad thing?

From what I've learnt, the main one who opposed Enlil was his brother, Enki. They fought because of their different attitudes towards the human race. Enlil wanted to enslave humans and have them worship him, Enki wanted humans to be free and enlightened by putting his own DNA into "Adam". Enlil won, and he became "God" and Enki was thereafter known as Satan/Lucifer" thereafter because he opposed him.

The brothers were not spirits but super intelligent and technology-advanced beings known as the Anunnaki, or "powerful ones/Elohim", who ruled over areas of land and sea on Earth. These powerful ones were worshipped as the gods we read about in the world's mythology. Enlil became the God of Religion, making himself out to be good and his brother the evil one, "Satan". He then projected all his own evil qualities onto him and those who followed his brother were thus called "fallen angels".

It is these inversions which have misled us into defining what is good as bad and vice versa. It's worth noting that everywhere different beliefs are demoted to myth-status. Never has this been as obvious as in this current period of our history.

DEVIL

The word "devil" comes from the Greek word "diabolos", which means "slanderer" from the Greek word "diabállein", which means "to slander". In Jewish, Christian, Zoroastrian, and Muslim traditions, the word "devil" refers to a spirit of evil that opposes the will of God.

This supreme spirit of evil is represented as the tempter of humankind, the leader of all apostate angels, and the ruler of hell often used as an interjection, an intensive, or a generalised term of abuse', a spirit enemy of mankind. So, Satan is supposed to be a real person, but the Devil is a spirit and yet people say "Satan the Devil" without knowing what they are saying.

See also *www.etymonline.com/word/devil*

If the story of Enlil and Enki is true, as I've come to believe, then the ruler of the world has never been

Satan the Devil but the God of Religions, Enlil/Yahweh. Anyone opposed to him has been called the adversary, "Satan" but who is the enemy of mankind really? The devious, lying person who has been in misleading the whole world, the one Jesus spoke against according to the Bible.

It hasn't been "Satan/Lucifer" ruling the world but the evil "God", so even the Apostle Paul may have lied. Anyone who opposed the Jews were demonised, the Qumran Community was one example. They proclaimed that they represented "true Israel". The others, they claimed, were colluding with the Devil and his entourage (Pagels 1996: 56-61).

> *[The brief history of the development of the belief in the Devil and fallen angels presented here should serve as proof that this belief cannot be classified as a pure "biblical belief". In one sense, it could even be argued that "[d]evils, hell and the end of the world are New Testament rather than Old Testament realities" (Barr 1966:149).*
>
> *...Christians and Muslims too easily claim to be on the side of the good and point fingers at others as being on the side of evil and the Devil. Concerning this, Messadié makes the following observation: In the mid-eighties, the world saw an odd and symbolic case of geographical transference.*
>
> *The president of the United States, Ronald Reagan, called the USSR "the Evil Empire" while the de facto leader of Iran, the Ayatollah Khomeini, called the United States "the Great Satan.]*

SATAN IN KABBALAH AND HASIDISM[33]

Kabbalistic texts offer a rich description not only of Satan, known as Sama'el, but of an entire realm of evil populated by demons and spirits that exists in parallel to the realm of the holy. Kabbalah even offers explanations of the origins of the demonic realm. The most common of which is that this realm emerges when the attribute of God associated with femininity and judgment, is disassociated from the attribute of God associated with grace and masculinity and becomes constrained.

If this is the case, it is the patriarchal men who have created this demonic realm by disassociating themselves from the Divine Feminine. To deal with these entities, they created formulas for exorcisms to free the possessed of an evil spirit, known as a "dybbuk". According to some scholars, this belief was born from the mixing together of Christian and Jewish thinking in the so-called "golden age" of Jewish culture in Spain during the Middle Ages.

Hasidic Judaism is a religious movement within Judaism that arose in the 18th century as a spiritual revival movement in contemporary Western Ukraine. And this is how many of the early kabbalistic texts, including the Zohar, emerged.

JEWISH –V- CHRISTIAN CONCEPTIONS OF SATAN

On the whole, Satan occupies a far more prominent place in Christian theology than in traditional rabbinic sources. The Book of Revelation, in the New

Testament, is most descriptive. It describes a red dragon with seven heads and ten horns that stands opposite a pregnant woman about to give birth to devour the child — that is, Jesus. Revelation further describes a war in heaven in which Satan is hurled to Earth, where he proceeds to lead the world astray. It compares the dragon to an "ancient serpent" who is the Devil and Satan commonly understood as the snake that tempted Eve in the Garden of Eden.

According to Christian prophecy, Satan will be bound by a chain for 1,000 years after the return of Jesus. However, in the Bible Satan is ultimately subordinate to God, carrying out his purpose on Earth.

Some think that he isn't real at all but is merely a metaphor for sinful impulses. Both the kabbalistic/Hasidic and Christian traditions describe the forces of the holy and the demonic as locked in a struggle that will culminate in God's eventual victory.

In Matt.23, we have Jesus who criticised the scribes and Pharisees for their hypocrisy and called them 'Serpents, offspring of vipers...' *[and these were the writers and teachers of the Hebrew Scriptures!]*

MUSLIMS BELIEVE IN SATAN[34]

Although some Muslims do not accept that Allah is also Yahweh, they share many of the same characteristics. Again, we can see the inversion in Islam which developed in the late 6th century CE, Muslims say [38]Satan is a title or a designation and "Iblis" is a name. The Qur'an uses the former 88 times and the latter 11 times.

[Iblis was of the Jinn and was somehow affected by Allah's command to angels to prostrate before Adam (about this we cannot say, nor speculate, more, as the only source for this knowledge is the revelation). However, Iblis refused to follow angels and prostrate before Adam, claiming that he was better than him because he was made of fire and Adam of clay.

At this point, Iblis became Satan, which means "rebel" and "arrogant". He exercised his freedom and chose to be Satan(ic). He was not created evil – indeed nothing is – but chose to be so. Iblis was proud and self-centred. He rebelled against Allah and became a non-believer. He became the chief of all the Jinn that were like-minded with him. Whoever follows Iblis in his arrogance, rebellion and wickedness is also called a satan. That is the case both among the Jinn and people (al-An'am, 112).

There are many "satans", but only one Iblis. Iblis as Satan is capitalized – because of him being the epitome as well as a source of all evil and mischief – whereas other "satans" are in lower case. The relationship between the two is one of a leader (godfather) and followers. It is truly enlightening to study how precisely the Qur'an uses the words Satan and Iblis, recognizing the contexts and giving each word its exact meaning and role.

For example, when a discourse is about prostration before Adam, the Qur'an uses the word Iblis, because solely in his personal capacity did he refuse to follow divine orders and to prostrate. However, when the discourse moves to the acts of deceiving Adam and his wife and causing them to fall, the Qur'an employs the word

Satan, because thus he acted in his capacity as the avowed deceiver...

Satan – supported by his army of satans from among the Jinn and mankind - is the source and incarnation of all sin. He even paved the way for today's most devastating forms of evil: rampant materialism, agnosticism, and pleasure-seeking.... Satan is what he is because he is jealous of mankind. He does not accept Allah's decrees concerning them – or him. He can't stand them and wants to destroy as many of them as possible.

Accepting man as Allah's vice-regent on Earth and an honourable being preferred over much of what Allah had created (al-Isra', 70), was not compatible with Satan's delusions and self-absorption. He was consumed by his iniquitous qualities to the point that he worshipped them (himself). There was no room in his personality for submitting to and worshipping Allah.]

MEANING OF THE WORD "DEMON"

www.etymonline.com/word/demon
states:

[c. 1200, "an evil spirit, malignant supernatural being, an incubus, a devil," from Latin daemon "spirit," from Greek daimōn "deity, divine power; lesser god; guiding spirit, tutelary deity" (sometimes including souls of the dead); "one's genius, lot, or fortune;" from PIE *dai-mon- "divider, provider" (of fortunes or destinies), from root *da- "to divide."

The malignant sense is because the Greek word was used (with daimonion) in Christian Greek translations and the Vulgate for "god of the heathen, heathen idol" and also for "unclean spirit." Jewish authors earlier had employed the Greek word in this sense, using it to render shedim "lords, idols" in the Septuagint, and Matthew viii.31 has daimones, translated as deofol in Old English, feend or deuil in Middle English. Another Old English word for this was hellcniht, literally "hell-knight.

The usual ancient Greek sense, supernatural agent or intelligence lower than a god, ministering spirit" is attested in English from 1560s and is sometimes written daemon or daimon for purposes of distinction, meaning "destructive or hideous person" is from 1610s; as "an evil agency personified" (rum, etc.) from 1712. The Demon of Socrates (late 14c. in English) was a daimonion, a "divine principle or inward oracle." His accusers, and later the Church Fathers, however, represented this otherwise. The Demon Star (1895) is Algol (q.v.)]

MEANING OF THE WORD "HELL"

JWs don't believe in hell as taught by other religions. They believe it is the grave not a place of torment as a God of love would never create such a place. They teach that in the Hebrew Bible, "sheol" is the place where the dead go after death and is often described as an underworld or subterranean realm.

It is a place of darkness, silence, and gloom, and is often referred to as the "land of forgetfulness" or "Abaddon" (destruction). In Greek, the word was "hades". Old English hel, helle, "nether world, abode of the dead, infernal regions, place of torment for the wicked after death", Proto-Germanic *haljō "the underworld" (source also of Old Frisian helle, Old Saxon hellia, Dutch hel, Old Norse hel, German Hölle, Gothic halja "hell"). Literally "concealed place" (compare Old Norse hellir "cave, cavern"), from PIE root *kel- (1) "to cover, conceal, save." Old Norse Hel (from Proto-Germanic halija "one who covers up or hides something") was the name of Loki's daughter who ruled over the evil dead in Niflheim, the lowest of all worlds (nifl "mist").

In Middle English, also of the Limbus Patrum, a place where the Patriarchs, Prophets, etc. awaited the Atonement. Used in the KJV for Old Testament Hebrew Sheol and New Testament Greek -Hades, Gehenna. The Old Testament word for the abode of the dead is Sheol. It is derived, as most scholars think, from a word meaning hollow.

To the Hebrew mind Sheol was simply the state or abode of the dead used figuratively for "state of misery, any bad experience" at least since late 14c. As an expression of disgust, etc. first recorded in the 1670s.

So, there have been many ideas about hell, but the main thing was that it put people into a state of fear at the thought of ending up there.

DEMONOLOGY & EXORCISM

My friend, Jan, was unfortunate enough to have lived in a very haunted house in Chigwell, Essex, which turned out to be a portal and resulted in an exorcism which generated her Interest to learn more. Coincidentally I was living in Woodford Green, Essex around the same time but we didn't know each other then. She kindly lent me her book, **Dominion**, by Fr. Chad Ripper, an American Catholic priest, theologian, philosopher, and exorcist, well-known in traditional Catholic circles.

The first part of his book is about **Angelology**, then from page 71-113 he writes about **Demonology**. He explains much more of course, obviously based upon Christian beliefs than I can write here, so I have only written the bits I feel relevant to explain what I've now come to believe.

On page 73-74, he quotes from another book, The Christian Faith in the Doctrinal Documents of The Catholic Church, 2001 he explains:

> [...that these are intelligent beings are "fallen angels" with the 'intellectual knowledge of God' also can have knowledge of the future, and even have their own hierarchy. They don't have bodies or emotions only metaphorical ones such as anger, having a hatred of natural things and their main sins were pride, envy, selfishness and malice, wanting to be like God...]

On page 85-89, he quotes St. Thomas saying that '...The first angel that sinned was from the Cherubim', not the Seraphim. He also refers to Lucifer...' On pages 90-91, he explains that:

> [...the Church believes that of demons or the damned (humans) will be subjected to eternal punishment by everlasting fire because of them

> *being evil in line with Thomas Aquinas's thought, whereas Origin believed the punishment was not eternal or perpetual...]*

Zoroastrianism, thought to have originated as early as 4,000 years ago is based on the teachings of the Iranian prophet Zoroaster. This was the first introduction to the concept of angels. The word angel means "a messenger of God", characterized as having human form with wings and a halo. The word suggests goodness and is often used to refer to someone who offers comfort and aid to others in times of trouble. (*www.vocabulary.com*)

According to Stephen Okey, (a theologian and assistant professor of philosophy, theology, and religion at Saint Leo University in Florida), the term "exorcism" is most associated with Christianity, especially Catholicism. This is partly because of the numerous explicit references to Jesus casting out spirits in the Gospels. His followers and others as well, drove out demons 'in his name.'

> *[In the first two centuries of the Christian era, the power of exorcism was considered a special gift that might be bestowed on anyone, lay or cleric. Then special classes of the lower clergy were called exorcists and were entrusted to carry out this special function. About the same time, exorcism became one of the ceremonies preparatory to baptism, and it has remained a part of the Roman Catholic baptismal service.*
>
> *Exorcism of persons possessed by demons is carefully regulated by Canon Law in the Roman Catholic Church, and the elaborate rite is*

contained in the Roman ritual. In some traditions, the "possessed" individual becomes ill and is regarded by his community as having committed some spiritual transgression; recovery is held to require expiation of his sin, often by a sacrifice. In other traditions, the "possessed" person is conceived as a medium for the controlling spirit and functions as an intermediary between spirits and men.]

Fr. Ripper's major role is usually to diagnose and heal other spirit-afflicted individuals. In this tradition the trance behaviour of the medium is often self-induced (auto-hypnotic); it may be stimulated by drugs, drumming, or collective hysteria. In his trance the medium appears genuinely insensible to ordinary stimuli. He explains:

[It seems that those who are heavy drinkers or take heavy drugs are more likely to be affected but it has been known that even pious people have been too. Some conditions historically termed demonic possession has come to be treated as epilepsy, hysteria, somnambulism, schizophrenia, or other organic or psychological forms of illness. Until recently, those who claimed to have had ET contact were also treated as mentally ill, demon-possessed*, ridiculed or just disbelieved.]

Many religious traditions believe that there are evil forces that can have a negative influence on a person's life and reports suggest that demand for exorcisms have increased since the turn of the century. In 2017, Pope Francis told priests that they "should not hesitate" to call on a Vatican-trained exorcist should they need one.

IS LUCIFER THE DEVIL?

Many refer to Satan as Lucifer, but some biblical scholars claim Lucifer isn't a proper name either, but descriptive. the Latin phrase meaning "morning star."

In a prophetic vision by the prophet Isaiah (Isaiah 14) the King of Babylon (Marduk, Nimrod etc) is condemned and is called (Helel ben Shachar, Hebrew for "shining one, son of the morning" (Hêlêl ben Šā-ar). So it seems that Marduk is Lucifer.

What I've learnt so far is that although Marduk aka Baal, Nimrod etc. left his father Enki to side with his uncle, Enlil, he opposed Enlil in the end by building the Tower of Babel. His intention, it seems, was to unite people under his rulership, not Enlil's and of course Enlil wasn't having that. So this made him an adversary in Enlil's eyes (ie. a satan).

SONS OF GOD

It seems that anyone who is termed the "son of God" is directly created by God. Thus, Adam was the "son of God" because he was directly created by God (Luke 3:38). Satan, like other angels, was created by the direct hand of God (Ezek 28:13), and therefore he too is a "son of God". (Job 1:6, 2:1). And we know Jesus was considered a "son of god". I always ask the question, "Which God?"

From my findings, Yahweh didn't create Adam, nor did he create the "angels" or anything else. He was known as the "destroyer". Therefore, the "Sons of God" were the Elohim who refused to follow Enlil and became known thereafter "fallen angels or demons". Those who opposed the evil Enlil/Yahweh, the "God of the Bible" were some who sided with Enki identified and were as "Satan", the adversary.

The Apostle Paul, according to the Bible in 1 Cor.10:20, says that 'the things which the nations sacrifice they sacrifice to demons.' This is true if you think that the world, via their religions are really sacrificing and worshipping the ruler of the world; and that '...*the god of this system of things has blinded the minds of the unbelievers...*'

The "God of the Bible" has deviously misled people whilst causing the death of millions of humans by creating wars and diseases in order to feed off the fear and stress which he and his non-human followers need in order to exist – known as "Loosh". I will write more about this in my next book and how I found out about "loosh".

WHAT IS THE DEFINITION OF EVIL?

The word "evil" means 'profoundly immoral and wicked' and people consider someone like Hitler or Ted Bundy to have been evil men. However, like "beauty" is considered as such by the beholder, so is evil.

One's perception of evil is based upon one's beliefs, just as beauty is. Is it really evil to love someone of the same sex? Is it evil to have second sight or heal people, or believe differently? Is there really such a thing as a "righteous war" or the killing of people who choose to follow different beliefs? Is it evil to have sex with someone you love and who loves you, outside of marriage? Is it evil not to be part of a religion?

Millions lost their lives because they refused to worship the God of the Bible and even those who did, died defending him. To me that is the ultimate evil and certainly nothing like the teachings of Yeshuah.

I now believe there are extremely evil people running our world who encourage others to think and behave the same way they do regardless of their victims. But I believe they are more afraid of those above them and each other, so that they are willing to sacrifice their own humanity and conscience.

I've listened to several interviews by Jason Reza Jorjani (See Sources of Information). He believes that the Satan/Lucifer of the Bible was the one on whom Prometheus was modelled. If the adversary of the evil god was Enki the good brother, then his trying to enlighten people, isn't this a good thing?

My own conclusion so far is that there have been two main characters called "Satan the Devil". Both opposed Enlil (Yahweh/Jehovah) one because he wanted power for himself (Marduk), the other because he wanted to free mankind from this god (Enki).

ALIENS AND RELIGION

In the book, **Aliens and Religion: Where Two Worlds Collide** by Jonathan M.S. Pearce (a philosopher) and Dr. Aaron Adair (a Scientist), many questions are discussed including:

- If there are ETs, what would their religions be and what would they think about ours?

- Would aliens be fallen creatures, requiring salvation through atonement and the resulting incarnation of God?

- Would one Jesus suffice, or would the universe require trillions of Jesuses, many existing simultaneously?

They mention on p.236 that, '...*When trying to explain the supernatural events of the Bible, some Christians have suggested that it was all aliens, and the angels of the Bible were aliens with their technology.*'

They then quote from p.49 of a book by Michael Dimond, **UFOs, Demonic Activity & Elaborate Hoaxes Meant to Deceive Mankind (1980):**

> *[...However, to test the world in these last days, God has allowed the Devil to have significant power to attempt to deceive mankind. These false signs, such as UFOs, are done by demons...fraught with theological issue and makes God look like a trickster, deceiving humanity, though (one assumes) for some greater good.']*

Some of the ETs drawn by Elena Danaan in her book, **A Gift from the Stars**, certainly look like some of the ones depicted by artists through the centuries. This truth has been hidden in the Bible because the best way to hide things is in plain sight.

It's the priest class of all religions who serve this god and deliberately mislead their followers, preaching one thing but doing the opposite. Telling their congregations they are sinful and needed redemption in the form of a human sacrifice. A truly loving God would never want the sacrifice of animals or humans He created.

There have been UFO sightings for centuries but since the late 1940s, there has been more and cases of ET contact resulting in new technology. There have also been warnings from these visitors to stop being so warlike, because we'll end up destroying this planet and affecting the rest of the universe.

The good thing is that people are waking up from these false teachings and learning the truth, which will free them forever from those who run this system. Yes, it's been God's Will – but the question is always, which God?

CONCLUSION

Having spent the last three weeks rewriting and formatting this book, I'm amazed at all the information I found with my research, a lot of which I haven't put in this book. So far, I have learnt that:

- Yahweh/Jehovah is the god of the Bible but has no love for mankind. He and his minions just want to control us whilst they live in luxury and we get poorer.
- There were different versions of paradise in the past and there will be in the future.
- Many of the earlier civilisations were more advanced than we have been taught.
- Humans have worshipped ETs as gods, some out of appreciation, others out of fear.
- The Source of everything, called The Origin by Guy Needler, the Source or Prime Creator, is an intelligent form of energy and frequencies, the highest being love. We are fractals of this energy and immortal. (See Book II for more information).
- We are more than our bodies – we are awareness, formless and incarnate into a physical form in order to have experiences.
- The Holy Spirit is not as taught by religions.
- The Logos is a frequency that causes things to be created.

- Yeshua/Jesus is likely a composite character of those who had the Christ-consciousness who did exist, such as Apollonius of Tyana. This character is a construct of those who wanted to create a religion to oppress us.
- "Satan the Devil" is not the name of any entity but a description of anyone who dared to oppose Enlil/Yahweh/Jehovah who is the evil one and ruler of the world.
- Humanity has been controlled and brainwashed into subjection by the words conveyed through the many secular and religious organisations, as well as the media. This was not the plan set up by the first Trinity or the first Creators.
- No matter how much I know, there is always more to learn. As much as I've discovered, there is still more research to do, especially when there are many conflicting opinions by "experts".

Many times, I wanted to give up, but I feel that if only one person finds this information useful then it will have been worth all the effort. If the information gets people talking, thinking or starting their own research, then that will be even better.

Don't just dismiss the idea that there are other humans and humanoid beings, physical and spiritual, on Earth and other dimensions, who hate not only themselves and each other, but humans even more. This is because we have many qualities and abilities they will never have and the greatest of which is the ability to love. At the same time there are far more who really care about us and I will share what I've found out in my next book.

What I've discovered and what I believe are two different things, hence more research and more books to write.

In **My Journey to Paradise (Book II)** I will include the following chapters:

- The Universe, Planets & Constellations Dimensions & Densities
- Souls, Starseeds & Reincarnation
- Creation of Living Matter & Humanoids
- Akashic Records & Universal Laws
- Why Earth is so Special
- Why we are so Special

Thank you for buying this book. I would love to have your feedback and review as this is my first book.

I know there is much more to write about as I try to sort out what is really true and what is not. Meanwhile, do make time to do your own research, so that you can see for yourself that a 5D Paradise Earth will be a reality.

Susan Hayward
November 2024

SOURCES OF INFORMATION

ALEX COLLIER
www.alexcollier.org
An Andromedan Contactee since 1985. The first contact was in the upper peninsula of Michigan in a place called Woodstock. In 1964 he was on a family picnic and went out to play with cousins. He laid on the grass and the next thing he found it was nighttime - he had been missing for several hours but didn't remember anything until age 14.

BILLY CARSON
www.4biddenknowledge.com
An American entrepreneur, author, music artist, TV host, producer, actor, director, and expert in Ancient Civilizations. He is the founder and CEO of 4BiddenKnowledge Inc, He often works with Paul Wallis and Matthew LaCroix.

CORINA PATAKI
www.thequestfortruthwithcorinapataki.com
She is a Minister, Author, Speaker, Writer, Podcaster, Light Worker, Truth Seeker, Teacher and Student with a very strong faith in Jesus and good knowledge of the Bible which she explains passionately. She immigrated to Chicago from Romania during Ceausescu's dictatorship and has written a book about this in her book, The Quest for Freedom.

DANI HENDERSON
www.galacticspiritualinformersi.com
Dani Henderson has had a lifetime of paranormal experiences, psychic/intuitive revelations, and extraterrestrial contacts. She has worked as a "spiritual therapist" in England for several decades, and in 2010 was tested by the British media who blindfolded her and took her to secret locations, one being the Old Vic Theatre, to successfully confirm her psychic/intuitive abilities. Dani has had direct contact experiences with extraterrestrials associated with the Galactic Federation of Worlds.

DOLORES CANNON
www.dolorescannon.com
Her 50 year career as a hypnotherapist specialising in past life regression took her on an incredible journey along countless fascinating destinations. She developed and refined her own unique method of hypnosis known as Quantum Healing Hypnosis Technique® (QHHT®)

DR. MICHAEL SALLA
www.exopolitics.org
He is a pioneer in the development of 'Exopolitics', the political study of the key actors, institutions and processes associated with extraterrestrial life. His interest evolved out of his investigation of the sources of international conflict and its relationship to an extraterrestrial presence that is not acknowledged to the general public, elected officials or even senior military officials.

EDGAR CAYCE
www.edgarcayce.org
He was an American attributed clairvoyant who claimed to speak from his higher self. While in a trance-like state Cayce would answer questions on a variety of subjects such as healing, reincarnation, dreams, the afterlife, past lives, nutrition, Atlantis, and future events.

ELENA DANAAN
www.elenadanaan.org
A French Archaeologist who spent many years working on diverse sites in Egypt and in France studying ancient cultures. Hereditary Shaman, she also studied Pagan spirituality, Magic and Alchemy. She was trained and ordained as a Druidess. An Extraterrestrial Contactee with Pleiadians since childhood, she became an emissary for the Galactic Federation of Worlds.

ERICH VON DANIKEN
www.daniken.com/en
Erich von Däniken is the award-winning and bestselling author of Chariots of the Gods, Twilight of the Gods, and many other books. He lectures throughout the world and has appeared in TV

specials and many episodes of Ancient Aliens on the History Channel.

FREDERICK DODSON
www.realitycreation.org
He is the author of 50 books, a success coach, consciousness researcher and international speaker, He believes everyone has their own version of the truth and the purpose of his life is not to get others to agree with him, but to have fun. His favourite activities include scuba diving, surfing the internet, writing, collecting movie, travelling and lucid dreaming.

FREDDY SILVA
www.invisibletemple.com/about.html
For over fifteen years Freddy Silva has been an author, and independent researcher of ancient systems of knowledge, alternative history and Earth mysteries. He has been a permanent feature in the international lecture circuit since 2003.

GRAHAM HANDCOCK
www.grahamhancock.com
He is a journalist who has travelled the globe hunting for evidence of mysterious, lost civilisations dating back to the last Ice Age.

GUY STEVEN NEEDLER
www.beyondthesource.org
Guy Needler initially trained as a mechanical engineer and quickly progressed to become a chartered electrical and electronics engineer. During his training as an energy healer (1999-2005) Guy discovered that he was able, via meditation, to traverse the frequencies above those associated with the auric layers.

JASON REZA JORJANI
www.jasonrezajorjani.com
He is a philosopher & author who received his BA , MA & PhD at State University of New York at Stony Brook. He has taught

courses on Comparative Religion, Ethics, Political Theory, and the History of Philosophy at the State University of New York.

JORDAN MAXWELL
A renowned researcher who had also been involved with Jehovah's Witnesses when a young man. He had discovered a lot of exciting stuff and new places in his own research which no one talked about until recent years, especially about the meaning of symbols and basis for religions around the world. He was only interested in those who desired and prioritized Truth and genuine spirituality over everything else and this was obvious from his talks. He died in 2022.

MATTHEW LACROIX
www.thestageoftime.com
A passionate writer and researcher. He worked as a writer/researcher at Gaia, appeared on shows such as Ancient Civilizations on Gaia, The UnXplained on the History Channel, and Mystery School of Truth on 4Biddenknowledge TV.

MAURO BIGLINO
www.maurobiglino.com/en
He is an Italian author, essayist, and translator. His work focuses on the theories concerning the Bible and church history, including conspiracy theories, ufology, and the Pseudo-scientific speculation of ancient astronauts. He has also been involved in producing Italian interlinear editions of the Twelve Minor Prophets for Edizioni San Paolo in Cinisello Balsamo, Italy. He admits having been a Freemason and member of the Italian Freemasonry for more than ten years until the 2000s when he left.

MICHAEL TELLINGER
www.michaeltellinger.com
He is a scientist, explorer and author of numerous books, and dozens of lectures available on YouTube. His research includes archaeology, mythology, human origins, religion, origins of money, spirituality, breakthrough science and consciousness. Also the Founder of the UBUNTU Movement. An authority on the ancient, vanished civilisations of Southern Africa, the

mysterious origins of humankind, resonance, cymatics, and the power of sound.

PAO L. CHANG
www.esotericknowledge.me
Author of Word Magic. A Born Again Christian and the creator of the Rumble channel Revelation Knowledge. In his early twenties, Pao became interested in finding the truth about 9/11. He studied many subjects, such as conspiracy, secret society, new age, science, religion, spirituality, esoteric knowledge, word-magic, etymology, and law, hoping to find the key to spiritual freedom. In 2020, after going down the rabbit hole for nearly 16 years, Pao felt an impulse to study the Holy Bible more deeply.

PAUL ANTONY WALLIS
www.paulanthonywallis.com
As a Senior Churchman, Paul served for 33 years as a Church Doctor, a Theological Educator, and an Archdeacon in the Anglican Church in Australia. He has published numerous titles on Christian mysticism and spirituality and is a popular speaker at conferences around the world. His books probe the world's ancestral narratives for their insight into human origins, human potential and our place in the cosmos.

SARAH BRESMAN COSME
www.theholistichypnotist.com
She is a Master Hypnotist, a Level 3 practitioner of Dolores Cannon's QHHT, and a student of Dr. Brian Weiss. Sarah began her unsuspected journey into the world of UFOs by regressing her clients with the use of past life regression hypnosis.

BIBLIOGRAPHY

AUTHOR	BOOKS
Sarah Breskman Cosme	A Hypnotist's Journey to Atlantis, A Hypnotist's Journey to the Secrets of the Sphinx
Frederick Dodson	Atlantis & The Garden of Eden, The Pleiades & Our Secret Destiny
Graham Hancock	America Before
Bruce Nixon	A Better World Is Possible
Nigel Warburton	A Little History of Philosophy
Barbara Marciniak	Earth: Pleiadian Keys to the Living Library
Jeffery Furst	Edgar Cayce's Story of Jesus
Paul Wallis	Escaping From Eden, The Scars of Eden, Echoes of Eden, The Eden Conspiracy, Invasion of Eden
Zecharia Sitchin	Genesis Revisited & The Lost Book of Enki
Francesca Stavrakopoulou	God: An Anatomy
Mauro Biglino	Gods of The Bible, The Naked Bible
George Kavassilas	Our Universal Journey
Guy Steven Needler	The History of God, The Origin Speaks, Beyond the Source 1 & 2, The Om

MY JOURNEY TO PARADISE (BOOK I)
BIBLIOGRAPHY

Lena Einhorn	The Jesus Mystery
Freddy Silva	The Lost Art of Resurrection
Robyn Faith Walsh	The Origins of Early Christian
Frederick Dodson	Our Secret Destiny, Atlantis & The Pleiades and The Garden of Eden
Lynn Picknett	The Secret History of Lucifer, The Masks of Christ
Elena Danaan	The Seeders, A Gift from the Stars, We Will Never Let You Down
Shapurji Aspaniaarji Kapadia	The Teachings of Zoroaster
Alexander Hislop	The Two Babylons
Dolores Cannon	Jesus & The Essenes, They Walked With Jesus
Sandra Daroy	Walk-in Case

WEB LINKS

1 – A PARADISE EARTH – FACT OR FICTION?

1. www.thesecret.tv/law-of-attraction
2. www.unacademy.com/content/nda/study-material/geography/origin-of-Earth
3. www.rsarchive.org/Books/GA011/English/TPS1911/GA011_index.html
4. www.morien-institute.org/interview1_MK.html
5. www.britannica.com/topic/New-Age-movement
6. www.findhorn.org
7. www.press.uchicago.edu/Misc/Chicago/256626.html#:~:text=First%20Great%20Awakening%2C&text=1730%2D60:%20Weakening%20of%20predestination,1830:%20Breakup%20of%20revolutionary%20coalition

2 - EARLY CIVILISATIONS, RELIGIONS & PHILOSOPHIES

8. www.aboriginalcontemporary.com.au
9. www.learnearnandreturn.wordpress.com/2011/04/25/bunyips
10. www.brown.edu/Departments/Joukowsky_Institute/courses/architecturebodyperformance/326.html
11. www.answersingenesis.org/genesis/the-original-unknown-god-of-china
12. www.biblestudytools.com/bible-study/topical-studies-what-is-the-meaning-of-the-name-shaddai.html

3 - THE BIBLE & OTHER BOOKS

13. www.britannica.com/topic/Huitzilopochtli
14. www.pbs.org/wgbh/pages/frontline/shows/jesus/evangelicals/vs.html
15. www.smithsonianmag.com/history/is-judaism-a-younger-religion-than-previously-thought-180981118
16. www.simonandschuster.com/books/Moses
17. www.ancient-origins.net/history-famous-people/moses-myth-or-history-002246
18. www.amazingbibletimeline.com
19. www.penelope.uchicago.edu/josephus/ant-1.html#:~:text=Now%20it%20was%20Nimrod%20who,of%20great%20strength%20of%20hand
20. www.independent.co.uk/artsentertainment/books/reviews/babylon-by-paul-kriwaczek-2063000.html
21. www.jbqnew.jewishbible.org/assets/Uploads/393/jbq_393_Hammurabi
22. www.learnreligions.com/lilith-in-the-torah-talmud-midrash-2076654
23. www.gotquestions.org/Job
24. www.biblestudytools.com/topical-verses/paul-in-the-bible/#google_vignette
25. www.ehrmanblog.org/was-paul-the-founder-of-christianity
26. www.philpapers.org/rec/TYMCWT
27. www.register-of-charities.charitycommission.gov.uk/Charity-search/-/charity-details/3966490/financial-history in 2023
28. www.chabad.org/library/article_cdo/aid/3347866/jewish/What-Is-thetalmud.htm#:~:text=The%20Talmud%20is%20a%20collection,the%20Holy%2

MY JOURNEY TO PARADISE (BOOK I)
WEB LINKS

oLand%20and%20Babylonia

4 – WHO IS GOD? – NO LINKS

5 – SOURCE, THE LOGOS & THE HOLY SPIRIT

29. www.jw.org/en/bible-teachings/questions/what-is-the-holy-spirit

6 – WHO IS JESUS?

30. www.historytoday.com/archive/history-matters/strange-christian-afterlife-pontius-pilate#:~:text=By%20the%20second%20century%20AD,portray%20Pilate%20as%20a%20convert.Testament

31. www.claudiamerrill.com/blog/who-were-the-atlanteans

32. www.qcc.cuny.edu/socialSciences/ppecorino/PHIL_of_RELIGION_TEXT/CHAPTER_2_RELIGIONS/Hinduism

33. www.greekreporter.com/2024/05/04/greek-jesus-christ-apollonius-tyana

7 - WHO IS SATAN?

34. www.history.com/news/what-did-jesus-look-likewww.myjewishlearning.com/article/satan-the-adversary

35. www.islamicity.org/77304/unveiling-the-deceiver-9-startling-facts-about-satan

INDEX

144,000, 282, 283, 288
3D, 5D and 7D, 24
5D Tara, 28

Aborigines, 65
Abraham, 13, 133, 138, 143, 144, 145, 146, 147, 148, 160, 169, 200, 209, 216, 236, 276
Abrahamic religions, 26, 27, 116, 119, 126, 157, 178, 218, 219, 221, 259, 288
Adam, 1, 23, 109, 125, 130, 131, 133, 148, 149, 150, 151, 152, 153, 196, 216, 217, 236, 276, 284, 285, 286, 289, 290, 309, 314, 315, 323
Adam and Eve, 1, 23, 109, 125, 151, 152, 153, 216, 217, 285, 286
Ain Ghazal, 63, 68
Akhenaton, 84, 128, 129, 130
Allah, 47, 169, 213, 217, 218, 314, 315
Alpha Draconis system, 30
Amilius, 290
angel, 13, 132, 174, 198, 299, 319
Angelology, 318
Anunnaki, 31, 76, 77, 152, 207, 208, 226, 228, 309
APOCRYPHA, 199
Apollo, 270, 274
Apollonius of Tyana, 269, 271, 273, 304
Apostate, 186, 189, 310
Apostle Paul, 163, 164, 165, 173, 267, 270, 301, 311, 323
Archimedes, 113
Archosaurs, 30
Arcturians, 302, 341
Aristotle, 85, 114
Ascended Master, 299

Ascension Cycle, 26, 27
Asherah, 211, 212, 246
Atlantis, 27, 34, 35, 38, 39, 40, 41, 42, 43, 44, 59, 81, 82, 103, 105, 109, 152, 207, 243, 257, 335, 340, 341

Augustine, 113
Avalon, 294

Aztec, 40, 63, 105, 106, 107, 108, 110,

193
Baal, 212, 322
Babylon the Great, 178
Bamber Gascoigne, 166
Bart Ehrman, 191, 269
BASIC TEACHING 1, 203
BASIC TEACHING 10, 181
BASIC TEACHING 11, 183
BASIC TEACHING 12, 184
BASIC TEACHING 13, 186
BASIC TEACHING 14, 187
BASIC TEACHING 15, 192
BASIC TEACHING 2, 120
BASIC TEACHING 3, 268
BASIC TEACHING 4, 268
BASIC TEACHING 5, 268
BASIC TEACHING 6, 268
BASIC TEACHING 7, 15
BASIC TEACHING 8, 306
BASIC TEACHING 9, 306
Bertrand Russell, 112
Bhagavad Gita, 258, 259
Bible, 1, 4, 13, 14, 16, 20, 35, 56, 107, 115, 116, 119, 120, 121, 122, 123, 124, 126, 133, 134, 135, 136, 137, 139, 140, 142, 143, 145, 148, 149, 153, 154, 157, 163, 164, 169, 171, 172, 173, 178, 179, 181, 182, 184, 185, 188, 191, 192, 196, 197, 200, 202, 205, 209, 210, 212, 214, 215, 216, 218, 225, 226, 228, 235, 236, 237, 246, 247, 248, 249, 254, 256, 258, 259, 260, 265, 271, 274, 275, 276, 278, 280, 283, 284, 286, 287, 303, 304, 308, 310, 313, 323, 324, 325, 326, 327, 330, 334, 338, 340, 344
Blood transfusions, 14, 188
BOOK OF THE HEAVENLY COW,

INDEX

194
Books of Chilam Balam., 90
BOOKS OF ENOCH, 197
Buddhism, 23, 94, 300

Caesar's Messiah, 259
Canon Law, 320
Caracalla, 272
Çatalhöyük, 63, 67, 70
Catholicism, 320
Cesare Borgia, 293
Chakra, 35, 53, 296, 297, 302
Cherubim, 319
Chinese, 39, 63, 70, 71, 94, 95, 97, 98, 99, 191, 194
Christ, 5, 16, 27, 50, 51, 52, 119, 121, 125, 149, 159, 161, 163, 164, 166, 167, 168, 172, 173, 184, 188, 219, 221, 261, 262, 263, 270, 272, 277, 283, 289, 290, 292, 293, 304, 307, 331, 341
Christendom, 178, 181, 188, 223, 240, 304
Christian, 5, 42, 51, 52, 70, 117, 153, 159, 162, 165, 166, 167, 169, 171, 173, 174, 180, 187, 197, 200, 203, 204, 210, 216, 219, 221, 224, 236, 252, 265, 266, 267, 273, 281, 282, 291, 299, 310, 312, 313, 318, 319, 320, 338, 341
Christian, 179
Christianity, 52, 91, 104, 119, 124, 125, 162, 163, 165, 176, 179, 181, 199, 201, 219, 220, 221, 238, 260, 261, 263, 267, 273, 286, 287, 297, 299, 300, 320

Church of Jesus Christ of Latter-day Saints, 224
Cicero, 114
Clive Prince, 292
Coatlicue, 108
CODEX SINAITICUS, 171
CODEX VATICANUS, 171
Constantinople, 167, 291
Cosmic Arena, 295
Council of Nicaea, 17, 167, 224, 291
Coyolxauhqui, 108
Cronus, 47
Cush, 139, 141

Daniel Rodriguez, 172, 173
Danubian culture, 79
Dead Sea Scrolls, 166, 197, 199
DEAD SEA SCROLLS, 197
Demonology, 318Demons, 102, 103, 132, 172, 312, 319, 320, 323, 324, 326, 327
Devil, 13, 27, 180, 252, 279, 306, 307, 309, 310, 311, 313, 327, 331
Dimensions, 4, 24, 26, 27, 55, 231, 232, 235, 326, 331
Dinosaurs, 30, 31
Disclosure, 57
Disfellowshipped, 189

Divine Feminine, 239, 240, 243, 244, 245, 312
Divine Masculine, 239, 240, 244, 245
DMT (Dimethyltryptamine), 297
DNA, 24, 30, 31, 101, 150, 188, 234, 276, 309
Dolores Cannon, 42, 278, 339, 341
Dominion, 301, 318
Donald Bruce Redford, 129
Donald Watkins, 282
Dr David Skrbina, 266
Dr. Aaron Adair, 326
Dreamtime, 64, 294

E. Valentia Straiton, 242
Ea/Enki, 22, 150
Earth, 4, 5, 13, 15, 16, 17, 18, 21, 22, 23, 24, 25, 26, 27, 28, 29, 30, 31, 32, 33, 37, 38, 39, 44, 45, 46, 50, 51, 54, 56, 57, 59, 60, 62, 64, 76, 77, 78, 83, 90, 92, 99, 102, 107, 108, 110, 111, 131, 132, 136, 142, 145, 147, 148, 151, 168, 179, 196, 201, 206, 207, 208, 209, 212, 216, 228, 230, 234, 235, 236, 241, 243, 257, 258, 268, 282, 283, 288, 296, 301, 302, 303, 305, 306, 309, 313, 315, 331, 332, 335, 340, 343
Edgar Cayce, 42, 290, 340
Egypt, 37, 40, 59, 60, 62, 71, 79, 80, 81, 83, 93, 103, 113, 126, 127, 128, 129, 130, 134, 147, 195, 199, 291, 335
Elena Danaan, 30, 44, 47, 150, 208, 241, 301, 303, 326, 341
Elohim, 26, 232, 235, 236, 237,

MY JOURNEY TO PARADISE (BOOK I)
INDEX

238, 249, 309, 323
Empress Julia Domna, 272
Enlil, 76, 78, 90, 101, 102, 107, 109, 119, 137, 138, 139, 147, 148, 151, 178, 213, 214, 215, 225, 226, 258, 271, 308, 309, 310, 322, 323, 327, 331
Enmeduranki, 132

Enoch, 83, 131, 132, 133, 197, 198, 199, 287, 291
ENŪMA ELIŠ, 196
Erich Von Daniken, 208
Eridu, 135, 152
Essenes, 166, 269, 278, 288, 341
Evangelicals, 120
Eve, 149, 150, 151, 284, 286, 313
Evil, 13, 27, 33, 66, 102, 107, 117, 131, 140, 149, 180, 217, 220, 222, 223, 282, 284, 285, 295, 306, 308, 309,
310, 311, 312, 314, 315, 319, 321, 323, 324, 325, 328, 331

Exorcism, 318, 320
Fallen angels, 309, 311, 319, 323
Feminine and Masculine frequencies, 243
Flavius Josephus, 129, 136, 139, 260
Founders, 30
Fr. Chad Ripper, 318
Frederick Dodson, 29, 37, 38, 340, 341
Frequency, 25, 52, 53, 118, 150, 229, 232, 238, 239, 331
Fundamentalists, 13, 121

Gad Barnea, 122, 125
Galactic, 26, 47, 234, 302, 335
Garden of Eden, 23, 38, 124, 152, 153, 313, 341
Genesis, 115, 116, 124, 131, 132, 136, 141, 149, 151, 152, 207, 236, 237, 246, 247, 249, 340
George Kavassilas, 46, 228, 252, 294, 303, 341
Gérard Nissim Amzallag, 213
God, 6, 1, 4, 13, 14, 15, 16, 18, 21, 23, 27, 30, 47, 51, 55, 62, 72, 77, 81, 99, 100, 102, 109, 115, 117, 118, 119, 120, 121, 123, 124, 125, 132,

134, 136, 139, 141, 142, 143, 148, 150, 152, 154, 155, 156, 157, 160, 161, 163, 164, 165, 166, 167, 168, 169, 170, 174, 178, 180, 183, 186, 187, 188, 193, 194, 195, 197, 198, 200, 201, 202, 203, 204, 205, 206, 208, 209, 211, 212, 213, 215, 216, 217, 218, 222, 223, 224, 225, 226, 228, 230, 232, 234, 236, 237, 241, 242, 243, 244, 245, 246, 247, 249, 251, 252, 255, 256, 257, 258, 268, 270, 275, 278, 279, 280, 283, 284, 285, 286, 287, 289, 290, 294, 296, 299, 303, 304, 306, 307, 308, 309, 310, 311, 312, 313, 314, 319, 323,
324, 325, 326, 327, 328, 340, 341
Golden Age, 57, 88, 241, 243
Graham Hancock, 110, 111, 208, 340
Great Arena, 295
Great Awakenings, 56
Great Flood, 90, 103, 193, 194, 195
Greece, 59, 80, 84, 85, 86, 88, 101, 263
GUN-YU MYTH, 193
Guy Needler, 230, 232, 234, 252, 330, 336

Hammurabi, 137, 142, 143, 196, 214, 344
Heathen, 220
Heaven, 4, 13, 23, 24, 76, 92, 93, 98, 99, 100, 103, 132, 140, 144, 145, 165, 166, 168, 169, 195, 198, 201, 206, 208, 235, 240, 268, 271, 272, 276, 283, 287, 294, 300, 313
Heavenly Government, 282
Helel ben Shachar, 322
Helen Bond, 281
Hemis Monastery, 277
Hermes, 83, 94, 133, 291
Hinduism, 23, 94, 95, 259, 345
Holy Spirit, 27, 50, 123, 124, 167, 168, 172, 174, 188, 236, 239, 240, 246, 247, 249, 250, 251, 252, 331
Homo sapiens, 96
Homo Sapien Sapien, 276
Homo sapiens, 31, 96
Huitzilopochtli, 106, 107, 108, 343
Humanoid beings, 331
Hybrid, 79, 150, 215

MY JOURNEY TO PARADISE (BOOK I)
INDEX

Iblis, 314, 315
Immanuel, 22, 290
IRENAEUS, 219

Ishtar, 76, 155, 200, 275
Islam, 6, 119, 132, 153, 201, 213, 220, 221, 241, 314
Jamshid, 103
Jehovah, 1, 3, 5, 10, 13, 15, 16, 17, 43, 47, 49, 50, 57, 78, 102, 121, 130, 153, 163, 164, 169, 170, 172, 178, 179, 181, 182, 183, 184, 185, 186, 187, 190, 191, 209, 210, 215, 216, 217, 218, 223, 224, 225, 226, 228, 255, 256, 268, 279, 280, 283, 285, 296, 300, 306, 308, 327, 330, 331, 336
Jehovah's Witnesses, 1, 3, 17, 43, 49, 57, 121, 169, 170, 172, 178, 181, 185, 186, 187, 190, 209, 210, 216, 255, 308, 336
Jesus, 13, 14, 15, 16, 47, 50, 51, 52, 119, 125, 148, 149, 151, 153, 159, 160, 161, 162, 163, 164, 165, 166, 167, 168, 169, 172, 179, 182, 184, 190, 197, 205, 209, 213, 216, 217, 218, 219, 223, 224, 225, 238, 241, 249, 250, 254, 255, 256, 259, 261, 262, 263, 264, 265, 266, 267, 268, 269, 270, 271, 272, 273, 274, 275, 276, 277, 278, 279, 280, 281, 282, 283, 285, 286, 287, 288, 289, 290, 291, 292, 293, 294, 299, 300, 303, 304, 306, 310, 313, 314, 320, 323, 326, 331, 334, 340, 341
Jiahu, 63, 70, 71
Job, 156, 247, 307, 323, 344
Johannes Greber, 173, 175
John, 37, 72, 120, 138, 161, 163, 174, 175, 179, 182, 204, 206, 211, 224, 247, 249, 250, 251, 257, 260, 262, 270, 278, 281, 292, 304
John Day, 211
Jonathan M.S. Pearce, 326
Jonathan Pritchard, 101
Joseph, 95, 128, 197, 259, 263, 275, 291

Joseph Atwill, 259
Joshua, 61, 154, 289, 291
Judaism, 119, 124, 158, 175, 188, 201, 211, 220, 221, 256, 259, 260, 278, 287, 291, 312

Kabbalah, 132, 198, 312
Karl Marx, 175, 177
King of Babylon, 322
Kingdom, 39, 40, 51, 135, 136, 137, 146, 168, 282, 283
Krishna, 267

Law of Attraction, 18, 19, 51
Lemuria, 27, 34, 35, 36, 37, 38, 39, 42, 59, 207, 243, 257
Lena Einhorn, 262, 341
Leonardo Da Vinci, 292, 294
Life for Ruth, 3, 188
Logos, 227, 239, 240, 241, 243, 289, 303, 331
Lucifer, 212, 284, 309, 310, 319, 322, 327, 341
Luke, 15, 51, 117, 159, 160, 174, 179, 246, 247, 276, 281, 283, 323
Lynn Picknett, 292, 341

Mahabharata, 259
Maldek, 24, 29
Mandaeans, 218
Manetho, 128, 129
Marduk, 77, 102, 119, 139, 143, 147, 155, 196, 214, 322, 327
Mark, 45, 159, 160, 166, 179, 281
Mars, 24, 29, 101
Martin Kähler, 263
Mary, 133, 168, 260, 275
Maryam, 133, 275
Matrix, 26, 299
Matthew, 59, 159, 160, 179, 224, 247, 276, 290, 334
Mauro Biglino, 158, 236, 237, 248, 340
Mayan civilization, 89

Melchizadek, 291
Merikare, 114
Merlin Stone, 201
Mesopotamia, 37, 71, 74, 75, 76, 79, 93, 95, 136, 138, 139, 140, 142, 143, 147, 152, 270
Michael Dimond, 327
Michael Tellinger, 208
Montauk method, 302

MY JOURNEY TO PARADISE (BOOK I)
INDEX

Moses, 13, 84, 100, 124, 125, 126, 128, 129, 130, 142, 148, 156, 198, 209, 210, 216, 344
Muslim, 133, 310
Myriam Batjoachim, 275

Nag Hammadi Scriptures, 166, 199
Naram-Sin, 75, 140, 141
Nebu Hive, 302
New Age, 18, 24, 44, 45, 48, 49, 50, 56
New Testament, 159, 163, 164, 172, 173, 174, 175, 182, 200, 205, 217, 224, 240, 254, 260, 261, 265, 273, 276, 289, 311, 313
Nibiru, 24, 147, 150, 208
Nicene Creed, 167, 168
Nigel Warburton, 112, 340
Nimrod, 131, 135, 136, 137, 138, 139, 140, 141, 142, 143, 144, 145, 146, 322
Ninhursag, 76, 108, 109
Noah, 102, 103, 130, 131, 134, 136, 139, 140, 142, 144, 146, 147, 193, 196, 200, 226

Original sin, 153, 154, 285

Pagan, 63, 161,
Paradise, 15, 17, 18, 22, 23, 24, 27, 28, 56, 63, 106, 112, 161, 187, 204, 220, 221, 259, 261, 287, 283, 330, 332
Pa-Taal, 30, 238
Paul Kriwaczek, 141

Pentateuch, 122, 158
Persians, 88
Peter Singer, 113
Phaeton, 29
Philo of Alexandria, 139
Philosophy, 66, 67, 69, 71, 74
Philostratus, 271, 272, 273
Pineal Gland, 297, 298, 299, 301
Plato, 40, 42, 112, 113, 114, 258
Plato, 40
Pleiades, 29, 32, 37, 340, 341
Pleiadians, 26, 32, 234, 302, 335
Pneuma, 246, 248, 249
Pontius Pilate, 162, 168, 254
Popol Vuh, 90, 91

Psalms, 156, 157
Ptah, 217
Ptahhotep, 113
Pythagoras, 88, 113, 270

Queen Hatshepsut, 126
Qumran Community, 311
Quran, 119, 120, 132, 191, 205

R. Joseph Hoffmann, 263
Reincarnation, 43, 44, 63, 65, 287, 288, 290, 335
Rene Descartes, 297
Resurrection, 165, 166, 168, 287, 288
Richard Abanes, 215
Richard Carrier, 262, 264, 265
Roger R. Keller, 223
Roman Empire, 100, 221, 263, 266, 269
Ron Rhodes, 216
Ruach, 246, 248, 249

Salvator Mundi, 293
Samaritan, 205, 279, 304
Sandra Daroy, 227, 341
Sarah, 42, 146, 148, 339, 340
Sargon, 75, 139, 140, 141, 142, 143
Sasha Lessin, 147
Satan, 13, 15, 21, 180, 211, 237, 279, 282, 284, 306, 307, 308, 309, 310, 311, 313, 314, 315, 322, 323, 327, 331
Seeders, 30, 31, 38, 150, 238, 241, 301, 341
Seneca, 114
Senenmut, 126, 127, 130
Seraphim, 319
Serpent race, 29
shachah, 278
Shambala, 294
Shangdi, 98
Shiva, 47, 73, 94, 245
Shroud of Turin, 292, 293
Socrates, 113, 114, 316
Son of God, 323
Son of Man, 165, 289
Source Entity One, 234
Sparta, 85
Spartan, 86, 87
Starseed, 26
Starseeds, 26, 27, 57, 332

INDEX

Stephen Okey, 320
Sumerian, 75, 76, 77, 78, 109, 110, 116, 119, 124, 130, 132, 134, 138, 139, 140, 142, 143, 150, 151, 152, 194, 195, 196, 207, 208, 212, 213, 215, 218, 287
SUMERIAN KING LIST, 195
Swastika, 94, 95

Tamil, 35, 36
TAOISM, 300
Terah, 131, 144, 145, 146
Tertullian, 219
Tetragrammaton, 210, 214, 215
THE AZTEC FLOOD STORIES, 193
The Black Goo, 301
THE EPIC OF GILGAMESH, 193
The Gnostics, 180
The Great White Brotherhood, 45, 47
The Matrix, 21, 296
The Merovingian's, 282
THE MYTH OF ADAPA, 194
The Naga, 30
The Nine, 301
The Om, 230, 232, 341
The Origin, 230, 231, 232, 233, 234, 235, 238, 242, 330, 341
The Supreme Cosmic Deception, 295
The Talmud, 119
Theos, 170, 204
Thoth the Atlantean, 83
Titus, 260
Torah, 122, 144, 149, 165, 198, 300
Tower of Babel, 139, 140, 144, 200, 322
Trinitarians, 281

Trinity, 167, 169, 172, 188, 224, 236, 240, 303, 331
Truth, 6, 25, 48, 59, 60, 83, 118, 123, 124, 145, 151, 157, 179, 181, 201, 206, 238, 243, 248, 251, 254, 265, 266, 279, 280, 281, 327, 328, 335, 338
Tula, 294
Tutankhamun, 84

UFO sightings, 325
Utnapishtim, 103, 193

Vaishnavism, 218
Valhalla, 294
Vespasian, 260

William Linville, 227, 341
Word Magic, 341

Yahweh, 1, 47, 78, 102, 107, 130, 163, 164, 210, 211, 212, 213, 215, 218, 225, 226, 236, 237, 246, 248, 249, 252, 271, 276, 280, 285, 289, 290, 296, 300, 304, 306, 308, 310, 314, 323, 327, 330, 331
Yeshua, 104, 151, 267, 274, 275, 289, 290, 303
YHWH, 137, 140, 141, 210, 214, 215, 223, 224, 225, 246
Yonatan Adler, 122

Zelophedad, 134
Zend (father of Zoroaster), 291
Zeus, 78, 101, 170, 203, 214, 271, 294, 300
Ziusudra, 135
Zoroastrianism, 101, 102, 104, 319

Printed in Great Britain
by Amazon